THE THEATRE NOW

By the same author

THE FIRST THREE YEARS OF THE WAR
THE DEVIL IN WOODFORD WELLS
THEATRE
THEATRE II
VERDICT AT MIDNIGHT

THE
THEATRE NOW

by

HAROLD HOBSON

THEATRE BOOK CLUB
48 Old Bailey, London, E.C.4

THIS EDITION

first published for the THEATRE BOOK CLUB in 1954 (by arrangement with Longmans, Green and Co. Ltd.) as one of the outstanding books of the theatre selected for their members to whom it is issued exclusively at a privilege price. Particulars of membership can be obtained from the officers of Theatre Book Club, 48 Old Bailey, London, E.C.4.

PRINTED IN GREAT BRITAIN
BY WESTERN PRINTING SERVICES LTD., BRISTOL

TO MARGARET,
with love

You sat beside me as we sped
   Through the wide harvest land,
While field by field the golden miles
   Slipped past on either hand.

Two long braids framed your young grave face,
   Its still, enchanted air;
Your eyes were on the stooks, but mine
   On your wheat-coloured hair.

We paused. In golden languor held,
   The sheaves drowsed head to head:
'They have a combed and silken look
   Like braided hair', I said.

You turned and leaned your face to me
   With listening, lovely grace—
Brighter than corn your aureoled head
   Made beauty in that place.

MADGE ELDER

ACKNOWLEDGMENTS

I am grateful to Viscount Kemsley, Editor-in-chief of *The Sunday Times*, for permission to quote passages that have appeared in that newspaper; to the Editor of *The Sunday Times*; and to Miss Madge Elder, who has allowed me to use the poem she wrote for my daughter after an August drive through the lovely country round Melrose.

CONTENTS

		page
1.	ELIOT	1
2.	FRY: ANOUILH	13
3.	SOME RELIGIOUS QUESTIONS	44
4.	THE INVOLVED THEATRE	86
5.	THE OLD AND THE NEW	128
	INDEX	173

Plays discussed in this book, in order of production:

1949

May	THE LADY'S NOT FOR BURNING	Globe
July	DEATH OF A SALESMAN	Phoenix
October	A STREETCAR NAMED DESIRE	Aldwych
October	BEFORE THE PARTY	St. Martin's
November	THE SEAGULL	St. James's
December	FALLEN ANGELS	Ambassadors
December	BONAVENTURE	Vaudeville

1950

January	VENUS OBSERVED	St. James's
January	RING ROUND THE MOON	Globe
February	LARGER THAN LIFE	Duke of York's
February	THE SCHOOLMISTRESS	Saville
March	HOME AT SEVEN	Wyndham's
March	MR. GILLIE	Garrick
March	THE WAY THINGS GO	Phoenix
April	THE TRIAL	Winter Garden
April	IVANOV	Arts

1950—cont.

May	THE COCKTAIL PARTY	*New*
May	THE HOLLY AND THE IVY	*Duchess*
May	CAROUSEL	*Drury Lane*
May	BACKGROUND	*Westminster*
June	MACBETH	*Arts*
June	SEAGULLS OVER SORRENTO	*Apollo*
July	MISTER ROBERTS	*Coliseum*
July	ACE OF CLUBS	*Cambridge*
August	SAYONARA	*New Lindsey*
August	THE LITTLE HUT	*Lyric*
August	CAPTAIN CARVALLO	*St. James's*
September	ACCOLADE	*Aldwych*
September	RELUCTANT HEROES	*Whitehall*
September	THE SECOND MRS. TANQUERAY	*Haymarket*
October	TOP OF THE LADDER	*St. James's*
October	WHO IS SYLVIA?	*Criterion*
November	TO DOROTHY A SON	*Savoy*
November	RETURN TO TYASSI	*Duke of York's*
December	POINT OF DEPARTURE	*Duke of York's*
December	LACE ON HER PETTICOAT	*Ambassadors*

1951

February	MAN AND SUPERMAN	*New*
February	GAY'S THE WORD	*Saville*
March	A PENNY FOR A SONG	*Haymarket*
April	WATERS OF THE MOON	*Haymarket*
May	A SLEEP OF PRISONERS	*St. Thomas's Church*
May	HAMLET	*New*
May	THREE SISTERS	*Aldwych*
May	CAESAR AND CLEOPATRA	*St. James's*
May	ANTONY AND CLEOPATRA	*St. James's*
May	THE LOVE OF FOUR COLONELS	*Wyndham's*
June	THE WINTER'S TALE	*Phoenix*
July	POOR JUDAS	*Arts*
July	STORKS DON'T TALK	*Comedy*

1951—cont.

August	ARDÈLE	*Vaudeville*
August	RIGHT SIDE UP	*Arts*
September	SAINT'S DAY	*Arts*
September	TEN MEN AND A MISS	*Aldwych*
October	FIGURE OF FUN	*Aldwych*
November	THE FLIES	*New*
November	MOMENT OF TRUTH	*Adelphi*
November	MARY HAD A LITTLE . . .	*Strand*
November	SOUTH PACIFIC	*Drury Lane*
November	RELATIVE VALUES	*Savoy*
December	INDIAN SUMMER	*Criterion*
December	PETER PAN	*Scala*
December	CINDERELLA	*Scala*
December	THE DAY'S MISCHIEF	*Duke of York's*

1952

January	THE HAPPY TIME	*St. James's*
January	THIRD PERSON	*Criterion*
January	MUCH ADO ABOUT NOTH-ING	*Phoenix*
February	RED LETTER DAY	*Garrick*
March	THE DEEP BLUE SEA	*Duchess*

Chapter One

ELIOT

THE period during which the four score or so plays mentioned in these pages were produced was, in the larger world, a time of moderate hopes and considerable disappointments, of rising prices at home and risen tempers abroad. The pound was devalued and rearmament begun, and one after another Korea, the Suez Canal, Persia and Tunisia became centres either of war or of acrimonious dispute, while the whole world hung fearfully on the lightest words spoken in Washington or Moscow.

Those words were carried to every nation by radio and newspaper as soon as they were uttered, and there was no part of the earth's surface where a man could shut his ears against them. The air rang with threats and counter threats, with accusations and insults. Judging from what the members of the victorious alliance of 1945 said of each other, one would have guessed that the Governments of all of them were composed exclusively of thugs, murderers and liars.

Some writers found themselves heavily oppressed by this atmosphere, and few could entirely free themselves from its influence. As early as February 2, 1946, even before the flush of victory had quite faded, the French novelist, Julien Green, whose books show a strange insight into the phenomena of cruelty and hatred, noted in his diary that he saw no one who did not talk to him of a new age of catastrophes into which the world was moving. A few months later he observed that there is 'talk of an armaments race which will start a new war in five or ten years' time', and he added that 'when I read of such things I wonder what there is to make us cling to the world'. Another time he remarked, 'Either war or revolution is what the future offers us, according to daily rumours which I observe without really knowing whether to believe them or not. There is a shadow over us all. To begin a

B   I

new book is to place in tomorrow a confidence it may not deserve.'

M. Green, naturally, was not thinking all the time of war, though his fine mind habitually casts a somewhat gloomy light on most of the subjects that occupy his thoughts. He is ever concerned over the number of the Elect, which the Saints disturbingly considered to be small, and he is not really comforted by the reflection that the Saints may have been wrong. He thinks much too on the moral problems of creative authorship, and finds them a difficult matter. 'Desire', he says on one occasion, 'is the impure source whence one draws one's sombre and poetic novels, and if one tries to purify the source, then the novels stop coming.' This is a question as close to his heart as the possibility of war, and one day the two themes unite. 'There is one inescapable fact', he asserts. 'I no longer wish to write a novel. What does this imply? Perhaps I am discouraged by the threat of war. But there is always this threat, even if the war doesn't come. . . . But there is something else: to fight against himself paralyses the imagination of the novelist, for the simple reason that the novelist's talent has its roots in sin, I do not say in a life of sin, but in the idea of sin.' And then he repeats, 'The source of the novel is impure'.

The idea that the creative impulse is allied to evil is not uncommon in European, especially in recent European, literature. It is one with which Thomas Mann, for example, has particularly identified himself, from his earliest short stories to the immense, discursive, ill-arranged, and powerful *Doctor Faustus*, whose theme is that artistic inspiration in its origin, even when it manifests itself in hymns to God, is literally devilish.

For reasons perhaps of political exemption, contemporary English literature is less troubled in spirit than that of the Continent. No foreign occupation has driven us to morbid introspection, or put into us the constant fear of accusation and death, whilst the bombing we endured was relatively mild. Recent English drama is not of the searchingly questioning kind, and it does not much manifest that distrust of art which is found in the work both of Mann and Green. It is however touched on in Emlyn Williams's *Accolade* (Aldwych, September, 1950), a circumstance that brings this play, though it is only a melodrama, into some sort of connexion with the distressed, probing drama of the Continent.

Mr. Williams's hero was a famous novelist, Will Trenting.

Trenting the Tramp, he is fond of calling himself in an unnecessarily playful phrase. Trenting's studies of vicious low life have won him the admiration of the cultured, and when the curtain rises he has been awarded the Nobel Prize, and is about to be knighted. But at this point it is discovered that Trenting's knowledge of evil is not only realistic but real. He not only writes about parties in Thames-side public houses where people take off their clothes: he goes to them; and at one of these he seduces an apparently mature girl who turns out to be under age. Blackmail follows, and after blackmail, exposure. There are unsavoury details in the newspapers, and the play ends with Trenting adopting a defiant attitude as a crowd of angry moralists throws stones through his Hampstead windows.

Mr. Williams told this story as we should expect: that is, with a full realisation of its dramatic excitement. Nothing could be tenser than the moment when Trenting learned with a freezing of the blood that the buxom young woman he had taken into a corner was really a schoolgirl; nor more thrilling than the second encounter with the blackmailer, when this man decided that what he wanted was not money, but prosecution; nor more finely and delicately handled than Trenting's confession to his son. Except in one instance (Anthony Nicholls's performance of Trenting's publisher), the play was finely acted. Mr. Williams himself had immense forensic force as Trenting, even though, in abandoning the sinister, he sometimes bordered on the immature, his face too smooth despite the greying hair; Mr. Noel Willman was skilfully disturbing as the cultured blackmailer with ambition but no talent, and John Cavanagh first-rate as the boy.

What the play surprisingly, and in the end, fatally, lacked was the sense of evil. It was hidden from Will Trenting that vice is vicious. Here is his defence of himself to his publisher, Thane Lampeter:

THANE: But your interest in this—you're not pretending it's healthy? (*Sitting, on the sofa*).

WILL: Definitely sordid. Didn't you once say everybody has one vice? It looks as if this is mine.

THANE: Go on.

WILL: Well, from the age of sixteen, I have been drawn towards promiscuous sex.

THANE: Towards loose women?

WILL: Women who will lean over in public and make an improper suggestion to men they've never met. And if the men look the women straight in the eye, wink, and order drinks all round, my heart warms to the men. Rowdy, communal, unblushing . . . sex—I'm sorry, but I'm fascinated by it. (*Catching Thane's eye*) Let's talk about existentialism . . .

THANE: Do you believe that the life you lead is right?

WILL (*carefully*): I believe that the life I lead is right, for me.

Later, to his wife, he says, 'And I *have* a conscience, about money, and loyalty and all that—you've often told me I had too many scruples. . . . But I've never felt that any of *this* was really wrong.'

Will Trenting, in fact, had no sense of spiritual perplexity or distress. Thomas Mann says of his Tonio Kruger that 'good work comes out only under pressure of a bad life'. This is an argument of which Mr. Williams was very fond in this play, and it is true enough that Burns drank more than he should, and Maupassant died disgracefully, and Proust had some reprehensible habits. But much can be said on the other side. What crimes did Wordsworth commit in the Lakes? Did Hardy rob the church poor box, and what were the misdemeanours of Jane Austen? There is however one word in Mann's phrase that cannot be gainsaid, and that word is 'pressure'. That good work, even the finest work, can come out of virtue as well as out of vice can be argued, but not that it doesn't come out of strain and stress of the spirit. 'Where did you find those colours?' someone asked the painter Opie in the old story. 'In Hell' was the reply.

Hell Will Trenting had never visited. Nowhere in this play did Mr. Williams show that what matters to the artist is not experience, but his own reaction to experience. And also his reaction from that reaction. One cannot believe that Trenting got great books out of his experiences, because those experiences did not disturb the placid surface of his soul. Mr. Williams may reply that he was telling a story, not exploring a character. But if he had explored the character, his story would not only have been admirably told, but also worth telling.

Since *Accolade* was about an author it not unnaturally contained frequent references to literature. Will Trenting's little boy had an infallible flair for crises, and even the most stupid members of the audience could easily tell which were the tensest moments in the play, because the climax of each act was plainly marked by this youngster's dashing in and asking, 'Do you think *Bleak House* is better than *Great Expectations?*' or something about *Macbeth.* It was in a literary manner that Will Trenting, at the time of his proposal, was said to have alluded to his double nature. 'Dr. Jekyll is anxious to marry you if you'll have him, but Mr. Hyde insists on being at the wedding.'

But though it talks much of literature, *Accolade* did not, like T. S. Eliot's *The Cocktail Party* (Edinburgh, Lyceum, August, 1949: Brighton, Royal, January, 1950: London, New, May, 1950), aspire to be literature. Its style might be called economical, or more honestly bald. Now Mr. Eliot himself in the drama also favours a style not too highly ornamented. The dazzling Mr. George Jean Nathan tells us for example that Eliot said of Christopher Fry, 'If the young man wants to be a poet, he must first learn to be less poetical'.

It is a lesson that has not come to Mr. Eliot himself as easily as many people suppose who too readily accept him as erudition's incomprehensible mouthpiece. There are moments when Eliot is as obviously poetic as the *Golden Treasury*. His

> Where the walls
> Of Magnus Martyr hold
> Inexplicable splendour of Ionian white and gold

rubs shoulders with Tennyson.

The tinkling Humbert Wolfe would have recognised poetry in

> The voice returns like the insistent out-of-tune
> Of a broken violin on an August afternoon:

and the romantic author of the second act of *Perchance to Dream* would hardly have been puzzled by

> Now that lilacs are in bloom
> She has a bowl of lilacs in her room.

The text of *The Cocktail Party* had none of this all-apparent magic. It discarded the singing robe and ignored the incantation. But without wholly being poetry, it created the effect of poetry. For an element in poetry is rhyme, which is a sort of echo: and the

play, even in its superficially trivial opening small talk, was full
of strange echoes, not of other poets, which is Eliot's customary
trick, but of itself. Consider this early passage, in the afternoon
party at Edward Chamberlayne's house, just after Edward's wife
Lavinia has left him.

ALEX: Delia Verinder?
  Was she the one who had three brothers?
JULIA: How many brothers? Two, I think.
ALEX: No, there were three, but you wouldn't know the third one:
  They kept him rather quiet.
JULIA: Oh, you mean *that* one.
ALEX: He was feeble-minded.
JULIA: Oh, not feeble-minded:
  He was only harmless.
ALEX: Well then, harmless.
JULIA: He was very clever at repairing clocks;
  And he had a remarkable sense of hearing—
  The only man I ever met who could hear the cry of bats.
PETER: Hear the cry of bats?
JULIA: He could hear the cry of bats.
CELIA: But how do you know he could hear the cry of bats?
JULIA: Because he said so. And I believed him.
CELIA: But if he was so . . . harmless, how could you believe him?
  He might have imagined it.
JULIA: My darling Celia,
  You needn't be so sceptical. I stayed there once
  At their castle in the North. How he suffered!
  They had to find an island for him
  Where there were no bats.

M. Green in his *Journal* says that ever since his childhood he has
been trying to discover and recognise the exact moment after one
has laid one's head upon the pillow when sleep comes. His efforts
now have been going on for more than forty years, and they have
never succeeded. Somehow that second when unconsciousness
lays its grip upon him always steals in unnoticed. There is a similar moment when one passes at the play from comparative indifference to absorbed interest, and often it is easier to isolate this
instant of transition from, as it were, sleep to waking than that
other from waking to sleep. At the first performance of *The
Cocktail Party* at Edinburgh in 1949, when Henry Sherek managed

the British theatrical side of the Festival, I can vividly remember the moment of this happening, when for the first time the play put a hold upon the imagination, and I knew that the evening was going to be memorable. It was when Cathleen Nesbitt as the supposedly gossipy and feather-brained Julia began to talk about the cry of bats. There stole over the theatre the feeling of something beyond the plain meaning of the words uttered, and one could hear in the far distance the faint whirring of obscene, dark wings.

This sense of vague disquiet should have warned even that first unaccustomed audience that *The Cocktail Party*, in spite of its lounge suits, its tinkling glasses, its gossip and its wit, was not another of those trifling comedies about maladjusted people who solve their problems by unburdening themselves to a psychiatrist. Edward Chamberlayne, a middle-aged barrister, fancied himself in love with a young woman, Celia Coplestone, but when his wife, on the afternoon of the party, left him, he discovered that this love did not amount to very much. He did not love his wife much, either: Edward, in fact, was incapable of really loving anybody. He was too centred in himself, too concerned with the convolutions of his own mediocrity to desire passionately the happiness of another. An interview with a psychiatrist, Sir Henry Harcourt Reilly, in the company of the returned Lavinia, soon put him more or less right. Lavinia, too, was not a deep or complex character. A few penetrating words from Reilly restored them, without great difficulty, to a marital road of jog-trot give-and-take.

The Edinburgh audience inclined to regard this anecdote as the substance of the play, whereas Eliot used it only as a means of off-setting, by its clever triviality, the depth and splendour of his real theme, which was martyrdom. Besides Edward and Lavinia, Reilly had another patient, Celia Coplestone: and she was quite different from these indifferents. Towards her Reilly's conduct was in some ways puzzling: it was both directive and aloof. He told her where to go, and at the same time he did not seem to know where she was going. He says to Julia (an inexplicable feature of the Edinburgh production was that Julia, the fluffy-headed, turned up in Reilly's Harley Street office as a uniformed nurse):

And when I say to one like her
'Work out your salvation with diligence', I do not understand
What I myself am saying.

Yet Reilly's conduct was such that Mr. Eliot, having already written *Murder in the Cathedral*, might at the first glance have called this play 'Murder in the Consulting Room.'

For it is certain that had not Sir Henry Reilly placed before Celia Coplestone, as an alternative to a commonplace, usefully happy life, the possibility of dedication to a high and perilous ideal, she would never have gone out into the wild places of the earth, and been crucified by fanatical natives, and devoured by ants. It is equally certain that when a doctor like Sir Henry, whose professional duty it is to know the character of those with whom he is dealing, indicates a course of conduct that may lead to pain and death, he cannot acquit himself of responsibility for the consequences. And it is certain that Sir Henry had no desire to be acquitted of this responsibility.

Sir Henry did not exactly despise (and we may suppose that Mr. Eliot does not exactly despise) the unambitious, spiritually compromising life that most of us live. Indeed, he said to Celia,

The form of treatment must be your own choice.
I cannot choose for you. If that is what you wish,
I can reconcile you to the human condition,
The condition to which some who have gone as far as you
Have succeeded in returning. They may remember
The vision they have had, but they cease to regret it,
Maintain themselves by the common routine,
Learn to avoid excessive expectation,
Become tolerant of themselves and others,
Giving and taking, in the usual actions
What there is to give and take. They do not repine;
Are contented with the morning that separates
And with the evening that brings together
For casual talk before the fire
Two people who know they do not understand each other,
Breeding children whom they do not understand
And who will never understand them.
CELIA: Is that the best life?
REILLY: It is a good life. Though you will not know how good
   Till you come to the end. But you will want nothing else

And the other life will be only like a book
You have read once, and lost. In a world of lunacy,
Violence, stupidity, greed . . . It is a good life.

But there is another kind of life, as Sir Henry says:

There *is* another way, if you have the courage. . . .
The second is unknown, and so requires faith.
The kind of faith that issues from despair.
The destination cannot be described:
You will know very little until you get there;
You will journey blind. But the way leads towards possession
Of what you have sought for in the wrong place.
CELIA: That sounds like what I want. But what is my duty?
REILLY: Whichever way you choose will prescribe its own duty.
CELIA: Which way is better?
REILLY: Neither way is better.
Both ways are necessary.

Reilly, it seems, and with him Mr. Eliot, tries to preserve a
strict impartiality. He does not urge upon Celia the higher,
braver course. He does not say that it is to be wished for rather
than the other. But the undertones of his speech, the rhythm of it,
the vague contempt in the first description, and the heightened
feeling of the second, show that in his heart Mr. Eliot thinks
that the way of martyrdom is the true but terrible prerogative
of the rarer spirits.

That first performance at Edinburgh was a very fine one. It did
in fact constitute one of the greatest evenings spent in a British
theatre since the end of the 1939–45 war. But *The Cocktail Party*
is not at any time an easy play, still less so at a first hearing, and at
a first performance, and there is no question that when the curtain fell for the last time many people in the audience had not
grasped Mr. Eliot's conception of martyrdom, and looked for the
main significance of the piece in the story of the Chamberlaynes.

Partly this was Mr. Eliot's fault. For he had written the
Chamberlaynes' part of the play extremely well. His dissection of
human weakness is as merciless, as finely accurate, and as malicious
as Jane Austen's. Miss Austen herself could not more neatly or
completely bring off a double deflation of a character than Reilly
when he dealt with Edward's alternate abasement and conceit.

EDWARD: But I am obsessed by the thought of my own insignificance.

REILLY: Precisely. And I could make you feel important,
And you would imagine it a marvellous cure;
And you would go on, doing such amount of mischief
As lay within your power—until you came to grief.
Half of the harm that is done in this world
Is due to people who want to feel important.
They don't mean to do harm—but the harm does not interest them,
Or they do not see it, or they justify it
Because they are absorbed in the endless struggle
To think well of themselves.

This was not what Edward had been expecting, and for a
moment he was taken aback. But he recovers, and one can almost
see his pride swelling as he begins to recognise himself as a villain
on quite a large scale.

EDWARD: If I am like that
I must have done a great deal of harm.

But Reilly does not allow him this considerable consolation,
but quietly knocks him down a second time with

(REILLY): Oh, not so much as you would like to think.
Only, shall we say, within your modest capacity.

Reilly is equally subtle and equally penetrating in dealing with
Mrs. Chamberlayne; and it was a heroic thing to watch the lovely,
almost Indian stillness of Miss Ursula Jeans's face as he planted in
her his arrows of precise perception.

The supreme excellence of the Chamberlayne scenes helped to
concentrate interest in the wrong place, and this was accentuated
by Robert Flemyng's remarkable performance as Edward.
Throughout the first act I was greatly moved by Mr. Flemyng's
beautifully judged presentation of a wronged husband. There
were some lovely cadences in his grave voice, and a slight jerkiness
of speech was in keeping with the subdued distress of a man
harassed to the point of breakdown. The play was more than half
over before one realised that Mr. Flemyng was running superbly
down the wrong course. For Edward is not a wronged husband.
He is, on the contrary, a shallow fellow incapable of virtue, and
the sincerity with which Mr. Flemyng invested him was as
inappropriate as the same quality in Iago.

Such were the positive influences that led the Edinburgh audiences into locating inaccurately the centre of gravity of *The Cock-*

tail Party. There were others of a negative kind. Sir Henry Harcourt Reilly is a difficult part, and it took Mr. Alec Guinness some time to solve the problems involved in it. Its central difficulty was this: if the drama is to be kept on an even keel Reilly must dominate the play, but a cardinal point in Mr. Eliot's philosophy is that he must not dominate the other characters. These have to make their own choice in life: they are not to be ordered about by Reilly. Whilst Reilly must hold the centre of the stage, he has equally to avoid the impression of being another Stranger in the Third Floor Back, with quiet but masterful fingers pulling the strings of his puppets. At Edinburgh Mr. Guinness avoided the second mistake, but he did not dominate the play. His whimsicalness in the first act had a Lob-like quality; he wandered in on the party unannounced from some land of humorous yet wise magic; and when he walked off, twirling his cane, and singing,

> As I was drinkin' gin and water,
>   And me bein' the One-Eyed Riley,
> Who came in but the landlord's daughter
>   And she took my heart entirely,

his jaunty, easy, quizzical manner fitted the preposterous song at once into the pattern of a realistic afternoon party and some beerhouse ritual of immemorial folklore. Even so, this act remained the powerful and mistakenly honourable Mr. Flemyng's; and in the second, when Edward's weaknesses were no longer able to be concealed, Mr. Guinness wanted authority.

This was at Edinburgh. When the play was put on for a fortnight at Brighton, before the company was taken for a triumphant visit to New York, Mr. Guinness's performance had matured. We knew how to rate Edward at his proper value, and in the second act Mr. Guinness was splendidly smooth, suave, and mysterious.

There still remained another difficulty. A new actor, Mr. Grey Blake, was brought into the company. Mr. Blake had the part of Peter Quilpe, a film scenario writer who is the only other character in the play built from the same metal as Celia Coplestone. Mr. Blake tended to utter his longer speeches as if they were recitations, but he did something that was not so much as suggested at Edinburgh: with great lightness of touch and apparent ease he communicated Mr. Eliot's difficult conception that

Quilpe is not a saint but has the quality of a saint in him, and yet is acceptable at Bloomsbury cocoa parties. When he talked, half-musingly, like a man exploring his own thoughts and experiences, of the peace that his love for Celia Coplestone brings to him, he established in the theatre a tranquillity that marked him out as an actor to be watched with lively interest.

But there was Celia Coplestone herself. Celia is the climax of Mr. Eliot's play. She is its supreme spiritual figure. And the truth is that Mr. Eliot manages Celia's spirituality far less consummately than the Chamberlaynes' futility. In her vital scene in the consulting-room her speeches are pharisaical; Celia is all the time smugly announcing that she is not as the other patients are. She does not, like them, pity herself nor blame her friends; she not only realises this, but talks about it. The impression left is not of righteousness, but of self-righteousness, and Miss Irene Worth, who played Celia, had not got it in her to cover up the deficiencies in Mr. Eliot's writing.

Miss Margaret Leighton, on the other hand, had, as she showed when *The Cocktail Party* was presented in London with a different company. This actress, one of the loveliest on the English stage, tall and sensuously supple, suggests a latent and sultry fascination better than most of her rivals can simulate a cold in the head. But spiritual distinction I would not have supposed, greatly as I admire her, to be within her range. Yet apparently it is. Mr. Eliot talked about, he wandered round, but he did not create saintliness, and Miss Leighton did. Maybe she accomplished it by the expression, the wan, searching, dedicated look upon her face; at any rate, the self-righteousness of which I have complained was wholly lacking from her performance.

Unfortunately Mr. Rex Harrison's Reilly was less good than Mr. Guinness's. We did not expect that it would come, like Guinness's, from the edge of fairyland, but Mr. Harrison's previous performances afforded reason for thinking it would suggest the best public schools. Yet it surprisingly lacked assurance, and when Mr. Harrison came to his little song, he seemed actually embarrassed.

To sum up: none of the performances of the play was perfect, and all had merits of the highest and rarest kind. On the whole, the most satisfying was that at Brighton.

Chapter Two

FRY: ANOUILH

WHEN he wrote *Venus Observed* (produced by Sir Laurence Olivier at the St. James's in February, 1950) Christopher Fry had certainly not learnt Eliot's lesson. Verbally the play was as brilliant as *The Lady's Not for Burning*. Diamonds shone out of every line: its glitter was such that it ought to have been read with dark glasses. It ransacked the heavens for similes as unexpected as the flash of lightning in a clear sky: 'I've a heart this morning as light as a nebula', says Reedbeck, the Duke of Altair's volubly dishonest bailiff, when he finds that his daughter Perpetua is coming home from America for the first time for many years. With a phrase, 'Equality is a mortuary word', the Duke, urbane, basking agreeably in the paling sunshine of late middle age, momentarily persuaded us that he had coffined the *Rights of Man* and the Declaration of Independence together. 'A blinding snowstorm of virginity': 'the leaves transfigured by the thought of death': 'over the mouldering rafters of the world' —the phrases fell illimitably out of God's plenty. Occasionally the verbal play, though exhausted, shammed inexhaustibility, and Fry, his brain uninspired but still tinkling with echoes, would talk of some such things as 'coruscating on thin ice'. But there were remarkably few of these counterfeits in a mint of true coinage.

When Sir Laurence Olivier commissioned him to write *Venus Observed*, Fry was still living in the tiny labourer's cottage on the edge of a farm just outside Shipton-under-Wychwood to which he had moved his family at the beginning of the 1939 war. The cottage, built of the enduring grey Cotswold stone, with uneven floors, looks out on to rough cobblestones, grass-grown and littered with wisps of straw. Its small spaces, like Mr. Fry's verse, are packed tight with romantic detail. There are odd pieces of porcelain, and gleaming old brass shines out of dark corners, there are ancient, rusty playbills on the walls, and the time is told by

13

immensely complicated and ingenious clocks under glass cases, clocks in which gaily plumaged birds dart out of luscious foliage to sing, and waterfalls glitter across brown, Victorian rocks. In these crowdedly picturesque surroundings, in which one can scarcely move without tripping over some palpably romantic reminiscence, Fry's fancy is nurtured. But it is in a study that he has built at the back of the cottage, a study in which he often writes from midnight until dawn, that this fancy shapes itself into the organised images he puts on paper. This room, with its hundreds of books and its writing-desk, is as neat and tidy as the others are gloriously spreadeagled. And it looks out across a level field of grass to an immense and empty and serene horizon. It is absolutely peaceful, and perhaps under the peace there is a slight tremor of apprehension, because of the vastness, and because one seems to be on the threshold of peering over the world's edge into unknown things.

Here Mr. Fry quite clearly, and in uninterrupted inspiration, saw the first act of his play: the scene, a room at the top of a mansion, once a bedroom, and now an observatory; the characters, a culturedly autumnal Duke, and three of his former mistresses, one of whom he intends to marry, the choice being made by his young son, Edgar, who is to present an apple to the fortunate lady when they are all gathered together for a total eclipse of the sun. At the first crisis of the play there enters Reedbeck's daughter, Perpetua, fresh from America, and both the Duke and his son fall in love with her. So much Mr. Fry saw in one continuous vision, which then faded. After that he had vague notions of something grouped round a decaying temple in a garden, but for a long time nothing more came to him. He did, in fact, complete another work for the stage before he could visualise the second and third acts of *Venus Observed*—the burning down of the Duke's house, the escape of the Duke and Perpetua through the window, and, under the light of Japanese lanterns in the gardens, the Duke's graceful surrender of Perpetua to his son.

Mr. Fry's scintillation of phrase early in his career won recognition, but a second characteristic, his deliberate bathos, was not so quickly appreciated. In one of the *Ego* volumes there is a lively correspondence between James Agate and the author of *A Phoenix too Frequent*, in which Fry did not really succeed in convincing

my brilliant predecessor on *The Sunday Times* that his descents
from Pegasus in that play were intentional. But Agate, I believe,
never saw a Fry play staged, and Mr. Fry's method is more clearly
recognised in acting than in reading. In *Venus Observed* it was
as strikingly employed as it was in *The Lady's Not for Burning*.
In the earlier play, in the old Chaplain who suddenly, to his
chuckling delight, realised that he understood Greek, Fry created a
character who speaks to our hearts more warmly than any in
Venus Observed. But I do not recall a passage even in *The Lady's
Not for Burning* in which the dazzling descent from the inspired to
the colloquial is made with such unruffled craftsmanship as in the
brief conversation of the Duke with the most vulgar and amiable
of his mistresses on the subject of the moon's part in the eclipse.

JESSIE: To think
  We're in the shadow of old Lunabella.
DUKE: To think.
JESSIE: When she moves over will she see us
  Coming out of her shadow? Are we really
  As bright as a moon, from the moon's side of the question?
DUKE: We have a borrowed brilliance. At night
  Among the knots and clusters and corner boys
  Of the sky, among asteroids and cepheids,
  With Sirius, Mercury, and Canis Major,
  Among nebulae and magellanic cloud,
  You shine, Jessie.
JESSIE: You're making me self-conscious.
DUKE: Here we're as dull as unwashed plates, out there
  We shine. That's a consideration. Come
  Close to paradise, and where's the lustre?
  But still, at some remove, we shine, and truth
  We hope is content to keep a distant prospect.
  So you, Jessie, and the swamps of the equator,
  Shine; the boring overplus of ocean,
  The Walworth Road, the Parthenon, and Reedbeck
  Shine, the dark tree with the nightingale
  At heart, dockyards, the desert, the newly dead,
  Minarets, gasometers, and even I
  Fall into space in one not unattractive
  Beam. To take us separately is to stare
  At mud; only together, at long range,
  We coalesce in light.

JESSIE: I like to think I'm being
A ray of light to some nice young couple out there.
'There's the Great Bear', they'd say, and 'Look,
There's old Jessie, tilted on her side
Just over the Charing Cross Hotel'.

This is a brilliant passage: and with feeling, too, both in the Duke's gentle teasing and in Jessie's kindly vulgarity.

Phrasing and designed bathos, however, are only means to an end. That end is the total impression that Mr. Fry intended *Venus Observed* to make. Time and again Mr. Fry stated that impression in a single speech, as when the Duke says,

I have to consider my years and decline with the sun,
Gracefully but gratefully decline:

and again

We're not, I hope, in this mellow October light
Getting ill at ease? We're here this morning to watch
The sun annulled and renewed and to sit affectionately
Over the year's dilapidation. 'Mellow'
Is the keynote of the hour. We must be mellow,
Remembering we've been on the earth two million years,
Man and boy, and Skerfontein ape.

'How bitter it is when youth is ended', exclaims de Ciz in *Partage de Midi*. There is no bitterness in *Venus Observed*, no struggle against the ripening process of time. But in it youth and summer are ending: it is a play of autumn.

We knew this at its first performance, with Sir Laurence as the Duke, George Relph as Reedbeck, Denholm Elliott as Edgar, and Heather Stannard as Perpetua. We knew it, but I doubt if we felt it, and in the theatre what we feel is more important than what we know. Sir Laurence watched life go by, with a sardonic air of quizzical amusement; his hair was greying, his moustache also, and there was a little stiffness, a brief suggestion of the ghost of sciatica, in his movements. There was perhaps, despite these things, more of September in him than of October; and there was not the least hint of pathos in the quiet irony, the beautiful grace of the tones in which he spoke Fry's verse. Miss Stannard had an enormous speech to make without taking breath, and she managed it like a virtuoso; it was a rare achievement, and the first night audience rightly burst into applause when it was finished. But simpler things have stirred me more. Roger Furse's scenery was superb, his telescope stared magistrally at the skies, and his garden temple had the patina of years upon it.

Is it possible that this partial disappointment was because Mr. Fry sowed his pearls too thickly? His imagination is so fecund, his head so stored with picturesque figures, he can so easily lay his hand on one shimmering phrase after another that it would hardly be surprising if he were tempted to produce a glittering series of isolated effects instead of a total feeling. His difficulty is always to make these flashing facets into a steady illumination. Not many of the greatest writers are so continuously brilliant. There are acres of dullness in Hardy, but they become at last integral parts of the Hardy landscape. People who, like Chesterton, make every phrase tell find at the end of their books that they have told little. One misses the pattern by too much ornamenting the detail.

This detail in Fry has been universally praised, but not even it has been appraised by everyone equally. All have admitted its brilliance, its curious learning, and its wit. But its claim to be poetry has been so widely challenged that Mr. Fry (the most good-humoured man in the world) has himself asked whether the question of nomenclature matters very much. Why not, he says, call his particular style 'sliced prose'? One objection to doing so is that this description would apply more accurately to the plays of other poets, to, for example, *The Cocktail Party* and *Partage de Midi*. The writing of Eliot and Claudel is simpler, less highly charged, less decorated than Fry's, more, in fact, like good 'sliced prose'. The taste of Fry's is heightened by all manner of succulent additions. If he insists on the phrase, it must be amended to 'spiced sliced prose'.

Mr. Fry's good-tempered offer to his detractors is generous, because the verdict in the end is bound to go in his favour. The notions of what constitutes poetry have in the last twenty-five years been considerably widened, or rather they have returned to the breadth of view that in the seventeenth century could include Donne as well as Spenser in the list of poets. It is still demanded that poetry should provoke the shiver of delight as well as the dazzle of admiration, but that shiver nowadays is the response to

C

stimuli that would have puzzled Palgrave. I do not see how it can be denied to the several passages I have quoted, or to this, the Duke's last self-communing talk to the drowsy Reedbeck, after the fire had been put out, and everyone else has gone to bed:

DUKE: Shall I be happy for myself?
In the name of existence I'll be happy for myself.
Why, Reedbeck, how marvellous it is to moulder.
Think how you would have felt when you were lying
Grubbing in your mother's womb,
With only a wall to look at,
If you could have seen in your embryonic eye
The realm of bryony, sloes, rose-hips,
And a hedge's ruin, a golden desuetude,
A countryside like a drowned angel
Lying in shallow water, every thorn
Tendering a tear. Think, Reedbeck,
Think of the wonder of such glimmering woe;
How in a field of milk-white haze the lost
Apollo glows, and wanders towards the moon;
The wind-blown webs are brighter,
The rolling apples warmer than the sun.
Heavens! you would have cried, the womb
Echoing round you: These are the heavens, and I,
Reedbeck, am stillborn. Would you not?
REEDBECK (*waking slightly*): And the Duchesse de Condé, I think.
DUKE: So with ourselves; imagine; to have the sensation
Of nearness of sight, shortness of breath,
Palpitation, creaking in the joints,
Shootings, stabbings, lynching of the limbs,
A sudden illumination of lumbago.
What a rich world of sensation to achieve,
What infinite variety of being.

This is no laboured warming up of dishes that have been served before in other poets' kitchens. It is a window thrown open on the world for the first time, stirring the imagination to explorations not yet thought of. If there was any lack of full communication at the first performance of *Venus Observed*, it may have been partly due to the coldness of Miss Stannard's Perpetua, to the guardedly ladylike presentation of some of the Duke's mistresses, even to Mr. Fry's prodigality of fancy, keeping the attention of

his audience uncomfortably taut—what it was not in any
measure due to was Fry's shortcomings as a poet. Those simply
do not exist.

His footing as a *dramatic* poet, however, is less sure. One of the
Duke's mistresses (Rosabel Fleming, she who burns down his
house, and ultimately marries him) accuses him of having no
feeling. When he tells her that she used to love the observatory
room at night, she replies tartly,

> How do you know?
> How can you tell who loves, or when or why they love,
> You without a single beat of heart
> Worth measuring?

The accusation was unjust. The Duke is no longer a young man,
and the heartbeats are slower than of yore. But they are still there.
Yet Mr. Fry does not always convince us of this. The Duke is
ready, like Richard II, to take any thought or feeling tossed up by
circumstances, and make of it a rather fine poem. A remark of
Rosabel's, for example, suggests to him:

> So Rosabel believes when the cold spell comes
> And we're compelled to enter this draughty time
> And shuffle about in the slipshod leaves,
> Leaves disbanded, leaves at a loose end,
> And we know we're in for the drifting of the fall,
> We should merely shiver and be silent: never speak
> Of the climate of Eden, or the really magnificent
> Foliage of the tree of knowledge,
> Or the unforgettable hushed emerald
> Of the coiling and fettering serpent:
> Pretend we never knew it, because love
> Quite naturally condescended
> To the passing of time.

Similarly Aumerle's remark that Bolingbroke is increasing in
power at once fires Richard's poetic imagination.

> Discomfortable cousin! know'st thou not
> That when the searching eye of heaven is hid
> Behind the globe, that lights the lower world,
> Then thieves and robbers range abroad unseen
> In murders and in outrage, boldly here;
> But when from under this terrestrial ball

He fires the proud tops of the eastern pines
And darts his light through every guilty hole,
Then murders, treasons, and detested sins,
The cloak of night being pluck'd from off their backs,
Stand bare and naked, trembling at themselves?
So when this thief, this traitor, Bolingbroke,
Who all this while hath revell'd in the night
Whilst we were wandering with the antipodes,
Shall see us rising in our throne, the East,
His treasons will sit blushing in his face,
Not able to endure the sight of day,
But self-affrighted tremble at his sin.

It is plain that both Richard and the Duke have large imaginations. One of them turns naturally for synonyms and metaphors to the solar system, and the other goes back to the Garden of Eden. But whereas Richard immediately and definitely identifies himself with the sun, the connexion between the Garden of Eden and the Duke is only a graceful affectation. There is a passionate conjunction between the sun and Richard, whilst the Duke merely makes a few fine observations about the Garden. The one poetry is highly personalised and dramatic, the other detached and fanciful. Mr. Fry does not always, perhaps not often, transmute his poetry into his people.

The merits of Mr. Fry's *Venus Observed* were thrown into sharp relief a few nights later, when *Larger than Life* (Duke of York's, February, 1950) reached London. *Larger than Life* was an adaptation by Guy Bolton of Somerset Maugham's *Theatre*, and its theme had affinities with *Venus Observed*. Both plays dallied with the amorous preoccupations of glamorous creatures who identify the first breath of middle age with the chill wind of waning physical attractiveness. Mr. Maugham's Julia Lambert, an actress, moved in a world as artificial and unreal as that of Mr. Fry's Duke, and on the first night of the second play I was interested to ponder why *Venus Observed*, despite some weaknesses, was a delightful and civilised entertainment, whilst the first part of *Larger than Life* was rankly offensive.

Julia Lambert, as I have said, was an actress. She was a leading lady of long standing who had been divorced from her husband, but continued to live with him partly because he was invaluable to her in the business management of her career, and partly because their reputation as the Darby and Joan of the British theatre was good for business.

Now, at forty odd or so, Miss Lambert became professionally alarmed, and looked round for reassurance that her bodily charm had not vanished. Whereas, at some such crisis, Fry's Duke proposed with airy grace to subside into marriage, Miss Lambert decided for a night to go on the streets, hoping to restore her confidence by finding that she had a reasonable market value still. Where the Duke showed, lightly and amusingly, a glancing knowledge of that vast, complex culture that has descended to us from the Greeks, the Hebrews, and the Renaissance, Julia Lambert appeared to believe that one of the most famous sayings of Jesus was an old proverb, as she called it, on which it was seemly to make an obvious jest.

Whereas the Duke talked gaily and with ease of love as something linked with and enriching all the other aspects of human life, Julia Lambert discussed it, with maddening reiteration, and a Basic English vocabulary, as if it were as separable from all else, and as negotiable, as a slab of meat on a butcher's hook. In the one play the characters had bright wits and sharp imaginations; in the other, not. The difference was in quality of mind.

Though everyone round me seemed to be having a glorious time, I felt I was in for a miserable evening, until halfway through the play improved. Indeed, when Michael Gosselyn, her former husband, had left Julia, and she was coping alone with a difficult new production, when she annihilated a young chit of an actress as unpleasant as herself, when before the curtain she gained a professional, and behind it a domestic, triumph, there were moments approaching liveliness.

Once there was something more. In the company was Laurence Naismith, a middle-aged, stocky little actor who, every few years, emerges briefly from obscurity, proceeds in a short scene to act everybody else off the stage, and then vanishes from view. In *Larger than Life* he was an old actor turned butler, and, when Julia was about to throw up the sponge, he revived her with an anecdote of Henry Irving on the night of his death, the moral of which, of course, was the platitude that at all costs the show must go on, the actor must never disappoint his public, never say

die, and so on and so forth. Nothing could be more trite. But Mr.
Naismith told his anecdote as if he believed it; you could have
sworn that Irving really was in that old man's mind that evening,
and that there had been something in Irving's behaviour that had
lit in it a flame of courage. A couple of years before, in Clifford
Odets's *Rocket to the Moon*, Mr. Naismith brought off a similar
small miracle. He should be seen oftener.

The end of the play was remarkable. The American leading
lady, Jessie Royce Landis, had come over to England with only a
middling reputation, but it was evident as the evening wore on
that her enormous vigour and energy were making a considerable
impression on the gallery. When the curtain came down for the
last time the roar of applause for Miss Landis was memorable, and
she was moved by its outstanding warmth. It was a response
to that quality which carried Dickens over so many dangerous
places—vitality—rather than to any particular skill or subtlety;
but that Miss Landis that night had a popular triumph cannot be
denied.

The play which Christopher Fry completed whilst waiting for
the idea of the second act of *Venus Observed* to dawn on him was
an adaptation of Jean Anouilh's *L'Invitation au Château*, which,
under the title of *Ring Round the Moon*, and directed by Peter
Brook, came to the Globe Theatre in February, 1950, a week after
the production of *Venus Observed*.

The presentation of *Ring Round the Moon* marked a turning-
point in M. Anouilh's fortunes in England. Sir Laurence Olivier
and Vivien Leigh had played in his greatly heralded *Antigone* for
the Old Vic a year or two before: its severity had won a rather
cold admiration. Later an adaptation of *Roméo et Jeannette*
at the Duchess, called *Fading Mansions*, caused such English playgoers as went to see it to wonder what the Parisian fuss over
Anouilh was about. But *Ring Round the Moon*, with its fairy-
tale delicacy, with that astoundingly solemn and ridiculous tango
which Mr. Brook invented for it, with Oliver Messel's crystal
winter-garden setting, and Fry's enchanting phrases established
itself soon after its opening as likely to run for eighteen months:
and run for eighteen months it did, since it was not withdrawn
until September, 1951; and even then it was taking £1,500 a week.
It was *Ring Round the Moon* which introduced into British minds

the thought that modern French plays, besides being striking, intelligent, and uncompromising, could also be entertaining.

That thought has had remarkable results in the English theatre. For twenty years after 1918 the dominating foreign influence on the West End stage was American. In the early 1930's an effort was made to temper the wind blowing from the west by bringing to London some of the plays of Marcel Pagnol, which were extremely popular in Paris. The effort failed completely. The American supremacy was not even challenged. In the sphere of musical comedy, of course, it remains unchallenged still. But in the serious theatre American influence in Britain, within six years of the ending of the war, became only a shadow of the French.

Jean Anouilh was born on June 23, 1910, at Bordeaux. He entered an advertising business in Paris as a very young man, and there, he says, he 'learnt lessons in exact statement and in ingenuity which have stood him in place of poetic studies'. At nineteen he wrote some small pieces that have never been played, and married the actress Monelle Valentin, who was his leading lady until illness prevented her from playing any more. Though he has known hard times, he declares, with a suspicion of boasting, that he has always succeeded in avoiding journalism. In 1930 he wrote *Attila le Magnifique*, and in 1932 had his first stage success with *Le Bal des Voleurs* (produced in Britain in Birmingham and Edinburgh, 1951). Since then he has written *La Sauvage* (1934), *Le Voyageur sans Bagage* (1938: Old Vic, Bristol, September, 1951), *Le Rendezvous de Senlis* (1938: Edinburgh, August, 1951), *Léocadia* (1939), *Eurydice* (1941: Lyric, Hammersmith, 1950), *Antigone* (1942), *Roméo et Jeannette* (1946: Duchess, 1949), *L'Invitation au Château* (1948: Globe, 1950), *Ardèle* (1949: Vaudeville, 1951), *La Répétition* (1950), and *Colombe* (1951: New: 1951).

Anouilh has a charming Bordeaux shyness of manner, and a low, quiet voice. He is thin and dark, he stoops a little, and wears glasses that give him the air of a thoughtful undergraduate. He lives in a moderately large white villa at Neuilly, on the edge of the Bois de Boulogne, and has Jean Gabin for a neighbour. Though this house is only at the other end of the Avenue de la Grande Armée from the Arc de Triomphe, no journalists penetrate into it. In the autumn of 1950 I secured admission; but that,

I think, was because French is to me a means of self-expression rather than communication, and I doubt whether Anouilh, who treated me with a courteously puzzled surprise, clearly realised what my profession was. He told me of his admiration for Paul Scofield's performance in *Ring Round the Moon*, and that he wished Jean Servais were less hard ('dur') in *La Répétition* and had more of Scofield's grace; that English audiences accept the supernatural in the theatre more readily than the French (he thinks that what he calls, in one of his rare English phrases, the Gosst in *Hamlet*, has had a great effect on them); and that, if he could combine the contradictory geniuses of Shakespeare and Racine into a single work, he would be a happy man. He talked with a quiet nervousness, and often paused, and during these pauses he looked at me, out of solemn, dark eyes, as if wondering how a strange Englishman came to be interested in a French dramatist.

Anouilh's quietness is said to be deceptive, and his shyness can be a fury of self-isolation. During the rehearsals of *Colombe* journalists would gather outside the Atelier Theatre, hoping to have a word with him as he came out. But when the rehearsals were over, Anouilh would rush from the theatre, leap into his car, and drive off as if the police were after him. Inside the theatre, too, his behaviour was difficult. He insists on being present at all rehearsals of his plays, and his sarcasm can be very bitter. Because of it, during the rehearsals of *Colombe*, Mary Marquet, Michel Bouquet, Beauchamp, and Tonia Navar, all of them players of talent, resigned from the company.

The curious thing is that, although Anouilh attends all rehearsals, though he can easily, despite his customary gentleness, get into a mood in which he cares nothing for the feelings of those he is dealing with, and has definite ideas of how he wishes his pieces to be played, those wishes often are not carried out. In the French productions of his plays his most careful stage directions are frequently ignored, sometimes in a way that makes nonsense of his plot, sometimes so as gravely to impair its fantasy and charm.

I was in Paris when *La Répétition* was produced at the Marigny by the Madeleine Renaud-Jean-Louis Barrault company at the end of October, 1950. This was the week when the Korean war took a more serious turn with the intervention of the Chinese, but no shadow lay over M. Anouilh's play, which immediately began to fill the house to capacity and to take 600,000 francs a performance.

The play is in five acts, of which the first three, to adopt the author's celebrated classification, are *rose* and the last two *noir*. The opening scenes are excellent comedy, in which a family of the French nobility, in costumes of the court of Louis XV, rehearse a play of Marivaux's. Anouilh has written *La Répétition* in the style of Marivaux, so that it is impossible for anyone but a theatrical scholar to tell where Marivaux's lines end and Anouilh's begin. It is a comedy of intrigue, and the hero, the Count, is in love with the governess who plays one of the parts, a circumstance that annoys the Count's wife a little and his mistress very much. These scenes are presented in a sumptuous salon. Presently there is a plot against the governess, in which the Count's drunken friend, Hero, compromises her by entering her bedroom at night. This is the fourth act, and Anouilh's stage directions for it are precise. The bedroom is a small attic, and in front of a meagre fire Lucile, the governess, in her dressing-gown, dreams vaguely, flickeringly illuminated by the flames. I could hardly believe my eyes when the fourth act at the Marigny showed the same salon as we had seen in the first three, and I have not yet discovered how it is possible for a woman to lose her reputation by the mere fact of conversing with a man in a drawing room. I ventured to put this point to Anouilh, who replied with a patient smile, 'Ah, unity of scene, you know'.

I believe that *La Répétition* is one of the few Anouilh pieces to be presented in a fashionable theatre. Hitherto his plays, at least up to 1948, had been given in the Atelier, which is a sort of tabernacle that juts out into a dankly romantic square on the southern slope of Montmartre. There are trees round the Atelier, but their green is darker, their trunks are smokier than those in the Champs Elysées that surround the gay, the brightly painted Marigny, whose crimson and gold make it a worldly jewel among theatres. Yet it cannot be said that Anouilh, by this ignoring of his wishes, was justly punished for transferring himself from the theatre of the *avant-garde* to the prosperous boulevard. For the director of the Marigny is Jean-Louis Barrault. Wherever the McLean is, there is the head of the table; and the *avant-garde* is where Barrault is. In other words, in going to the Marigny, Anouilh had not deserted the *avant-garde*. He had merely moved with it.

If Barrault's neglect to provide *La Répétition* with a new set in the fourth act made the plot incomprehensible, some of the productions—largely, be it remembered, put on under the author's supervision—that André Barsacq had given Anouilh at the Atelier robbed his plays of much of their charm. Barsacq is a theatre director deserving of great respect. He took over the Atelier from Charles Dullin in 1940 and, without reducing the standard of playwriting there, he brought the theatre a popularity Dullin had never been able to win for it. He founded the Compagnie des Quatre Saisons, and gathered round him a company, including Maria Casarés and Robert Vattier, of great merit. Yet I am not putting the matter too strongly when I say that the production of *Le Bal des Voleurs* which he brought to the Edinburgh Festival of 1951 horrified me.

I am well aware that the standards of French production are different from ours. In Britain, as in the United States and in Germany, the theatre is regarded as a union of all the arts, and a presentation of such a play as *Ring Round the Moon* is something to which actors, author, director, musician, and scene designer contribute on more or less equal terms. This is a view of the theatre which, though to the London playgoing public it seems obvious enough to be banal, is vigorously repudiated by the best minds in Paris. The notion that the director's task is to interpret and to enrich what the author has written was wholly inacceptable to men who, like Giraudoux and Jouvet, have played no small part in the French theatre's recent glory. To them—and they represented the general Parisian view—the author has a unique importance in the theatre, and the director's duty is simply to serve him, not to serve him up.

French audiences go to the theatre, unlike the English and Americans who flock to the Casino de Paris, to hear rather than to see, and to talk rather than to hear. The consequence of this is that French players in general speak with extreme clarity, partly in order to cut through the buzz of conversation in the auditorium, and partly in accordance with the theory that the great crises of the heart and soul, as Giraudoux says, express themselves in words and not in claps of stage thunder. One of the things that most impressed Londoners about the Madeleine Renaud—Jean-Louis Barrault company when it made its visit to England in September, 1951, was the to us amazing clearness of its diction. With a French company the word is all-important.

With the word goes the gesture. The hands are extraordinarily expressive instruments of the French histrionic genius. The love scene between Mesa and Ysé in the second act of *Partage de Midi* in the Chinese cemetery, as it was played by M. Barrault and Mme Edwige Feuillère, reminded me of nothing so much as of the dazzling play of Sergeant Troy's sword round the motionless body of Fanny Robin in *Far from the Madding Crowd*. As the point of Troy's sword wove an invisible garment of steel round Fanny, so did M. Barrault's hands, flickering from the thighs to the shoulders over Mme Feuillère, swaying in ecstasy, clothe her in passion. English players, attempting to take the scene in this way, would become self-conscious; and self-consciousness brings ridicule. With Mme Feuillère and M. Barrault the effect was breathtaking.

To speaking, and to the auxiliaries of speaking, therefore, Parisian directors pay close attention. But to a degree to which I cannot accustom myself they neglect scenery and the stage grouping of characters. Now, in *Le Bal des Voleurs*, the grouping and movement of characters are of great importance, for the author describes the play as a Comédie-Ballet. It was as such that it was presented by the Birmingham Repertory Company in the spring of 1951, in a production in which several amusing little dances charmingly accentuated the mood of the play. That it was Anouilh's intention to have such dances is clear from the text, for in it he describes them with affectionate care. But it was equally clear at Edinburgh that M. Barsacq had not given them him, that his scenery was shabby, and that M. Barsacq's devotion to the sanctity of the word was such that silent scenes of great importance to the atmosphere of the play were entirely omitted. The most striking of these was that which precedes the love scene between the conscience-plagued thief and the enterprising young lady of the house. The entry of the servant into the drawing-room, the turning out of the lights in the grand chandelier, the closing of the windows, the sound of the departing motor-car, all these things that should soften and sentimentalise the atmosphere, were

missed out. The transition from the absurd farce of the disguised
thieves ridiculously cavorting on their way to the ball—the transition from this to the lightly troubled affection of Gustave's talk
with Juliette, became a sharp, unprepared break. I was, I say,
horrified. I cannot understand why Anouilh, who is so far from
accommodating on other points, permits it.

In contrast to what, in spite of my admiration both of the French
theatre and of M. Barsacq, I can only call this travesty of *Le Bal des
Voleurs*, Mr. Brook gave to *Ring Round the Moon* in London a
production as nearly perfect as one could desire. Everybody in it
had style: the old lady in her wheeled chair, with her fantastic re-
miniscences, had style: she had been ridiculous, but only in the
best society. The crumbling old butler, Joshua, had style: he had
served, with affectionate zeal, in the highest families. The conquering, gaily heartless Hugo had immense style: and the shy
brother, Frederick, in needing to have no style at all, had almost
more style than anyone. They were all preposterous, yet the universe with which Mr. Brook surrounded them was itself so preposterous, and so beautiful, that everything they did was beautifully right. They were all impossible: they were all inevitable.

The piece was excellently played by Margaret Rutherford as
the amiable dragon in the wheel-chair, by Claire Bloom as the
grave young ballet dancer whom Hugo invited to the ball without any thought that there she might lose her heart, and by Paul
Scofield in the double part of the dashing Hugo and his retiring,
gentle brother, Frederick. There was a scene in the third act in
which Mr. Scofield was particularly fine. Isabelle, the dancer,
is tired of the masquerade, and sick at heart at Hugo's treating her,
not as a human being, but as a player in the comedy he is getting
up. She turns on him, and upbraids him in a long speech, during
the whole of which Mr. Scofield stood absolutely motionless. His
head was half-bowed, and his left arm hung at his side, the fingers
loose and parted. They did not move by a fraction of an inch,
until at the end of Isabelle's tirade Mr. Scofield raised his head,
and one saw from the sad, concerned look on his face that he was
not Hugo, but Frederick. There was something extremely touching in this still and mute acceptance of undeserved reproach, and
at the first performance it produced a great effect. So did the
scene in which Isabelle and the dyspeptic millionaire, Messer-

schmann, in a gay hysteria, tore up millions of pounds of bank-notes, sitting on the stage, and letting a snowstorm of paper gold float round their heads.

This scene, too, was in the third act. On the first night it was not until this act was halfway through that it became evident that *Ring Round the Moon* was going to be more than an average success. That acute critic, T. C. Kemp, had seen it during its preliminary run in Birmingham, and I gathered that it had puzzled Birmingham audiences more than it had delighted them. Its charade-like character seemed to deprive it of weight and significance, and in London, during both the intervals of the play, there was some questioning of its quality. My own complete surrender to it was hindered by my sitting immediately behind the film actor, Herbert Marshall, who was afflicted with a cough. Mr. Marshall was justifiably embarrassed at the disturbance he was causing, and every time he coughed he muttered an apologetic 'Damn!' This showed Mr. Marshall's agreeable and considerate nature, but it added to the distraction rather than lessened it. The next night I went again. Second nights are notoriously flat and dull, but this was a triumph. Already one foresaw the long succession of 600 performances.

Now it is not the most controversial people who arouse the most controversy. Mr. Fry is, in his public character, the least argumentative of men. He has learnt, unlike Mr. Priestley, that what will determine his reputation is his work, and not what he himself says about it. He keeps modestly silent in the disputes that arise whenever a new play of his is produced. But, though we are aware that Mr. Fry cannot be drawn, those disputes come along as regularly as the plays. Over *The Lady's Not for Burning* the question was, Is Fry a poet? Over *Venus Observed*, Is Fry a dramatist? Its reception by the public showed that *Ring Round the Moon* had strong dramatic quality: and it was in prose. Only one question, therefore, remained: and it was duly asked. Was the theatrical force of this latest play due to Fry the translator, or to Anouilh the original author?

Anyone who compares Anouilh's text with that of Fry will see, first, that the changes Fry has made in it are small, and, second, that they are important. It is almost a literal translation. But, though Mr. Fry has carefully weighed every word and phrase

that Anouilh wrote, he has subtly heightened a large proportion of
them. Anouilh calls Josué a 'maitre d'hôtel', and Fry translates
this into Joshua, 'a crumbling butler'. Mlle Capulat, 'lectrice
de Mme Desmermortes', becomes 'Capulat, her faded companion'. The gain in atmosphere in these two small changes—
and atmosphere is what, in *Venus Observed*, I accused Fry of
failing to create—is surely enormous. In the first minute of the
play Anouilh's Josué, in reply to a question of Hugo's, says that
the shy, infatuated Frederick had slept all night under a young
lady's window. Joshua's answer to the same question is, 'Yes, Mr.
Hugo—under both her windows': and this happy exaggeration
more than doubles the fun. There are such changes in almost every
line, changes so small that the eye at first slides over them unob-
servant, yet their cumulative effect is great. An aspiring dramatist
who feels that his potential strength, if he has any, lies in the delicate and subtle rather than in what Scott called 'the big bow-wow
strain', would find a careful comparison of the text of *L'Invitation
au Château* with that of *Ring Round the Moon* an invaluable lesson
in finish, in how successfully to paint the lily, in how small a
flick of the wrist is needed to give an extra turn of the screw.

I did not see André Barsacq's production of *L'Invitation au
Château* in Paris, but it seems likely that the total gesture of the
play at the Atelier was different from what it was in London.
The Atelier is only about half the size of the Globe, but even so
the play's run of 333 performances in 1947-8 seems to show that
it satisfied the taste of the Parisian public. It pleased the critics
also, but it left them with reservations that appear strange to
those who found *Ring Round the Moon* an evening of undisturbed
and happy enchantment. The Paris critics found the play, which
they called a comedy of intrigue, to be written with a wit and a
grace not unworthy of Molière and Marivaux: and they praised
its ingenuity of effects. But Francis Ambrière, then critic of *Opéra*,
expressed a general feeling when he wrote that the dominating
character of the play's comic action was 'the ambiguity of its
appeal, which is never that of unmixed gaiety. M. Anouilh's
laughter is a pessimist's: it is not the best kind of laughter. Essen-
tially it wants the feeling of healthiness, of generosity which . . .
is in authors as different as Rabelais, Molière, and Marivaux—or in
Labiche and Feydeau, to come down somewhat from the summits.'

Serge Radine, in his study, *Anouilh, Lenormand, Salacrou*, is harsher still. He says that Anouilh is the least suitable man in the world to write such a would-be gay artificial comedy as *L'Invitation au Château*, whose bitterness, if it has any, ought to be light and fleeting. But the bitterness of Anouilh is always present, insistent, even when he tries resolutely to disguise it. How can it be otherwise, when bitterness is at the root of his character? *L'Invitation au Château*, M. Radine concludes, leaves the spectator uneasy. Its smile is wry. It is an uncomfortable play.

I doubt if anyone felt like that about *Ring Round the Moon*. I do not think that English spectators were disturbed by Isabelle's mother, who so distressed M. Ambrière. Where he thought her a degraded woman who was willing to sell her daughter for the highest offer, the worst impression she made in London was that she was nearer to being a bore than any of the other characters, except, perhaps, Romainville, the lepidopterist. I do not believe there was any underlying uneasiness in *Ring Round the Moon*.

If there were, it is possibly true that we were not on the look out for it. French critics, on the other hand, if not French audiences, were watching keenly for signs of bitterness in *L'Invitation au Château*. It was Anouilh's first play since *Roméo et Jeannette*, which during 1946 and 1947 had had a comparatively short run of 140 performances at the Atelier. *Roméo et Jeannette* had come as a great shock to the intelligent Parisian public. It seemed to them unspeakably depressing. The drunken, Bohemian father, the bitter and desperate elder brother, the soiled young girl, and the double suicide struck them as horrible. They remembered that Anouilh had written of such people and such things before, so at first they said merely that this time he had produced a poor play, a play of unconvincing characters and tedious analysis. But by the time that *L'Invitation au Château* came along they had changed their ground. *Roméo et Jeannette* remained in their minds as a sign of misery and mental disarray. To explain it they invented for M. Anouilh a formidable 'interior crisis', and began to look for indications whether he was coming out of it, or plunging deeper in. For myself, I believe this 'interior crisis', as an acute contemporary feature of M. Anouilh's personality, to be a myth. Either this 'interior crisis' does not exist, or it seems to me that Anouilh has been in it all his life. It is not so much he who has changed as his public and the Parisian critics. The reason for the change in these latter people is not obscure. It is simply this. The war, in which France had been subjected to an ignominious Occupation, ended in 1945.

The story of the French theatre during the Occupation has never been fully told in this country, though it is one of which all who are concerned with the drama may be proud. There was no factor in social life between the collapse of 1940 and the landings in Normandy in 1944 which did so much as the theatre to sustain hope and courage among the French people. In life the French in those days were humiliated and defeated: in the theatre, listening to the majestic alexandrines of Racine at the Comédie, they were able to remember their former greatness. Hungry and cold, smarting under their submission to a correct but arrogant foreign invader, they flocked night after night into the theatres of Paris to see plays that uplifted their spirit with notes of defiance and heroic self-sacrifice. One of the first plays seen in Paris after the Occupation began was Péguy's *Jeanne d'Arc*, of which the pedantic and unimaginative German censorship approved because it contained frequent references to driving the English out of the country. But every time Joan said 'English' the audience understood 'German', and the play became a rallying point of stout hearts which each performance served to exercise and strengthen.

Many of the plays put on in Paris between 1940 and 1944 were, naturally enough, no more than pleasant trifles: and these also accomplished their purpose. But others, like Sartre's *Les Mouches* and Barrault's superb production of Paul Claudel's *Le Soulier de Satin*, were the beginnings of the Resistance. Béatrix Dussane, in *Notes de Théâtre*, puts the matter thus: 'At that time there was a widespread attitude of refusal and disobedience, which was, according to the individual temperament, a purge, a discipline, a frenzy, or a superstition, and which, among philosophers, poets, and artists, developed into a system, and even into an inverted ethics. Through them a vast *no* hurtled its way through the metaphysical heavens, but it had its humble roots in the thousand daily *noes* of ordinary people.'

Now, to these *noes*, to this defiance of the occupying Power, there were some authors who contributed deliberately, and some by chance of temperament. Among the first was Sartre, with his devotion to the theory of *la littérature engagée*: among the second, Anouilh. Anouilh, crisis or no crisis, is by nature a man who rejects: his plays are a steady refusal of life, and an acceptance of death. To Creon's defence of conformity in behaviour, his Antigone replied steadfastly, 'I am not here to understand, but to say *no*'. Those words were taken up by by the defiant people of Paris, when the play began its long run just before the invasion of Europe, as a battle cry of resistance. But they were not so intended by the author. He wrote them as an expression of his customary and habitual philosophy. It was a happy accident of history that made them embody the deepest feelings of a people rediscovering its soul.

The point I am trying to make is that Anouilh, in writing as he did in *Antigone*, was writing in his usual vein of emotionally philosophic pessimism. The spirit that refuses is normally a gloomy spirit. But, during the Occupation, the refusing spirit was the spirit of all those who still nurtured the hope of freedom. By the chance of events it became for a brief time indistinguishable from a spirit of optimism.

But when the war ended, the need for refusal ended, too. The desire for affirmation came instead. It was a desire that Anouilh had never been able to satisfy, and could not satisfy now. He continued to write as he had always written, and, in the new temper of the time, Paris saw that he was a man bereft of hope. Instead of seeing that he had always been bereft of hope, there was invented for him an entirely imaginary 'interior crisis', in order to account for the disappearance of an optimism which had, in fact, never existed.

London, of course, knew little or nothing of the emotional tension of Paris during the Occupation. It had no notion that in 1944 Anouilh had seemed something like an optimist. It had not regarded *Roméo et Jeannette*, which it had seen as *Fading Mansions*, as evidence that the author was falling into a pit he had avoided in *Antigone*. It did not scrutinise Anouilh's latest play with anxious eyes as if it were an involuntary symptom of his state of mental health. It went to it as to an ordinary entertainment; and it found it more than ordinarily entertaining.

But among those who knew him best, the nervous inquiry into Anouilh's mental condition continued. It reached its most dis-

D

tressed point with the production of *Ardèle* (Paris, Comédie des Champs-Elysées, November, 1948: Birmingham Repertory, October, 1950: London, Vaudeville, August, 1951). In its London presentation, with Isabel Jeans, Ronald Squire, and George Relph at the head of the cast, the critic John Barber found *Ardèle* too sketchy. He wanted more information about the characters than Anouilh gave him. This, I think, was because in London *Ardèle* was offered as a full-length, three-act play, with two considerable intervals. Now, in a three-act play there is room to turn about; the author can fill in the background of his people, and indeed is expected to do so. In *Ardèle* Anouilh does not fill in this background. But *Ardèle* is not a three-act play. It is a one-act farce, and was so presented at the Comédie des Champs-Elysées, where it was played at immense speed, seeking only laughs, to be got through in about an hour and a quarter. The night I saw it there was a long curtain-raiser, and *Ardèle* did not begin until nearly half-past ten. Yet we were out of the theatre before midnight.

It was not the brevity or thinness of *Ardèle* that distressed M. Anouilh's thoughtful admirers in Paris, but what they took to be the play's appalling pessimism. M. Radine calls it 'the blackest of Anouilh's black pieces'; and adds that in this play the author has reached the last degree of despair. M. Ambrière says that Anouilh's world is one in which men, like dogs, like insects, like plants, are ruled only by the coupling instinct. This conclusion, he asserts, is of an evident falsity, for the real world is not populated only by sexual maniacs. He refers to a character in one of Charles-Louis Philippe's novels, who, in reading Zola, exclaimed 'How true that is!' every time he came upon the word *merde*, as if the rose were not just as real as the dunghill.

But is this doctrine that a dramatist must reflect the real world tenable? Who knows what the real world is? Does it not vary with the personal viewpoint of every one of us? The world of Barrie was a world of lovable women. In Strindberg women are hateful. But this irreconcilable contradiction did not prevent either dramatist from writing good plays. Ambrière says that the real world is composed of good people and of evil people. The naïve who see only angels here below and M. Anouilh, who appears to see nothing but animals, are spirits equally mistaken, and describe universes equally false.

This is a reasonable proposition, but as a guide to a judgment of the drama it is, of course, useless. No playwright peoples his world only with good people, or with wicked people, or with people who are wholly wicked or wholly good. There are evil people in a comedy like *Dear Brutus*, as there are good people in a tragedy like *Lear*. And there is self-righteousness in Cordelia as there is a remnant of better feeling in Mrs. Dearth. In determining the nature of a dramatist's universe, the question is not whether all the characters are good or bad, but what are the relative proportions of goodness and badness. And about those relative proportions there is room for infinite legitimate divergence of opinion.

I do not for a moment admit that there is only evil in the world of *Ardèle*. M. Anouilh's characters are soaked in a stew of passion. This indeed cannot be denied; nor can it be denied that it makes some of them sick, and some mad. Upstairs is the woman crazed for love, screaming in raucous tones which the peacock mocks: darting from bedroom to bedroom in search of the insolently accommodating maid is the debased and pitiful and ridiculous old general who, by attempting a greater kindness to his mad wife than his nature warrants, has fallen below even what he might have been: in the foreground are the flippant count and the ageing countess and her absurd embarrassed lover. It is true that in these people Anouilh dissects love, or lust, with an incisiveness beyond the capacity, or the desire, of an English dramatist.

The case can be built up still further. For Anouilh's horror culminates in a last terrible scene in which the madwoman bursts out of her bedroom, and, leaning over the staircase, whimpers, rails, shrieks, and gabbles a dreadful curse on the world's concupiscence, which makes even the flowers foul to her. Ambrière took this scene to be the summary of M. Anouilh's intention in *Ardèle*, and if it were so, the play would be truly frightening. But it is not. Though even the young people who move through the play are tainted, there are Ardèle herself, and her lover. Both of these are hunchbacks. Whilst everyone else talks, thinks, dreams about, and sullies love, these misshapen beings, whose behaviour shocks all but the Count, actually feel it; and the answer to the madwoman's screams is the pistol shots that show that two people, if everyone is determined to stop them from living for love, can at least die for it. This suicide is a terrible thing, but it is also heroic, and, in its way, an affirmation of values.

There is, too, the Count. No one can claim that the Count, with his indulgent complaisance and his mistress, is another Bayard: he is neither Chevalier nor Dobbin. But he has a fine pity, and has learned not to judge harshly. A great deal of fuss has been made over Anouilh's bitterness, yet there are few dramatists with a deeper fund of pity. He retches at the obsessional thought of sin, but for the sinner his heart aches. He is aware of the pathos of the Countess's fading youth, and that the General's degradation is partly due to the intolerable strain of his kindness to his demented wife. And there is great tenderness in the scene in the second act in which, after her relatives have abused and ridiculed the deformed Ardèle, the Count tries to speak to her more sympathetically through her locked bedroom door. Here is one brief incident from it:

THE COUNT: You have all your life in front of you, aunt Ardèle. And life is full of simple little joys for every day. Think of your piano, of your flowers, of your water-colours. Things like that are very good. (*He listens.*) No, no. We all ask too much, aunt Ardèle. Life is made up of halfpenny pieces, and there is a fortune for those who save them. Only we look down on them. We always expect that life will put us right with a five-pound note. And so we remain poor in the midst of wealth. Five-pound notes are rare, aunt Ardèle. (*He turns towards the others.*) I have no confidence in these commonplaces. I do it merely to help you. (*He listens.*) Pardon, aunt Ardèle?

THE GENERAL: What does she say?

THE COUNT (*coming down the stairs*): She says, very sensibly, that when you find a five-pound note you would be foolish to let it go.

At Birmingham Eric Porter played this scene exquisitely, not less admirably in the aloof ironic gentleness of his voice than in his variety of gesture: it was a dance as much as a speech, and it was perfectly in the mood of the play. Mr. Squire took it more quietly in London, but with equally touching kindness.

The compassion in this scene cannot, in my opinion, be squared with the contention of some critics that Anouilh has declined into a festering misanthrope, in whose skies there is now no gleam of hope. In fact, I should say there is actually more hope in *Ardèle* than in some of his earlier plays, such as *Eurydice* (Paris, 1941: as

Point of Departure, Lyric, Hammersmith, October, 1950: Duke of York's, London, January, 1951).

This play was translated by Miss Kitty Black, who as a young girl had been a student in Paris, and had seen the early productions in the Place Dancourt of several Anouilh plays. Her work had great sensitivity, and in spite of omitting a few scenes, preserved effectively the spirit of *Eurydice*, a spirit I am bound to call both strange and terrible, as beautiful as the *White Devil* but not a little frightening.

Point of Departure revealed many of Anouilh's theatrical merits. First, Anouilh has an unfailing eye for a romantic situation. A railway station, with the scream of engine whistles and the flash of carriage windows past an empty waiting-room, is as irresistible in the advanced French drama as it was in *The Ghost Train*. In the first and third acts of *Point of Departure* the long drawn out whine of a distant train was as heart-bursting as the wail of a violin. Second, Anouilh writes very fine speeches, notably that exuberant outbreak of Orpheus when, in the early tide of young and triumphant love, his eyes are suddenly opened to the astonishing qualities, the essential chairfulness, of chairs: and that other in which the old and battered and sensual and defeated but very far from downhearted wandering harpist rolls his tongue over the consolations of life, the succulence of a good meal or an exciting glance from a pair of pretty eyes. (In Paris, Anouilh told me, this speech always failed, but in London Hugh Griffith delivered it with such relish, with such a rich savouring of pleasure, the apotheosis of apéritifs and cheap cigars, that it was one of the evening's immense successes.)

Equally in this play Anouilh showed himself a master of the simple phrase, as when the mysterious M. Henri looked out of a window over Marseilles, and said meditatively, 'It is a fine town. There aren't as many suicides in the old port as they say, but it is a fine town', charging a good half of his author's philosophy into the unexpected conjunction. Then there was M. Anouilh's inventive richness in character, which extended even to the creation of two separate waiters, one with a suspicious moustache and the other as distinguished as a *sociétaire* of the Comédie Française, who were as different from each other as Falstaff and Hamlet. And, on top of all, there was the skill in narrative that enabled him to make so poignant the sad and poetic tale of a soiled, modern Eurydice, grimed by the life of a touring player, and her strolling musician, Orpheus, who nearly brought her back from death, and died himself.

The play was acted by Mai Zetterling with a frail, weeping softness marred by her incapacity to speak two consecutive phrases with a native intonation; and Dirk Bogarde's Orpheus was not as moving as its expenditure of passion deserved, or as Peter Finch's later performance in the same role. The director, Peter Ashmore, modulated the production like a piece of heart-breaking music, and the play itself seemed, too, like the music of a broken spirit. The meaning of *Point of Departure* is that young physical love is the only thing that matters, and that it is better that lovers should die than that love should become degraded. (In *Ardèle* the lovers die, not because love cannot last, but because it is frustrated: which is a very different matter.) To the Anouilh of *Eurydice* life degrades inevitably: men grow foul, belching, and dirty, women coy and floppy-chested.

It was with a cruelty that would be horrifying were it not the manifestation of a revolted heart that Anouilh here matched three scenes of lyrical affection with three others of love coarsened and defiled. It was not only the French who were distressed by *Ardèle*. John Gielgud told me he was disgusted by such scenes in it as that in which Natalie revealed her physical bondage to a husband she did not love. But it seems to me far more reasonable to protest against the temper of *Point of Departure*. The middle-aged lovers, played with bravura by Brenda de Banzie and George Hayes, and the reprehensible old father, at any rate had courage and vitality; and it appears as if it was for this cause only that Anouilh, in love with surrender and collapse, shrank from them in a refined loathing.

The upshot of *Eurydice*, despite its beauty and its magic, was as Hubert Gignoux, one of Anouilh's best critics, puts it, just this: 'To the question, Is .it possible to live? it seems that Anouilh replies, after consideration, no; and, convinced of the powerlessness of love, perceives no other issue, for the man who wishes to remain faithful to its primary demands, than death.' This dreadful thing *Eurydice* said with a most seducing accent; it was altogether lovely, but it would not be unjust to call it a blasphemy against life.

I hope that by now I have shown that Anouilh was no more despondent in 1948, the year of *Ardèle*, than he had been in 1941, when he wrote *Eurydice*. If he seemed so, it was because of a change in the atmosphere of Paris, not because of any deepening pessimism in himself. The play, however, which, when compared with *Ardèle*, is generally used to prove Anouilh's developing interior crisis is not *Eurydice*, but *Le Voyageur Sans Bagage*, a still earlier play (Paris, 1936: Bristol, Old Vic, September, 1951).

The argument that *Le Voyageur Sans Bagage* shows a saner, healthier, more optimistic outlook upon life than some of the later works of Anouilh has this much to support it, that it is one of the author's *black pieces*, and yet has a happy ending. Its hero, Gaston, is a returned prisoner of war who has lost his memory, and does not know who he is. He has spent many years in hospital, where finally a doctor, having made inquiries all over France, narrows down to five or six the possible families to which Gaston may have belonged. One is a lamplighter's, another a dairyman's, a third is part of the well-to-do bourgeoisie. (That these three so diverse possibilities should be feasible is an interesting indication of the homogeneity of French society and speech.) The bourgeois family, the Renauds, is the home that the psychiatrist tries first, and it is there that the action takes place.

Two things become certain as the play proceeds. One is that Gaston truly is Jacques Renaud. The second irrefutable fact is that Jacques Renaud had been a young man of very unpleasant character. He had killed animals, large and small, cats, dogs, squirrels, out of sheer love of cruelty. He had cheated at examinations. In a quarrel, he had pushed his best friend down the stairs and crippled him for life. He had seduced his brother's wife. As one dreadful thing after another is revealed about Jacques, Gaston shrinks in increasing disgust from the increasingly inevitable identification. The scene of final proof is very short, and very moving, and is an almost insolent example of Anouilh's mastery of theatrical technique. Anouilh chooses to clamp down upon Gaston the past of Jacques by one of the oldest and stalest devices in the world, the strawberry mark on the back of the shoulder. Yet the effect of it in this play is as though it had never been used before. Servants are peering through the fanlight of Gaston's bedroom. They mutter bewilderedly as Gaston, standing in front of a long mirror, with trembling fingers, tears off his shirt from his shoulder: and they stare at each other in uncomprehending surprise as, after one look in the glass, he flings himself on his bed weeping terribly. The effect of this scene at Bristol—it is hardly more than a dumb-show—was tremendous; it was one of the big moments in my theatrical experience.

My visit to Bristol for this production, which was directed by Denis Carey, with an admirable setting by Hutchinson Scott, is one I shall remember for a long time. I am sometimes asked if a critic can do justice to a play on those occasions when he comes to the theatre tired or worried or ill-humoured. I never felt less inclined to enjoy a play in my life than on the Thursday night in the first week of September, 1951, when I saw the fourth performance of *The Traveller Without Luggage*. On the previous Monday I had seen the unsatisfactory production, in the Lyceum Theatre, Edinburgh, of *Le Bal des Voleurs*, which I have already spoken of. On Tuesday I drove south from Edinburgh to Melton Mowbray, arriving just as dusk was falling, only to find that none of the four hotels there could give my wife and myself a bed for the night. We had come three hundred miles, and were very tired, and it looked as though we were not only not going to have anywhere to sleep, but also nothing to eat. There is not much late dining in Melton Mowbray, and the coffee rooms of all the hotels were closing as we came into the town. But with extreme readiness a waitress at the George, an old and charming hotel, with a local artists' exhibition in the bar, agreed to serve us in the dining-room, where the last resident, a lady, was just finishing her meal. This lady, noticing our dispirited appearance, engaged us in conversation. We talked of Trollope, and the big estates round about, and the Edinburgh Festival, and the fullness of the George Hotel, in which not a single room was vacant that night: and at the end of our conversation, this lady sought out the proprietress, who began to telephone on our behalf the hotels in neighbouring villages, one of which happily had a bed to spare.

The next day we came to London, and at night I saw John Whiting's much attacked and defended £700 Arts Theatre prize play, *Saint's Day*. Many of my colleagues treated this piece with ridicule: John Gielgud, Peter Brook, and Christopher Fry, on the other hand, spoke warmly in its favour. I shall discuss Mr.

Whiting's work later. All I need say here is that, good or bad, *Saint's Day*, in its involved structure and its elaborate symbolism, was not the kind of play to soothe the brain. Returning home after the performance I congratulated myself that, for the rest of the week, my work was done, and I could recover from the fatigue of the tiresome journey from Edinburgh.

But then I remembered something I had forgotten, namely, that on the previous Monday the Bristol Old Vic had given the first performance of an English translation of *Le Voyageur Sans Bagage*. My conscience pricked me. I have a warm feeling for the Bristol Old Vic. I have twice gone as far as Paris to see plays by Anouilh. It seemed indefensible not to do for the Old Vic what I have always been ready to accomplish for the Marigny and the Atelier. So the next morning found me on the road again, bound unwillingly for the west. I arrived late in the afternoon; my hotel was pretentious and scruffy, with standards of attention and service far below those of the excellent George; I lost my way to the theatre, and drove round several corners in annoyed frustration. At one crossing I had an animated but unprofitable argument with a traffic policeman. When the curtain went up, I was both tired and angry. I could hardly have been in a worse mood for seeing a play.

Yet these weary and irritated feelings were dispersed almost at once. By the time that Laurence Payne as Gaston was standing at the top of the stairs in the Renaud house, listening with controlled, grieved face to the story his brother was reluctantly telling him about the laming of his friend, I was entirely refreshed. A good play brings its own magic; it creates the conditions, however unfavourable the circumstances, in which it can be best judged.

One question that naturally occurs to an audience of *The Traveller Without Luggage* is why, if Jacques were so unpleasant, his family should want him back. This question occurred to Anouilh also, and he answered it in two of the best scenes of the play. His mother wished to see him return because, on account of some quarrel, she had not spoken to him on the day he left for the army, and she had never seen him since. Her conscience troubled her. I would not have thought that that gentle and charming actress, Helen Haye, could have found in herself so much bitterness as she finely showed when she revealed to Gaston this episode from the past. And Jacques's elder brother, Georges, wanted him back because he had never forgotten how as a small child Jacques had trusted him, and put his hand in his when he wished to be led across a busy street. This was a most touching scene, played beautifully by both Mr. Payne and Mr. Michael Aldridge.

The best scene came in the third act, at the conclusion of which Anouilh contrived the happy ending of which French critics have made much capital in their effort to prove that he used to be mentally healthier than he is today. This act opens very finely. Gaston is asleep, and his family have surrounded his bed with the stuffed bodies of the animals that Jacques has hunted and killed. Their idea is, of course, that these mementoes of youth shall revive in Gaston recollections of his childhood, and so stimulate in him some recognition of his identity. But all they do is to fill him with horror: his tenderness towards these poor stuffed creatures is one of the most moving elements in the play. Nevertheless, that Gaston is Jacques is abundantly evident. It seems only a matter of time before he must make his formal admission. Then, at the last moment, Anouilh introduces another family that claims Gaston as one of its own members. It is an English family of title, and its only representative is a young boy. Every one of this boy's relatives has been drowned. There is no one left who can furnish the slightest recollection of the man who might, in his youth, have been Gaston. Gaston is thus offered at the last moment the possibility of identifying himself with a character of whom nothing is known. He can begin a new life completely untrammelled by the past. 'Tell me,' he says to the boy, not unkindly, 'you are quite sure that everyone in your family is dead?' 'Everybody', the boy replies. 'It is perfect', says Gaston, and blandly accepts the relationship which cuts him off from the Renauds. He is free of Jacques at last. He has escaped the trap that threatened him. He finishes the play a happy man.

But does he? Is he free of Jacques? Of course he is not. How could he be, when he *is* Jacques? If everybody in the world thought him to be a relative of young Lord Madensale, he in his heart still knows that he is Jacques Renaud. This is a fact that he cannot escape by running away from it. His true salvation lies in recognising his identity and refusing to be distressed or governed by it: in admitting that he was Jacques once, but in now remaining

Gaston. This would be the real victory and the only veritable happy ending. What is offered to us as a happy ending is a sham.

In other words, the Anouilh of *Le Voyageur Sans Bagage* is not above a pretence. He no more believed in the avoidability of misery in 1936 than he did in 1948. But in 1948 he admits his pessimism. Between the two years he did not decline in healthy cheerfulness, but grew in intellectual honesty.

Chapter Three

SOME RELIGIOUS QUESTIONS

M. RADINE, in his assessment of Anouilh's aesthetic balance-sheet after the production of *Ardèle*, declared him bankrupt. He was, of course, speaking of Anouilh's spiritual condition, for even M. Radine does not maintain that there has been a decline in his technical dramatic skill. I have tried to argue that, even in the field of psychology, Anouilh is no more bankrupt today than he ever was, and that M. Radine, and those who agree with him, are wrong in their adverse judgment. Nevertheless, a substantially mistaken play may contain several good scenes, and one of M. Radine's observations is exceedingly acute. He expresses an illuminating truth when he says that Anouilh is a rebel but not a revolutionary. A revolutionary has a new faith to put in place of the old one he destroys, but to the rebel the rebellion is everything. In order to be renewed, adds M. Radine, Anouilh must escape from himself into some great hope of collective salvation, whether its inspiration be Socialist or Christian.

It is true that Anouilh might attain serenity of mind by accepting one of the great salvationary doctrines. This doubtless would add to his own happiness, but it would not necessarily make him a better dramatist. It would destroy the bitter, grotesque, disillusioned, and witty universe which is Anouilh's literary creation, and it might not give anything in its place. We should hesitate before we demand too vehemently that someone should do for Anouilh in the spiritual realm what Watts-Dunton did for Swinburne in the material. We might gain a soul, but lose a lot of poetry.

That Anouilh, though he formally calls himself a Catholic, really has no religion does not seem to trouble him, though if he had religious belief most of his troubles would be cured. There is a surprising number of dramatists today who know that this is true, if not of Anouilh, at any rate of themselves. Those who have the firm faith of Eliot or Claudel may be few, but many times in the contemporary theatre one hears a cry whose utterance is the desolate signal of an empty soul yearning to be filled.

We heard such a cry, for example, in Ken Attiwill's *Sayonara* (New Lindsey, August, 1950), and it was the most striking thing in it. Mr. Attiwill's play was set in a prison camp in Japan, in which the chief characters were an objectionable glutton, a man crazed for lack of a letter from home, his friend, whose serenity of spirit is hardly touched by the fact that both his legs have become paralysed, a doctor, and a clergyman. Now and again Japanese Guards wandered in, screamed, and wandered out. The heat sweltered, the flies buzzed, there was an endless monotony, there was greed, there were quarrels, and always at the pit of the stomach hunger gnawed.

Into this framework Mr. Attiwill fitted a confused, congested, constricted, and unconstructed play that occasionally was very moving. The defect of the piece was that Mr. Attiwill seemed to have about as much notion of how to put a drama together as an average cuckoo of building a cathedral. He introduced episodes, such as the making of a concealed radio, for no reason at all, and dropped them just as arbitrarily. Apart from this, the chief faults of *Sayonara*, as I said at the time, were begotten by materialism upon America.

First, for materialism. It is due to materialism that the play's sympathetic character, to whom the others turn for help and sustenance, was not the priest but the doctor. Down at Bart's and up at Guy's, they may see nothing wrong in this, since every man should stand up for his own profession. Yet it is a symbol of a warped sense of values (which was not without its indirect influence upon even so fine a work as *The Cocktail Party*), a sense of values that ranks the body higher than the spirit. Now, that Mr. Attiwill should get his sense of values not only right, but rightly translated into theatrical terms, was extremely important, for they were of the essence of the best thing in his play.

From America Mr. Attiwill took the noise that so often degenerates into unintelligibility. A great deal of the dialogue in *Sayonara* reminded me of the ecstatic slobberings that the Palladium sometimes passes off on us for singing. From America too Mr. Attiwill took the sentimental toughness which decrees you should never do a man a good turn without at the same time spitting in his eye. The manners of his doctor were such that to die under his care would have been an agreeable escape from his society.

Amidst all these mistakes and defects the play occasionally flashed a bright light. Somewhere stirring inside it, giving it potential life even at its clumsiest, was a deep and troubled emotion. Mr. Attiwill had heard that piteous cry, They have taken away my Lord, and I know not where they have laid him. When his Jack Seacombe, agonised at not knowing whether his wife is alive or dead, blindly groped for faith, the feeling was strong as when Job lamented, O that I knew where I might find him, and was ennobled with all sorts of sad and magnificent associations. It was at this point that Seacombe called for a miracle, and Mr. Attiwill provided him with a puling little hallucination miserably recalling the second act of *Dear Brutus*. It was a pity, but Mr. Attiwill had at least tried. The seven-league boots did not fit him, but one admired his reluctance to be satisfied with carpet slippers.

For the ending of the play, when Seacombe, now physically as well as mentally exhausted, heard what had happened to his only friend in the camp, I felt nothing but admiration. It is a risky thing to bring the whole of the 23rd Psalm into a play, but here it was beautifully, heart-rendingly done.

Peter Madren, who played Seacombe, laboured under the handicap of resembling one of our greatest actors, but he had a dark force of his own, and his speaking of the psalm seemed to me quite perfect. Daniel Wherry was excellent as the odious Sibley.

I have remarked that when the author of *Sayonara* wished one of his characters to be friendly and helpful to others in their distresses, he made this man a doctor and not a clergyman. This is a point worth some consideration, for it illustrates the connexion between the theatre and life. Nowadays it has become a theatrical cliché that when one is troubled, it is to a psychiatrist, to the man who knows about man, that one goes, and not to a priest, the man who knows about God. T. S. Eliot's Harcourt Reilly was a doctor: once he might have been a bishop; and in Thomas Heggen's curious *Mister Roberts* it was again the doctor to whom the supposedly more intelligent members of the ship's company turned when life went sour in their mouths.

This is partly a reflection of the current popularity of psychiatry: it is due to the fact that doctors are fashionable, as well as to the other fact that clergymen are not. But it does not mean merely that doctors have gone up in the scale, whilst the clergy have remained stationary. The clergy have not remained stationary. They have gone down. They have gone down (I personally regret it) fast and far, and to the accompaniment of derisive jeers and whoops.

The treatment of the clergyman in *Saint's Day*, the play to which the Arts Theatre Club gave a prize of £700 in September, 1951, and which I shall discuss in more detail later, is in this connexion very interesting. The author of *Saint's Day*, John Whiting, is a young actor of promise. The play was obscure, and there came into the second act a distraught and stuttering parson, half beside himself with panic and remorse, who had, apparently from cowardice, allowed some marauding soldiers to burn the valuable library of his church. The total meaning of this parson was difficult to get, but it seemed that for half a night he had defended the church's treasure by keeping the men locked up. There was perhaps here some complicated parallel with Mr. Whiting's view of the Church's history. Possibly Mr. Whiting considers that for half its lifetime the Church defended the things of the mind but that it has now betrayed them? Perhaps so, perhaps not. Anyway, there was no doubt about the immediate impression made by this clergyman. There was pity for his wretched terrors, but there was contempt also, and more contempt than pity.

The contemptuous treatment that Mr. Whiting gave to this parson, reminded me of something in B. Seebohm Rowntree's and G. R. Lavers' recently published *English Life and Leisure* that I had found more than a little disturbing. In the extraordinary pattern of behaviour revealed in the 200 case histories of people over the age of 20 with which the book begins, one strand appears again and again. This is an almost virulent animosity towards Christianity, the Church, the clergy, and churchgoers. There is, for example, the middle-aged woman manager of a drapery store whose son had been killed in the war, and to whom a 'silly fool' of a parson had tried to give some conventional comfort, with the result that she 'told him to get to hell out of here'. There is the spinster of 50 who never goes to church, and almost splutters with fury whenever she sees a clergyman, and the elderly naval pensioner who says contemptuously, 'The parsons have a bloody fine job. I don't blame them. They've got a good racket, and make the most of it.'

I do not suggest that this bitterness is altogether typical of the treatment of the clergy in the contemporary drama. Nevertheless, the figure of the clergyman, who, as the representative on earth of the love and the knowledge of God, is ready to aid and comfort, has faded, terribly faded, even among the sympathetic. It was a sad and reluctant recognition of this fact that led Wynyard Browne to write *The Holly and the Ivy* (Lyric, Hammersmith, March, 1950, and Duchess, May, 1950). This was a gentle, understanding, unambitious, and touching play, which began as though it was going to be the familiar story of the young woman who gives up marriage in order to care for a possessive and selfish parent, in this instance a scholarly clergyman. But it turned out other and better than we thought. On the one hand, it was a wise and friendly commentary on the notion I have been talking about, the notion that a parson is the last man in the world to be taken seriously, as a man to be turned to in the hour of distress. Almost the only idea that all the members of the Reverend Martin Gregory's family had in common was that in front of him they must pretend to be nobler, less complicated than in reality they were. Their feeling, at bottom, was a kindly, civilised version of the contempt I have mentioned. They would have denied that they either despised or disliked Mr. Gregory. They did in fact love him, and they respected his character and his learning. But they felt instinctively that both fitted only the undisturbed seclusion of a country parish, that he was living in a quiet backwater where he could not possibly have acquired any of that skill in navigation which would have helped them to sail their own stormy waters.

This was one theme of the play. The other was the attempt which Mr. Browne made to create the feeling of Christmas—not the Christmas of wassail and Dickens and overeating—but that happy yet solemn feeling of Christmas morning, that a new world, a world in which church bells are not an alien sound, is trembling into birth.

Had Mr. Browne really established this feeling, his play would have had that underlying poetic spirit which is the chief merit of

Chekhov, and of which some glimpses are caught occasionally by André Roussin. But, in performance, his imagination was translated into too humdrum terms. The clergyman's second daughter, who had gone to London, become a fashion correspondent, taken to drinking too much at cocktail parties, had an illegitimate baby, and was now returned, broken and contrite, to the vicarage, belonged to melodrama, not to a serious play. There were defects, too, in the clergyman's scholarship. It was not of the right kind. It had nothing in it of the pure serene, of the realms of Arcady. Most of it seemed to come out of *Pears' Encyclopaedia*, an admirable publication, but not, I take it, the daily food of poets. Mr. Gregory was an Irishman educated at Cambridge, and Herbert Lomas gave to his speech the rhythm of Lancashire. But this, fortunately, mattered hardly at all in comparison with Mr. Lomas's fine and rugged integrity. Jane Baxter, Maureen Delany (as a mountainous and irritable aunt), and Patrick Waddington admirably supported Mr. Lomas's performance, and helped to give the play the long run it deserved.

I have suggested that Mr. Lomas's performance in *The Holly and the Ivy* wanted something in realism, since men brought up in Dublin, and educated at Britain's second university, do not talk as if their youth had been passed in Rochdale. Yet this is a trivial want when an actor, like Mr. Lomas, has power and strength and honesty. There was a similar lack of realism in one of the most exciting performances I have ever seen in my life. This was Alexander Knox's in Henry Sherek's presentation of Benn Levy's *Return to Tyassi* (Duke of York's, November, 1950). Before I saw this play I had heard of Mr. Knox. I knew he had played Wilson in the film of that President's life. I was aware that he had appeared in London in Shaw's *Geneva*. I knew these things as many members of the Drury Lane audience at Kean's first performance in *The Merchant of Venice* doubtless knew that Kean had acted much in the provinces. I do not suppose that this knowledge greatly keyed up expectation on that foggy night in 1814: I certainly went to the Duke of York's in a state of unanticipatory calm. I left it convinced that I had seen a great actor. This, of course, was uncommonly rash. When all the world hailed Elizabeth Bergner as a great actress on the strength of a single performance, James Agate refused to be rushed. What else can she do besides Gemma Jones,

E

he asked. Is she up to Hedda Gabler? Has anyone seen her Milla-mant? Or words to that effect. Nevertheless, when Hazlitt saw Kean that night in 1814 he said he was not one who, when he saw the sun, needed someone to tell him that it was not the moon. Mr. Knox is not the moon, either.

Not many people gave themselves the opportunity of agreeing with me. I saw the play three times in three weeks, and, apart from the first night, the theatre was half-empty on each occasion. At the end of three weeks the play came off, and a light of brilliance was extinguished.

I tried to account for this cruel failure of a performance which, towards the end of the play, achieved a fierce spiritual grandeur rarely encountered on the stage, by suggesting that the public was deceived by an obvious, but superficial, aspect of Mr. Knox's acting. Mr. Knox's part was that of a high Civil Servant, named Gilbert Cotton, who had married, as her second husband, one Martha Hubbard, the widow of an archaeologist. The legend had grown up during the years that this archaeologist had treated Martha badly by insisting that she should stay with him and his excavations in Tyassi, even when she was having a child. But the truth was that Martha had deserted him, he had been neglected, and he had died. So that Martha, though she wore a crown of martyrdom, wore it with a secretly troubled conscience.

The essential facts in this situation were expounded, with mathematical deliberation, in a first act completely devoid of emotion. It had no wit, either, and the characters were somewhat forbidding. Mrs. Grenfell (Helen Haye) was a grandmother who furtively read her daughter's diary. Martha, the daughter, had obviously not behaved well to her first husband. Her own daughter, Susan Hubbard (Tilsa Page), disliked her bitterly and to dislike one's parents is not even yet a certificate of charm. And the carefully shaved and neatly dressed Cotton had the cold cleanness of an iceberg.

The temperature rose a little with the entrance of Francis Hubbard, the dead archaeologist's brother. For Francis was troubled with a genuine and in its way an unselfish emotion. He was indignant that Martha Cotton should have deserted her first husband, that she should have left him, weak and ill, to the heat and discomfort of a foreign land. He happened to intervene when Martha was about to leave for the opera. Then, magnificently gowned, Martha made a long speech in which she recounted, with a sharp irony, the story of her married life, and, in a dry, deliberate voice that throbbed with self-scorn, and with eyes too smarting for tears, exposed the record of her own shortcomings. Constance Cummings, who played Martha, was here very fine, and the timing of her last few words, which she spoke like the slow placing of one lash after another across her back, was particularly impressive.

Mr. Levy had now got his play going, but only, alas, to run it off the road. Martha realised that it was her first husband she really loved, which, dramatically, was satisfactory enough. She then, that very night, had an affair with Francis, which, despite the attractiveness of John Justin's performance, was surely silly. Even in an age of jet-propelled aircraft, things do not happen quite as quickly as that, whilst, from the philosophical point of view, to return to a deserted love is one thing, and, with metaphysical dolling up, to hop into bed with the dead love's brother is something quite else. In short, the scene at the end of this act, in which Martha and Francis clasped each other in a concupiscent embrace, was incredible. Either Mr. Levy or Miss Cummings or Mr. Justin realised this, for, in the later performances of the play's brief run, they merely, in a singularly weak and ambiguous gesture, held each other's hands.

This was not a happy device, for it was essential to Mr. Levy's finest scene, which came in the third act, that Martha and Francis should commit adultery. Mr. Levy had thus got himself into the unlucky position of making his master-stroke depend on a psychological impossibility, and he did not make the matter any better by shuffling past the impossibility with averted gaze.

But, granted this ridiculous adultery, Mr. Levy's third act was certainly fine. Cotton was a deeply religious man, and, beneath his frozen exterior, passionate and proud. He hated Francis for betraying him, and he hated himself for hating him. His charged bitterness surged icily against the shore of his sarcastic self-possession. Of this scene Mr. Knox made something truly magnificent. He sat at a small breakfast-table, brushed and bathed and shaven, eating his morning egg; and from this inadequate position he scourged Francis: and the triumph of his performance was that he made it perfectly clear that he despised himself for his hatred and his scorn. For, as I have said, he was a religious man. As *The Holly and the Ivy* was a study of a religious man in orders, so was *Return to Tyassi* a study—and not an unsympathetic one— of a religious layman.

Mr. Lomas's Gregory was not realistic in speech, and neither was Knox's Cotton. I suggested that this was what bothered London audiences. In Charles Morgan's *The Voyage* there is a profoundly interesting passage about the heroine's version of the call of the binetu. This had in it an inaccurate double note, it was not a good imitation; but also 'it had herself in it, her own sadness and gaiety'. Mr. Knox's Civil Servant was not a good imitation. Upper Civil Servants do not speak with a strong Canadian accent. If the actor is a photographer, it was not a good performance; only if the actor is an artist, with his own sadness and gaiety, was it superb. Mr. Knox had his own sadness and gaiety, his own passion and scorn, of magnificent, of earth-shaking intensity. But London never noticed.

The obvious answer to this argument is that Mr. Lomas's Lancashire rhythms did not seem to worry anyone, and *The Holly and the Ivy* ran for three or four hundred nights. But rhythm is one thing and accent another; and in any case Rochdale is more familiar than Toronto. Yet it is probable that the weaknesses of Mr. Levy's play, the lack of sympathy in the characters, and the author's slow direction of it were stronger factors in its regrettable failure.

Return to Tyassi brings us to a point which seems to me to be of considerable social significance. Of the plays mentioned up to now in this chapter, only *The Holly and the Ivy* made much impact upon the ordinary playgoing public. If the verdicts recorded by Rowntree and Lavers are correct—and they are arrived at after careful investigation and inquiry—it would be unreasonable to expect a high proportion of theatre-goers to be interested in religion or in religious people. There is a general impression that the number of church attenders has markedly declined during the last fifty years, and the statistics in *English Life and Leisure* support this view. In 1901, for example, the number of people who attended Anglican places of worship in York on a given day in October was

7,453: on a given day in November, 1948, it had fallen to 3,384. Between the same dates attendances at Nonconformist churches dropped from 6,447 to 3,514, and at the Salvation Army from 800 to 249. Only the Roman Catholic churches in York managed to maintain their position. These figures apply to one city only, and from area to area there are probably regional variations. But there is no reason to suppose that there is a vigorous flame of religious enthusiasm in Mayfair, Bloomsbury, Bethnal Green, and Walthamstow, or wherever it is that the West End gets its audiences, to burn up the increasing paganism of York.

These facts give a particular interest to the growing concern with religion that the modern western European theatre displays. For the theatre does not merely hold an ordinary mirror up to nature; it is on occasion a Hallowe'en mirror in which the future can be dimly discerned. If anyone doubts this, let him consider how the Labour electoral victory of 1945 was foreshadowed a generation earlier when the London theatre was intellectually dominated by what then seemed the Socialist paradoxes of Shaw and the humanitarian sentiments of Galsworthy. It pleased Shaw to say that the theatre was always thirty years behind the times; but there have been periods when it has been, in the strictest, most accurate sense of the term, thirty years in front of them. This, I think, makes the present connexion between the theatre and religion worth discussing on a broader basis than the strictly dramatic.

In politics Lord Keynes noted a distinction between public opinion and informed opinion. Today's public opinion dictates how today's public votes, but it is informed opinion that decides how tomorrow's public will vote, for the simple reason that contemporary informed opinion becomes the public opinion of a generation hence, by which time, of course, it stands a very good chance of no longer being the current informed opinion. For it is a fact, at least in a social organisation like Britain's, that, with the passing of time, informed opinion percolates downwards into ever-widening circles of the population: and that informed opinion periodically changes. Perhaps it would be well to point out here that by informed opinion I mean no more than the opinion of informed people, and that the opinion of informed people often turns out to be wrong. There was a time when it was the opinion of informed people that it was a good thing to sleep with closed windows, just as there was a time when it was the opinion of informed people that it was a good thing to live with closed minds. But, right or wrong, it is the opinion of the informed people of today that settles the uninformed opinion of tomorrow or the day after. To put the matter concretely and perhaps in an oversimplified form, it was the informed opinion of Thomas Henry Huxley in 1860 that kept away from church in 1948 millions of people who had either never heard of him or who vaguely supposed that he was Secretary of the Regent's Park Zoo.

Probably at no time since the Reformation were English churches better attended than in the last quarter of the nineteenth century and the first decade of the twentieth. Yet the foundations on which that attendance was based had already been undermined. Public opinion enforced an attendance that informed opinion (or the opinion, with all its fallibility, of informed people) condemned. In 1860, in a famous meeting in Oxford, Bishop Wilberforce had sarcastically asked Huxley, then as later an ardent supporter of Darwin, whether it was through his grandfather or his grandmother that he claimed descent from the apes. To which Huxley made a retort which no one seems to have been able to remember with accuracy, but which everyone who heard it agrees was one of the most tremendous ever delivered, to the effect that the question of Evolution was not one to be discussed with levity, but that if the Bishop insisted on talking of it lightly, he would not be ashamed to be descended from an ape, but he would be ashamed to be connected with a man of great abilities who used his high gifts to bring ridicule on humble seekers after truth.

Those whom Huxley justly regarded as humble seekers after truth soon ceased to qualify for that description. Victory is usually an enemy to modesty, and before long it seemed that victory was entirely on the side of Huxley and his friends. The doctrines of Evolution and Natural Selection won almost universal acceptance among the informed, and their effect upon belief in the literal inspiration of the Bible, which had always been the rock on which English Protestantism was based, was disturbing and profound. The humility that characterised Huxley became the

materialistic cocksureness of people like Wells. It penetrated
downwards into the main body of the population, and church
attendances progressively declined, and have not since shown any
sign of recovering.

The extraordinarily interesting feature of this is that informed
opinion began to modify personal behaviour on a large scale just
about the time that this informed opinion was called upon to
adjust itself to a number of new considerations. The broad lines
on which Darwin worked remain, but it has now to be admitted
that there are phenomena which they do not explain. The usual
method of development may be evolution, but in Nature jumps
and leaps are not now held to be impossible; and though the process of natural selection may result in the giraffe's long neck, it
does not account for the behaviour of atoms and electrons. As
biology has been pushed further and further into the background
by the emphasis laid on psychology and physics, an entirely
materialistic explanation of the universe has had to be abandoned
by informed opinion. Such an explanation is, of course, at the
base of much public opinion, which is still busily making its own
the then up-to-date notions of half a century ago. But it is confined to those many millions of old-fashioned people, who never
think of going to church.

How long the characteristic habit of not going to church will
persist we cannot say. The question is complicated by the fact
that though the materialism of fifty years ago is shaken, the old
orthodoxy has not been restored. Informed opinion is not as certain today as it was in 1900 that some particular theological specu-
lations are impossible; but this is a long way from saying that they
are now to be admitted true. Nevertheless, the certainty of infide-
lity has been destroyed, as earlier was destroyed the certainty of
faith. An appreciation of this fact too will slowly seep downwards
and its effects on Sunday behaviour be interesting to watch.
Meanwhile, and this is, for us, its immediate importance, it is
already affecting the theatre.

Especially in France. In her magistrally organised history of the
French theatre in the recent past, which she modestly calls *Notes
de Théâtre*, Mme. Dussane contrasts the Parisian stage of today
with what it was forty years ago. The leaders of thought in 1910
were not to be found in the theatre. The youth of the day came

to enjoy and be moved by the work of Hervieu, of Bataille, and Bernstein, but they sought their philosophy elsewhere, in novels, in essays, and in poems, but not in plays.

In our own days the theatre has been conquered by philosophers like Sartre or Gabriel Marcel, by a moralist like Camus, by a haunted poet like Anouilh, and these have behaved in it like masters of thought. So much so, adds Mme Dussane, that the contemporary French theatre cannot be judged without putting on trial the ethics, the moralities, and the philosophies which now exert the strongest influence on French thinking.

The situation in Britain is not quite the same as this. From the intellectual point of view, one would not speak so harshly of the London theatre of 1910, when Shaw, Galsworthy, and Maugham were its principal authors, as Mme Dussane does of the Paris theatre of the same epoch; and the theatre of today in London, the theatre of Rattigan (which, all the same, is a very good theatre), even the theatre of Priestley, Fry, and Eliot is not a dominating influence upon contemporary thought. Nevertheless, it is affected by the change we have noted in informed opinion, and is one of the means by which that change spreads out in widening circles.

There is, then, a sense in which the modern drama of France and England is becoming increasingly religious. I do not mean that there is an increase in the number of plays whose object is to make men and women better by the advocacy of some form of religious belief, but that more and more plays are being produced that are the work of men whose minds are exercised by specifically religious problems. The great religious questions are raised again and again in the contemporary drama. To what extent, when in a position of great danger, can we rely utterly and exclusively on the goodness of God? This problem, which was raised in the fiery furnace, underlies Mr. Fry's *A Sleep of Prisoners*. How can we come to the love of Christ, asks Paul Claudel in *Partage de Midi*. Behold, I show you a mystery, and a frightening one at that, declares André Gide in *The Trial*.

Indeed, not all these plays are reassuring. They are not all, like *Partage de Midi* and *A Sleep of Prisoners*, established in faith. The authors of some of these plays have asked, and not been answered; they have knocked, and the door has stayed shut in their faces. One of them, M. Sartre, in *Le Diable et le Bon Dieu*, has knocked, and then turned on his heel. But their plays are not for this reason the less religious in atmosphere and in motive. They deal with the religious questions, as they would not have done fifty or even twenty years ago, even where they are unable or unwilling to give the religious replies.

Amongst the most striking of them was *The Trial* (Paris, Marigny, October, 1947: London, Winter Garden, April, 1950). In London it was presented by an American-Swedish actor, Frank Sundstrom, and his wife Jacqueline, who were rumoured to have spent on it the large sum of £12,000, and to regard it as one of the major masterpieces of the age. The English translation, by Mrs. Sundstrom, was from the French adaptation made by André Gide and Jean-Louis Barrault from Kafka's novel, which M. Barrault had produced at the Marigny with considerable success.

As it was presented to us by the well-meaning but apparently not over-gifted Sundstroms, nothing would have been easier than to dismiss *The Trial* as the higher pretentiousness sometimes degenerating into the lower ludicrous. That, in fact, was exactly how many people did dismiss it; yet even in the unskilful Sundstrom production it merited rather more considerate treatment.

It was a despairing cry from a man who was comforted neither by belief in religion nor by the philosopher's resignation. That the sun shines, that young men and women fall in love, that the heart leaps at the sight of a rainbow in the sky are facts so recondite and unusual that apparently Franz Kafka never observed them. He saw that good men suffer, that evil falls alike on the just and the unjust, and his soul revolted in a puzzled, desperate, protesting sorrow. Some Jewish commentators, I am told, have suggested that Kafka's torment was a transposition of the crushing minutiae of the learning of the Talmud, with its mingling of literal explanation and mystical fervour. But wherever it came from, it was a real and distressing thing.

Now, the facts that troubled Kafka have been noted ever since the world began, and men have found three refuges from them. The ultimate reality of evil may be questioned: it may be held that somehow good will be the final goal of ill; or in an ecstasy of abnegation man may resign himself to another will than his own,

Not so Kafka. He did not submit; nor believe; nor question. He saw only that mankind is judged by a divine judgment that is not the same as human, and he was like a man groping in a thick fog on the top of a high mountain, edging towards precipices he cannot see, with terror and protest in his heart.

There could be no easy success for a play like this. You cannot take Leviathan on a bent pin, nor sail the deep waters in a seaside dinghy. *The Trial* could not just pass the time between dinner and a dance. It was a question of greatness or nothing.

What is a great play? Let us say perhaps rashly that greatness comes in a play when an intense experience in a fine mind is translated with ecstasy into effective theatrical terms. The quality in this definition which does not indicate any fineness of spirit, theatrical effectiveness, is the one quality that is common to all plays, from *Hamlet* to *Abie's Irish Rose*, that have ever succeeded in holding the stage. In any scheme of values except the dramatic, it is not comparable with depth of experience or splendour of mind; but a play can exist without either of these, whilst without theatrical effectiveness Socrates and Sir Isaac Newton combined could not hold an audience's attention for ten minutes together. With all three qualities one gets *Othello*; with the last two, *The Importance of Being Earnest*; with only the third, *Charley's Aunt*. With the first two only, one gets *The Trial*.

For the glimpses that it affords of a distinguished spirit sorely distressed, *The Trial* should have been sympathetically received, but it is difficult to admit that, in the London production, it had any theatrical quality whatever.

Joseph K. is arrested on a charge he does not understand, and subjected to processes of justice which bear no relationship to any reality he is acquainted with. The source of his terror and protest is not that the law is unfairly administered, and that he is found guilty when he is innocent. It is rather that he cannot find out what the law is, nor comprehend such fragments of it as he from time to time thinks he has discovered, so that he has no notion what crime he is accused of, nor whether he has in fact committed it. This is that vague feeling of guilt of which the western world has never freed itself since the Versailles Treaty, a feeling raised in Joseph K. to nightmare power.

At times washing was hung out on the stage; at times people

ran up and down flights of stairs that doubtless were meta-
physically significant; at times Joseph K. put his head on an
executioner's block in the middle of a public thoroughfare. It all
meant nothing to this bewildered man, who despite Mr. Sundstrom's frenzied performance, was never half as bewildered as the
audience. For myself, I passed the greater part of the evening in
the state of mind of a child vainly endeavouring to understand
something that might be the differential calculus, but which the
unwary could easily mistake for the hieroglyphics of an imaginative
moron.

Probably Mr. Sundstrom had seen, and been excited by, M.
Barrault's production at the Marigny. Now Barrault's production
had not received unqualified critical praise. It was one of those
presentations that are immensely impressive to the eye, with
crowds of players surging through, and over, and round elaborate
and rapidly changing scenery. Barrault, in fact, made the performance what French critics appear so much to dislike, a director's evening. The judicious Dussane sums up the general
impression by saying that 'this was the first occasion when Barrault the virtuoso, Barrault the commander of men and things,
the Barrault who sets up difficulties for the sheer joy of knocking
them down, Barrault-Bonaparte, put into the shade Barrault the
loyal servant of the work he loves.'

But though this judgment passed uncontradicted, there were
other things that had to be said to supplement it. In particular,
though Gide's adaptation was criticised as lacking creative force,
it was considered that the play served as an excellent initiation
into Kafka's universe for those who had not read the novel.
'These performances of *The Trial*', said M. Ambrière, 'will do
a great deal to spread the work of Kafka beyond the little circle
of intellectuals to which up to the present it has been confined.'
This was a compliment no one could have paid to the English
production, which confused everything and explained nothing.

There were some things in it that, with a mighty effort, I
thought I could understand. I thought I could understand why
the parson was presented as an enemy, enlisted on the hostile side
(that, as we have seen, is almost common form today). I assume
that Enoch, who was translated, was among the legendary figures
whom Geoffrey Dunn's indiscreet artist regarded as one of the

'absolute acquittals'. And the books no one can see were written, presumably, by the Recording Angel. But these few flashes of comparative lucidity hardly pierced the circumambient fog.

No effort, no process of divination, served to explain to me why the screaming children came in; nor why the artist's word influenced the judge; nor why the laundress, who is also the magistrate's consolation, was literally carried off; nor why Mrs. Sundstrom, as the judge's nurse, suddenly through the gloom appeared in her knickers; nor why such an enormous cast, with so many changes of scenery, should spend so much time, with so much to say, in communicating so little. This was a play that gambled for high stakes, and failed for an immense sum.

Similarly, in Tyrone Guthrie's *Top of the Ladder* (St. James's, October, 1950) we were given another statement of the position of a bewildered man. But a bewildered man who, this time, in the end found God.

Mr. Guthrie's treatment of his theme reminded one, in form, but not in spirit, of Lytton Strachey. Strachey, in a famous passage, imagined the dying Victoria thinking back through the mists of eighty years to her mother's feathers bearing down upon her, and the trees and the grass of Kensington. Guthrie's Bertie, too, had a dying vision, and this vision was the play that Mr. Guthrie both wrote and directed.

Bertie's mind, however, was less orderly that the Queen's, and in place of her poignant simplicity we had a wild jumping about in time and space. At times John Mills's Bertie was a boy, at times a young man, now the head of a great business, and now a child again. But always and everywhere perplexed in the extreme, seeking for the security that comes from a trusted father, or from God. His mother was with him all the time, but grew no older, which perhaps meant that Bertie himself never grew up. Perhaps it meant something quite different, or possibly nothing at all. His wife and his secretary, by the way, aged considerably. Sometimes the scene was his father's middle-class home, sometimes his own huge mansion, sometimes a business office, yet always simultaneously it was in a dark abysm of creation where an old woman sat cosmically knitting, and commenting with good-humoured grumpiness on the follies and inadequacies of the pattern she was weaving.

These scenes shifted and dissolved, faded into each other, with a dream's independence of logic, and in this they resembled more than a little *The Trial*. But, unlike *The Trial*, there were moments when they achieved a dream's beauty, and its feeling of inexpressible significance.

One of them was when Toke Townley's limping and repellent tout saw all the kingdoms of the earth, and the poor people in them; another, when Mary Kerridge, as the secretary, in a small sad voice sang a child's lullaby; another, touchingly played by Miles Malleson and Mr. Mills, when a foolish old director was cruelly forced to resign by the rising, ambitious Bertie; and another still, when Bertie, at the end of his life, searching for the key to existence which had always eluded him, frantically turned to his wife, and she replied, 'You know I never had it'. Into those six words Rachel Kempson put all the pathos of the sense of marital inadequacy which had been building up throughout the play.

There were times also when Mr. Guthrie brilliantly illuminated the truth that, from generation to generation, events, motives, and compulsions repeat themselves; for, by his destruction of the consecutiveness of time, he was able, with occasionally most moving effect, to make these repetitions simultaneous.

Nevertheless, the play, as an artistic achievement, was a failure. The episodes in the first act were too short to be anything but bewildering and boring. Mr. Guthrie was tediously preoccupied with psychiatric theories that are as outmoded as last year's hats. His characters were types. The beginning was pretentious, and the end as drawn-out as a guerrilla war. Mr. Guthrie was, in fact, like Mr. Sundstrom, another who shot high and missed.

At the end of his life, as he lay dying, Bertie (rather sentimentally) found God. A light shone on him from the roof of the St. James's, and a voice spoke to him from on high.

Another and more troubling aspect of the search for God is revealed in Armand Salacrou, the author of *Les Nuits de la Colère*, one of the plays that the Renaud-Barrault Company brought to this same theatre in the autumn of 1951. Salacrou is one of the great figures of the modern French theatre. He was born in Rouen in 1899, and spent his youth in Le Havre, where his father was a chemist. He came to Paris as a young man, and at the Sorbonne he studied medicine, law, and philosophy. As a writer, he says that he is purely a man of the theatre. He began three novels, but they all turned in the end into plays. He declares that he gets fogged in descriptions and detests psychology, so that his natural bent is towards that form of writing which absolves him from describing, and enables him to show action without commentary.

M. Salacrou lives in a glittering apartment in the Avenue Foch, the most fashionable spoke of the wheel whose centre is the Arc de Triomphe. The entrance hall is bathed in a translucency of green which recalls sunlight playing upon the surface waters of a lagoon; and the walls of his drawing room are bright with pictures by Braque and Picasso. M. Salacrou radiates brightness and light; his inventively exuberant gestures, which are famous in Paris, are the symbol of an intellectual vivacity which was not extinguished even by the three years he spent as a schoolboy eating steak and kidney pie in Salisbury. In loyal memory of those days before the 1914 war he still eats steak and kidney pie on his rare visits to London.

Salacrou's intellectual activity is so great, and so manifest in his social behaviour, it gives him such an air of gay endeavour, that one would hardly guess—what is exceedingly apparent from his work—that he is a man haunted, as Mr. Guthrie's Bertie was haunted, by the necessity of finding God. Yet he is obsessed by a single thought—the destiny of a humanity that has ceased to believe in God. I do not mean that his plays are solemn, or that he is given to denouncing mankind in the accents of an ancient and angry prophet. On the contrary, his work sparkles with humour and wit. Yet he is always conscious that men have taken away his Lord, and that he knows not where they have laid him. In one of his plays, *Un Homme Comme les Autres*, a woman is reproached for drinking rum. 'You have taken God away from me', she replies; 'what is left if you take rum as well?' In *Histoire de Rire*, which would have been seen in London in the early 1940's but for the war, two men have been left by their wives. 'What have we to complain of?' says one. 'Today people no longer marry for eternity. Do we go to Mass? No. Very well then. For all their morality our wives have only a single word: love. And it is the vaguest word in the world, the least precise.'

Does M. Salacrou himself go to Mass? Probably not. His is the dilemma of the man who feels the necessity of faith, and lacks the capacity for it. He is convinced that there can be no salvation without God, and yet cannot convince himself that God exists. He longs for the mystic experience, and finds it alien to his nature and his reason. His most sympathetic critic, José van den Esch, says that Saul on the way to Damascus was not rent by a greater anguish than Salacrou. But for Saul there was the thunder-clap, and the lightning flash, whilst for Salacrou the sky remains empty.

This is a matter that M. van den Esch has twice discussed with M. Salacrou. On both occasions Salacrou went back to an incident in his childhood which he has made use of in *L'Archipel Lenoir*. 'One day, at the age of seven,' he said to van den Esch, 'I realised that I existed. It was terrifying!' In *L'Archipel Lenoir* one of his characters says, 'Do you remember, M. Lenoir, the exact moment when, suddenly, as a little boy, you thought to yourself, "I am alive, I could not avoid existing, and I am some day going to die"? No? I do! And I was terrified. It was an intolerable weight for the shoulders of a little boy.'

M. van den Esch adds that M. Salacrou found comfort in reading a book called *Le Catéchisme Républicain*, the sort of book that might well have been given as a school prize to young children in 1905 or 1906. It contained the pure milk of the then fashionable scientific doctrine, and explained to children the secrets of the Universe according to Lamarck and Darwin. It raised scientific atheism to the level of mysticism, and, says van den Esch, it brought 'to young Salacrou an interior peace that lasted until his adolescence. Though he belonged to a Catholic family, he refused both confession and communion, resting himself on the great revelation . . . he had just received.'

But this peace did not last beyond his early manhood. A universe constructed on purely mechanistic principles became unbearable to him. His heart and his soul yearned for God, but his mind could not believe in Him. This way lies despair. 'He searches for faith,' says van den Esch, 'but, by a contradiction in which is to be found all the tragic mystery of his destiny, he has no hope of finding it. Hence the permanent anguish that distresses him. For this unbeliever, this "atheist", remains convinced that, outside faith, there is no salvation.'

This feeling underlies even his lightest comedies. There could hardly be a play gayer or wittier or apparently slighter in texture, for example, than *Histoire de Rire*. It is a story of double adultery among these smart and clever and amusing people who alternate between the cafés of the Champs Elysées and the Côte d'Azur. It is studded with epigrams. It sparkles with wit. Yet its lightest dialogue has a resonance, and its echoes are disturbing. It is a comedy about people who have no religion by a man who has no religion, who feels, desperately, that they all ought to have religion. Another of M. Salacrou's plays, *La Terre Est Ronde*, has for its subject Savonarola and his tremendous doctrine that all is either God or the Devil, debauchery or piety, with nothing in between. Salacrou does not believe this, because he cannot. His soul is thick with doubt. But he would like to believe it. And again his gaiety keeps breaking in. Over these abysses his wit dances airily. *Histoire de Rire* is the sort of play that might result if Savonarola, disturbed by the misgivings of Robert Elsmere, had taken up the pen of Noel Coward. It is something to which, in modern English comedy, there is no parallel.

It is important to understand Salacrou's outlook and temperament, and the bearing of his other plays, before *Les Nuits de la Colère* can be properly appreciated. *Les Nuits de la Colère* is the only contemporary play that Jean-Louis Barrault included in his repertory at the St. James's. Except in its theatrical effectiveness, it is not typical of M. Salacrou. It opens in the living-room of a chemist's shop in Chartres, near the cathedral, in April, 1944, two months before the landings in Normandy. There is a round-up of the Resistance. There is shooting. Rivoire, a member of the Resistance, is killed. So are Pisançon, a French collaborator, and Bazire, who has tried to keep himself clear of complicity with either side, wanting to be neither hero nor traitor. Their ghosts talk to each other, Pisançon and Bazire resenting their death, which they think could easily have been avoided, but Rivoire exulting in his fate. Their wives enter, still living, and then the spirit of Jean Cordeau, Bazire's friend of long standing, whom he has, reluctantly, unwittingly, betrayed to the enemy, comes to them out of his prison, where his gaolers have blinded him. These characters, some dead, some alive, and one absent, speak to each other, and the scene shifts, fades, and transforms itself, passing through space and time, till the whole story is told of Cordeau's blowing up of a German ammunition train, his seeking of refuge in the Bazires' home, and their handing him over, so as not to endanger their children, to Pisançon and torture. 'And yet', says Bazire, with both sadness and truth, 'under Louis-Philippe I should have been quite a decent fellow.' I have mentioned the Surrealist pictures on the walls of M. Salacrou's apartment in the Avenue Foch. In *Les Nuits de la Colère* there is surrealism in his technique.

But the quality that distinguishes *Les Nuits de la Colère* from the other plays of M. Salacrou is the note of hope that sounds through its sombre story. *Les Nuits de la Colère* is a tragedy, and *Histoire de Rire* a comedy, yet while the comedy despairs, the tragedy looks forward to a future of happiness and nobility. In this play Salacrou appears for a moment to have ceased looking for a God whom he has not seen, in order to love and to admire the brother whom he has. He describes it himself as his only optimistic play. The fraternity of the Resistance roused in him hopes for the brotherhood of man, and for the duration of the play the brotherhood of man seems a sufficient ideal, and a justification of the whole earthly travail. In the first few minutes of the opening scene, M. Salacrou unfolds this flag of hope, and it will be seen that he waves it boldly, without any self-consciousness about heroics:

PISANÇON: Don't you understand that you are finished, just like me?
RIVOIRE: It isn't the same thing.
PISANÇON: But you are done in, just as I am.
  (*Gun-shots outside*).
RIVOIRE: No! My comrades go on. And one day, men will be free and happy. They won't know that I died for them, and I don't want them to know. What counts, is my certainty that they will be happy. So I have no despair in my heart, and I die with a smile on my lips.

There is no irony here. Vershinin also hoped that one day men would be happy, but Chekhov was not so easily persuaded. I do not know whether M. Salacrou shares Rivoire's confidence today, but he certainly did so in 1946. It opens the play, and it closes it. It is the last thing that M. Salacrou leaves in our minds as the curtain falls. The blind Jean Cordeau separates himself from

F

his friends, comes to the front of the stage, and, realism rebuked and defeated, speaks straight to the audience:

'You who will survive us for a few years; tell your children who grow up around you, never to despair of life, for, in the confusion of a time like this, we were able to live honourably.'

There was a time when English actors could walk right out of a play, and consciously speak a set piece with every device of beauty of tone and perfection of intonation of which they were capable. That was in the days when poets wrote soliloquies. Our English actors have no longer the opportunity, nor perhaps the desire, to speak with this rhetorical loveliness. In France it is different. Even in a realistic play an actor will suddenly realise that the words the author has put into his mouth are of more than ordinary pathos or impressiveness. He will then forget the play, forget his fellow-actors, and address the audience directly with all the artifice at his command. The words he speaks may be a reply to something that someone else on the stage has said to him. No matter. The interlocutor will be ignored, and the words launched directly across the footlights. There was a striking instance of this in Mme Elvire Popesco's performance in André Roussin's *Nina*, which, after its Paris run was over, I was lucky enough to catch during my holidays in 1951 in a one-night presentation in the Municipal Casino at Biarritz.

Nina is a middle-aged woman whose lover is beginning to tire of her, and whose husband, Adolphe, is ludicrously involved in the affair. In the last few minutes of the play, the lover, Gérard, is determined to leave Paris, to go anywhere to escape, even to Mexico. In a series of admirable speeches, full of a fantasy at once realistic and poetic, Nina almost, but not quite, persuades him to stay. She makes these speeches whilst they are both sitting on a couch, and when Gérard at last departs, her husband sits down beside her. She watches Gérard go out of the room without a word, and then, with a strained face, feeling an intolerable need for reassurance, she says, 'Adolphe, tell me that I am always beautiful'. An English actress, keeping within the conventions of realism, would stay upon the sofa, and look at Adolphe. But not Mme Popesco. These are the most affecting words in the play, and Mme Popesco was not going to throw them casually away.

She rose from the couch, marched to the footlights, at the absolute halfway mark between the two proscenium pillars, gazed straight at the middle of the dress circle, and spoke with her back to the forgotten Adolphe. The effect might easily have been absurd. As a matter of fact, it was very moving, because the climate of the French theatre allows players to do this sort of thing without self-consciousness, and to speak with a carefully studied beauty.

This is what M. Barrault did with Cordeau's last words in *Les Nuits de la Colère*. He spoke them with heart-rending simplicity and quietness, and the last phrase fell on the air, nobly and softly, like an autumn leaf whose sadness is mitigated by the knowledge that spring will come again.

The idea for *Les Nuits de la Colère* came to Salacrou on the night of Thursday, May 2, 1946, at Courval. By morning the whole plot was in his mind, and the treatment of it, and he set himself to write without delay. When he had finished his first draft he set out, as his custom always is when he has a play on hand, for the Pyrenees, and completed the final version at Luchon. He chose Chartres as the setting for the action of the piece as a compliment to the R.A.F. He says that the Germans in the early days of the war placed their stores close to the cathedral, and it was due to the courage of the men of the R.A.F. in flying low so as to bomb accurately that the cathedral still stands. In two months the play was ready, and on August 7 he returned to Courval. The next day, in the Cheval Blanc at Honfleur, he handed over his manuscript to Madeleine Renaud and Jean-Louis Barrault. It was eleven o'clock in the morning, and he left the Barraults to read the play, whilst he and his wife went, rather nervously, to look over a Norman museum in the neighbourhood. It was a critical moment in the career of both Salacrou and Barrault. Salacrou had not allowed any of his plays to be presented in Paris since the fall of the city in 1940. The Barraults had just taken the momentous step of leaving the Comédie Française, where Mme Renaud had been a great star for more than twenty years. They had assumed management of the Marigny, and were composing the programme of their opening season with trepidation and care. They were going to do *Les Fausses Confidences* and *Hamlet*. At twelve Salacrou returned, and Barrault told him that he would present

Les Nuits de la Colère at the Marigny somewhere round November 15. Honfleur is not famous for its hotels, and the Cheval Blanc is not the most elaborate of those that this small Normandy town has got. Michelin grants it a pleasant view, but does not suggest there is anything special about the food. Nevertheless, how succulent, exclaims M. Salacrou, were the soles à la crème that day, and how well browned the chicken!

Barrault was taking something of a risk. Salacrou was warned by many of his friends to leave the Resistance alone as a subject for a play, and he was himself a little uneasy when he recalled Racine's rule that the theatre should not deal with contemporary events and people, because the author cannot then acquire the necessary aesthetic detachment. The first-night came on December 12, 1946, and never, says M. Salacrou, did he so long for a play of his to succeed.

Succeed it did. Francis Ambrière said that in its 'astonishing second act' the Barrault company reached the peak of their achievement, and Mme. Dussane called it the most brilliant, the most widely representative of all the plays that deal with the period 1940–5. M. van den Esch thinks that it is less 'written' than some other of Salacrou's work, and that at times the dialogue, in its intense naturalness, has the air of being overheard in shops and on buses. But I can hardly believe that casual conversation reaches such poignancy as the play attains in the scene in which Bazire, badgered and reproached by the friends he has betrayed, rises out of his cringing self-contempt to make his pitiful defence. He had wished to live like the cathedral that he can see from his shop window, serene, untroubled. 'And now', he cries bitterly, 'the cathedral is still standing—and I am wiped out, assassinated.' Here, when for a moment fear is expelled by a sudden vision of life's irony, Jean Desailly was especially moving. And there is more than realism in those last words of Cordeau's of which I have already spoken: 'Et vous qui serez nos survivants pour quelques années, dites à vos enfants que vous verrez grandir, de ne jamais désespérer de la vie, puisque dans la mêlée d'une telle époque, nous avons pu vivre honorablement.' Whether *Les Nuits de la Colère* will be accepted in the future as the representative drama of the war of 1939–45, whether it will, in fact, live, as so few war plays do, may be debatable; but it can be claimed justly that it would be a remarkable shop-girl, or general, or Prime Minister, or even poet, who could, casually and without preparation, throw off such a speech as Cordeau's, with its unaffected nobility, its classical restraint, its exquisite, subtle rhythm, and its beautiful falling close.

Like Salacrou, there is another of France's famous contemporary writers, perhaps the most famous of all beyond the borders of his own country, who does not believe in God. Unlike Salacrou, however, Jean-Paul Sartre has no desire to do so. He is a happy atheist. He is a wealthy atheist, too, but it is not from this that his happiness derives. No doubt he has the natural pleasure which any man must take in reflecting that the product of his brain earns him £54,000 a year, has spread his celebrity all over the world, and identified him with the creation of a new philosophy. But he has not turned this fame and money into luxury. He continues to live within sight of the clock of St. Germain-des-Prés, the church which, among the Existentialist wits, is known as the cathedral, not of Chartres, but of Sartre. At the turn of the century the Faubourg St. Germain was the fashionable residential area of Paris. The great gateways of the district close off from the street the courtyards round which are built the grey palaces in which the Duchesse de Guermantes lived and visited her friends. But much of this glory, which was always hidden, has now vanished. The big doorways are as secretive as ever, but the paint is old, and beginning to peel.

Sartre, however, does not live amidst the declining remnants of this ancient, concealed splendour. His apartment is in the Rue Bonaparte, a few hundred yards to the north of these old, aristocratic dwellings. The Rue Bonaparte is a narrow street that runs from St. Germain-des-Prés to the Rive Gauche and Notre-Dame. It is crowded with little shops that are full of curious treasures. One of them is among the best three theatrical bookshops in the world, the other two being in the Rue Marivaux, off the Grands Boulevards. This area is a paradise of old prints, of mouldering bindings, and of ancient, black-lettered books. It also has small hotels, with narrow staircases, yellow lace curtains, and, till recently, strange notions of sanitation. The unambitious brothels of the district were closed down just after the war.

Short-sighed, a bachelor, middle-aged, Sartre, from these sur-

roundings, carries on a strenuous intellectual warfare with both
Right and Left. The invigorating air of Paris is sharp with controversy. There are men of letters on the Left Bank who have
so exalted themselves in the heady battles of literary quarrels,
and have acquired from them so extravagant a notion of life's
sensationalism, that they bid their friends good night as if they
were dispatching them on some Saracenic Crusade. M. Sartre's
enjoyment of controversy is not of this exuberant kind. But enjoyment it is, nevertheless. The struggle is as dear to his heart as
the triumph.

In the sixty-ninth chapter of Frazer's *Golden Bough* there is a
passage that is very pertinent to the philosophy of Sartre. 'If then
we consider', writes Frazer, 'the essential similarity of man's
chief wants everywhere and at all times, and on the other hand,
the wide difference between the means he has adopted to satisfy
them in different ages, we shall perhaps be disposed to conclude
that the movement of the higher thought, so far as we can trace
it, has on the whole been from magic through religion to science.
. . . In the acuter minds magic is gradually superseded by religion,
which explains the succession of natural phenomena as regulated
by the will, the passion, or the caprice of spiritual beings like man
in kind, though vastly superior to him in power.

'But as time goes on this explanation in its turn proves to be
unsatisfactory. For it assumes that the succession of natural events
is not determined by immutable laws, but is to some extent
variable and irregular, and this assumption is not borne out by
closer observation. On the contrary, the more we scrutinise that
succession the more we are struck by the rigid uniformity, the
punctual precision with which, wherever we can follow them,
the operations of nature are carried on. Every great advance in
knowledge has extended the sphere of order and correspondingly
restricted the sphere of apparent disorder in the world, till now
we are ready to anticipate that even in regions where chance and
confusion appear to reign, a fuller knowledge would everywhere
reduce the seeming chaos to cosmos. . . . In short, religion,
regarded as an explanation of nature, is displaced by science.'

It is, of course, the argument of this chapter that the view here
expressed by Frazer, whose great work was published between
1890 and 1915, in the heyday of philosophic materialism, is not

now tenable, at any rate in its entirety. It is questionable from two viewpoints: first, in its firm basing of religion upon irresponsibility: second, in its ignorance of the philosophic uncertainty produced by the principle of indeterminacy. Its confident rejection of religion, however, is accepted by Sartre: who must, on this account, be considered somewhat old-fashioned.

But Sartre carries the rejection of religion further than Sir James Frazer presumably was willing to do. The Professor of Social Anthropology at Liverpool may not have believed in Christ, but I have no doubt that he loved his neighbour as himself, was kind to the poor, did not answer back, in short, that he admitted the general validity of Christian ethics. But the plays of Sartre's we have seen in London—*Huis-Clos*, *Men Without Shadows*, *Crime Passionnel*—and his latest, longest work for the stage, *Le Diable et le Bon Dieu* (Paris: Antoine, June, 1951), throw out the ethics along with the religion. When the baby has gone, Sartre does not wish to retain the bath water.

Sartre's position is clearly stated by M. Marc Beigbeder in his study, *L'Homme Sartre* (Paris, Bordas, 1947). 'The Existentialist', says M. Beigbeder, 'is strongly opposed to a certain kind of lay morality that tries to suppress God at the least possible expense. When, round about 1880, French professors attempted to construct a secular philosophy, they said something like this: God is a useless and costly hypothesis which we throw overboard, but it is necessary however, in the interests of morality and society, to say nothing of the police, that certain values should be admitted to exist *a priori*: it must *a priori* be necessary to be honest, not to tell lies, not to knock one's wife about, and to keep the world peopled, etc., etc. . . . we will therefore show that these values exist all the same, written intelligibly in heaven, although there is no God. In other words . . . nothing will be changed if God does not exist; we shall find the same ideals of honesty, progress, humanity, and we shall have made God into an outworn hypothesis which will die quietly by itself.'

This, I take it, would, had he defined it, have been the position of Sir James Frazer, as it is today the tacit assumption of millions of excellent people who stay away from church. But it is not the position of M. Sartre.

'The Existentialist, on the other hand,' continues M. Beigbeder, 'thinks that it is distinctly a bore that there is no God, for with Him disappears the possibility of finding values in an intelligible heaven; there cannot any longer be any good *a priori*, since there is no infinite and perfect conscience to conceive it; it is nowhere established that good exists, that one must be honest, and not lie, since we live in a world where only man exists. Dostoievsky said: "If God does not exist, all things are permissible." That is the starting-point of Existentialism.'

This is what M. Sartre's latest play, *Le Diable et le Bon Dieu*, comes to in the end, though the end is a long time in coming. The curtain went up at the Antoine at eight o'clock, and did not come down till ten minutes before midnight. Even so, much of the original play was cut, and there are said to have been vigorous arguments between Sartre and his producer, the late Louis Jouvet, before he would allow certain passages to be omitted. The official reason given for these cuts was the play's great length, but the gossip of Paris asserts that the omitted passages were blasphemous. Some of those left in are striking enough, though Sartre maintains that the most shocking are quotations from respectable authorities. He takes a malicious pleasure in ascribing the least reverent phrases in the play to saints and Fathers of the Church. 'L'église est une putain, says one of the characters, who is named Nasty (without any ulterior motive, for Sartre does not speak English well). This is a phrase of Savonarola's. 'You are a bastard'— 'Yes, like Jesus Christ', is the reply. That, says Sartre, was a remark of Pope Clement VII.

These observations, and others like them, were tossed to and fro in the course of a bloodthirsty and turbulent story, interspersed with theological and political argument, set in the wars of the Reformation. Captain Goetz was a soldier of fortune who lived like a devil, and then, for a wager, behaved for a year like a saint. But as a saint he did more harm than as a sinner, for the city he ruled over prospered, its enemies grew jealous and attacked it, and 25,000 men, women, and children were killed. The tale is full of sensationalism. It was on a game of dice that Goetz staked his sanctity. A Pope was murdered on a balcony. Goetz took into his arms the repulsive and scaly body of a leper. Under a white and tormented Crucifix, he stabbed a knife through his hand in order to make the crowd below believe that he had received the stigmata. In the eleven scenes of the play, there was always something violent happening, generally the kind of thing that would have delighted Alexandre Dumas, who would cheerfully have ignored the piece's philosophy and revelled in its blood, horrors, and orgies.

It is difficult to give an adequate impression of the zest and exuberance that Pierre Brasseur brought to his performance of Goetz. Goetz is a tremendous fellow, at one moment a savage killer, at another embracing a leper, all the time feverishly trying to provoke God to take notice of his existence, either by blessing or by blasting him. By temperament M. Brasseur is well suited to this sort of tempestuous character. In his first leading part in a school play M. Brasseur played an old man, and at the end was so overcome with enthusiasm and excitement that he jumped in the air. The parents of the other pupils (like the critics later on, adds Brasseur) said, 'You overdo things'. To which he replied, 'If I don't overdo things, no one will notice me'. He certainly ran no chance of not being noticed in *Le Diable et le Bon Dieu*. Richly black-bearded, blackguardly, plump, and bounding, he played Goetz with blood-curdling geniality. His exuberant delight in crime gave him an inner excitement that would not let him be still for a moment, and his step had an extraordinary elasticity. He did not seem to walk across the stage so much as bounce from one end of it to the other. He had the darting vitality of those celluloid balls that leap gaily up and down on jets of water in fairground shooting galleries. If those jets of water were jets of blood the comparison would be even closer.

Nevertheless, it would be inaccurate. The celluloid balls are controlled by a force outside themselves. But to the Existentialist there is no force outside Goetz. 'Man', says Sartre, 'is only what he makes himself. That is the first principle of Existentialism. Man is fully responsible for what he is.' At the end of the play God had given no sign, and Goetz was left, not in the least depressed, to make out his own life in perfect freedom from any force beyond humanity.

There are French dramatists whose work has been seen in London who do not approve these doctrines. In an interview with Paul Guth, Paul Claudel exclaimed, 'Look at Sartre! He has plenty of talent. But how hideous it is! It is hell. Dante's is nothing to it'. Claudel, too, as well as Sartre, is now known in London. His *Partage de Midi* was presented by Barrault in his St. James's season. It is a play with a curious history. Claudel has had a long and distinguished career in the French diplomatic service. He has served as Ambassador in Hamburg, Pekin, Tokyo, Rio de Janeiro, Washington and Brussels, and wherever he has been in the world he has written plays. For more than a score of years the manuscripts of Claudel plays came regularly into Paris from the ends of the earth. Claudel wrote in the early mornings with the pertinacity and steadiness of Anthony Trollope, another but less eminent public servant. For many years these plays were considered unactable, though when he published *Le Soulier de Satin* in 1924, Claudel, never despairing, put in some stage directions with the words, 'After all, it is not absolutely impossible that one day it will be played'. Yet *Le Soulier de Satin* had to wait almost a score of years before Barrault solved the problem of making the long poetic Claudelian line speakable without monotony in his production at the Comédie Française during the war.

In this chapter we have found many examples of dramatists whose thoughts are preoccupied with religion. But Claudel is the first of them to be, like Eliot, a convinced and devout Christian. That revelation for which Salacrou has waited in vain came to Claudel long ago, at a definite moment in time. He can fix the place of it with touching, yet almost ludicrous, exactitude. It was Christmas Day, 1886, and he was standing behind the second pillar in Notre-Dame, on the right, at the entrance of the choir, when he recognized that the gates of the Christian church had closed, and he was inside them. This has not mellowed his spirit. When he was asked if he thought the growing influence of religion in literature would lead to more charity and gentleness of manners, he responded, 'What do you mean by charity? Charity towards evil-doers, or towards their victims? I am reading the Psalms. There is not a psalm that does not talk of enemies. David's hand wasn't nerveless. The Fathers of the Church weren't easygoing.' Julien Green records that when Gide said of Claudel that he was a man who thought he could go to heaven by Pullman, Claudel promptly retorted that Gide was travelling to hell by Metro.

It was in 1906 that Claudel first published *Partage de Midi*. He issued it in a limited edition of 150 copies only, because it was a record of a personal experience that he did not wish to share with the general public. It was not until the late 40's that he allowed an unrestricted edition to appear. This gave Barrault the chance to argue that if all the world could read the play, there seemed no reason why audiences at the Marigny should not be permitted to see it. Claudel, a logician as well as a mystic, agreed, and it was presented at the Marigny on December 17, 1948, with Edwige Feuillère as Ysé, Pierre Brasseur as Amalric, Jacques Dacqmine as de Ciz, and Barrault himself as Mesa. In the audience was the lady who had been the original Ysé, her youth now fled like the author's.

M. Claudel is not, as a dramatist, universally admired in France. He has been criticised in terms that in England we usually reserve for young men writing their first play. Claudel's 'sort of literature', says Paul Léautaud, 'with its hodge-podge of images, its verbal delirium, and its basis in bigotry does not give the idea of a great intelligence'. 'What is called the genius of Claudel', another critic remarks, 'is only aphasia. He is given to making powerful noises, some of which are true and the others unintelligible.' It has been said of his *Satin Slipper* (*Le Soulier de Satin*), 'Thank heaven there isn't a pair'.

Claudel's characteristic faults are easily discernible in *Partage de Midi*. These are verbosity, turgidity, cloudiness, and bathos. It is a formidable collection. Yet, anywhere but in a play, he can write with excellent directness. His statement of the situation out of which *Partage de Midi* arises, given in his preface to the play, is admirable. 'A man, ill prepared by his upbringing and temperament, has received, in spite of himself, a call from God, a call he cannot deny. After a long resistance that has led him to the ends of the earth, he decides to respond to it. Controlling his trembling will, he presents himself at the altar, and it is from God that he receives an answer. Sharp and clear. A rejection pure and simple, a peremptory No without any explanation whatever. He is flatly shut out, yet without any knowledge that the inexorable call has ceased. Once again he seeks solitude, exile. In actual fact, he finds it in the sea, and, during interminable days, in a certain position between the sky and the ocean outside everything. It is noonday.' In the actual play of *Partage de Midi* there is hardly anything so

admirably clear as this. The long speech in the middle of the first
act in which Mesa, on board the baking ship in the middle of the
Indian Ocean, with the hot sun blazing down on his white tropic
suit and on Barrault's bony, agonised countenance, tells the lan-
guid, lingering Ysé of his unhappy rejection by God, was superbly
spoken by M. Barrault; but it does not set the situation with the
sharpness of M. Claudel's preface. There are many moments in
the play when one does not exactly know what is happening,
and not all these are as deliberately arranged as the author's curious
omission to inform us whether his heroine is or is not a child-
murderess.

These defects, if defects they are, count for very little against
the play's splendid and shining qualities. Of all the plays that I
have seen since I became dramatic critic of *The Sunday Times*,
Partage de Midi furnished me with the most impressive, the most
memorable experience I have had in the theatre both in the intensity of its spiritual awareness and no less in its mastery of the small
change of melodramatic effectiveness.

Consider the use of the ship's bell. Ysé, crushed by the heat, is
lying in her deck chair, shaded by a parasol, listlessly rocking to
and fro, the strong, sensual Amalric stands beside her, and Mesa
leans over the ship's rails at the side of the stage, facing the audience. 'The sun is killing me', moans Ysé, 'I can no longer support
its strength.' 'The full strength of the sun', exclaims Amalric in
the confidence of his immense vitality. 'It is good to be able to
stare death in the face, and to have strength enough to resist it.'

There is a long silence, and the blaze of light through the white
awnings of the ship is so intense that it seems that, despite Amalric,
the sun has burned the life out even of time itself. Then, on this
interminable solitude both in time and space, sonorous, round,
and clear breaks the sound of the vessel's bell. Mesa's face seems
to shrink, and then he says, as if to himself, 'Noonday in heaven.
Noonday at the centre of our lives.'

There is a famous passage in de Quincey about the knocking
on the door in *Macbeth*, the breaking in of the commonplace
noises of every day on the murderers' guilty bedchamber. The
effect of the Porter's knocking always seems to me more exciting
in de Quincey's feverish prose than it does on the stage, where
indeed it is generally a very ordinary rat-tat-tat. But the sound

of the ship's bell in *Partage de Midi* made my heart stand still.
It seemed fraught with destiny and challenge, a destiny and a
challenge that the heat-exhausted bodies of Mesa and Ysé were
powerless either to meet or to control.

The credit for the sounding of the bell at this point in the play
belongs to M. Barrault, for Claudel's stage directions make no
mention of it. But with Barrault's performance as Mesa a certain .
dissatisfaction was expressed in London. In the first place, it was
felt that he was too small, probably on the theory, very widely
held by the ignorant, that God can speak only to men six and a
half feet tall. I also detected in the theatre a suspicion that M.
Barrault looked too intelligent, too clear-eyed to have a mystical
experience, a suspicion based on the companion theory that such
an experience can come only to the manifestly half-witted. These
objections to M. Barrault's performance I regard as too trivial
for discussion, but the feeling that he contorted his face too much
in speaking certain of his lines has more ground to stand on. Certainly there were moments when the working of M. Barrault's
jaws exceeded the licence that we should instinctively allow to an
English actor. But the sounds that he was able to produce by this
mobility of his face were, to my ears, ravishing; and the rhetoric
with which he brought the play to a close, advancing to the footlights as in *Les Nuits de la Colère*, and offering himself to the
Almighty 'in the supreme splendour of summer, the Spirit conquering in the transfiguration of noonday', had the real, choking
excitement of the greatest theatre.

But to judge M. Barrault only as an actor is a considerable
mistake. It is like judging Shaw exclusively as a political pamphleteer, or Shakespeare as a writer of sonnets. In other words it is a
howler, even though he is a sufficiently dominating actor to have
caused some French critics, Mme Beatrix Dussane being one of
them, to compare him, point by point, with Sir Laurence Olivier.

His powers of mime give a fluidity to his performances rare
on any stage. But it is as an animator, what one of his authors
more picturesquely calls a bomb, that his chief mark on the
theatre has been made. He is not only excellent in himself, he
is the cause that excellence is in others. Like John Gielgud, he
habitually surrounds himself with the best players, so that his
productions are a Milky Way of coruscations. No one is likely

to underestimate the immense services that Mr. Gielgud has
rendered to the theatre, services for which no conceivable honour
would be too great a recognition. His productions of *Hamlet*, of
Richard II, of *The Seagull*, and of *Three Sisters* touch the high-
water mark of the theatre. Nevertheless, there were, before Mr.
Gielgud, first-class productions of these plays. But before Barrault there were no productions at all of *Partage de Midi* or of
Le Soulier de Satin. Barrault has taken plays which everyone
thought unplayable, and shown them to be of the stuff of classics.
He has brought new planets into the sky of authorship.

It was in 1949 that Viscount Kemsley, recognizing, as was rarely
done at that time, the great importance of foreign drama in its
relationship to the English stage, and to western culture, gave me
on his personal initiative the opportunity of visiting Broadway;
and since then he has afforded me many chances of studying
the Continental theatre on behalf of *The Sunday Times*. Of all
the experiences which these opportunities have brought me undoubtedly the most important has been that of seeing the work
of Jean-Louis Barrault and Madeleine Renaud at the Marigny
Theatre.

If the sounding of the bell belonged to M. Barrault as producer,
M. Claudel can claim the central and original merit of *Partage de
Midi*. The play is about a soul's salvation. After his rejection,
Mesa finds himself, on the hot decks of the ship in which he is
travelling to the East, tempted to adultery with the attractive
and sultry Ysé, a married woman, whose husband, de Ciz, is on
board the same boat. Now, few things could be more banal or
foreseeable than Mesa's attainment of salvation by resistance to
this temptation.

It is M. Claudel's brilliant theatrical achievement in this play,
and it outweighs all his defects, that he springs on us the surprise,
which he makes absolutely convincing, of saving Mesa, not by
resisting temptation, but by falling into it. The very fine third
act takes place in a port in Southern China during the Boxer
rebellion at the turn of the century. In the first act Claudel has
shown Mesa and Ysé tempted. In the second, at night in a Hong-
Kong cemetery, they are plainly succumbing, and Mesa, who is an
important colonial official, sends off de Ciz to his death by offering
him an appointment in the cholera-ridden hinterland pretty much

as David dealt with Uriah the Hittite. Francis Ambrière justly remarks that the third act ought to reveal the culmination of the passion between Ysé and Mesa, and its subsequent breakdown. This is what the construction of the play calls for, but does not get. Instead the third act takes place after Ysé deserts Mesa, and joins the physically strong and decisive Amalric. There are the cries and shots of the rebels in the streets, and the high, thin voices of the actors in some nearby Chinese theatre, and Amalric and Ysé are trapped, unable to escape. At this moment Mesa breaks in, with a safe-conduct which Ysé refuses without a word, preferring to die with Amalric rather than live without him. But in a fight between Mesa and Amalric, Mesa is stunned, Amalric and Ysé get away with his pass, and he is left to be blown up in the dark and disordered room, which has been mined.

It is now complete night, but, as Mesa wakes, the stars in the sky shine brilliantly through the windows, and the moon throws a great silver beam across the floor. For a long time Mesa remains silent, thinking, and then he breaks into the immense and impressive canticle which is the crown and the solution of the play. For, until this moment, Mesa has never been really capable of love, of giving himself entirely to another. Some personal preoccupation has always stood in the way of complete surrender. It is this egoism of his, this self-centredness, that caused his rejection by God, and his desertion by Ysé. For the first time in his life, in the terrible agony he suffers at being now twice refused, first by God and then by a woman, this egoism disappears, and he thinks of something else besides himself. Specifically he thinks of the Crucifixion, and he cries, 'Ah, now I know what love is! And now I know what you endured on your cross, in your Heart, since you loved each one of us as terribly as I loved this woman.' This scene, the culmination of the play, is among the two or three really tremendous things of the modern theatre.

All this time I have said nothing of the remarkable actress, Edwige Feuillère, who played Yés. Mme. Feuillère I consider to be, without exception, the greatest and most moving player I have ever seen. She is the only actress I know who unites absolute mastery of her art with utter physical beauty and radiance. Yet in the past she used to worry unnecessarily over the thought that she was not pretty. When she appeared before the theatrical jury of the Conservatoire in Paris, she heard someone whisper, 'What a pity she is so ugly'. And the reply—'Réjane was ugly, too'—though kindly meant, might have been more reassuring.

She had been brought up in Dijon, a strict Protestant, by parents who thought the theatre derived from Babylon and Gomorrah. Her real name, before she married, was Vigette Cunati; it was her grandmother who first began to call her Edwige. When she was nineteen, it looked as though she would have to become a provincial typist. Instead, she took the train to Paris, and arrived at the Gare de Lyon with 35 francs in her pocket. Her biographer, Robert Kemp, adds that other authorities (less reliable) say 30 francs.

She had with her an introduction from a Dijon clergyman to the manageress of the Union of Christian Young Women, 22 rue de Naples, and it was from this address that she started her theatrical career. She had been organist in the Protestant church in Dijon, and at first she studied music as well as acting. One day, when she recited in one of the classes at the Conservatoire, a voice from the back exclaimed, 'Elle est formidable!' This voice belonged to another student, Pierre Feuillère, whom a few years later she married.

In reviewing Noel Coward's *Relative Values*, and applauding the author for having the courage to make his hero a peer of the realm, Beverley Baxter protested against the contemporary cant that only a truck driver can fall in love. Equally ridiculous is the notion, much fostered by gossip writers, that every eminent figure of the theatre or screen is a hearty, back-slapping, hail-fellow-well-met, jolly, companionable extravert. When Mme Feuillère arrived in London, a considerable effort was made to represent her as the sort of friendly young woman who calls everybody, from the first meeting, by their Christian name. I have never spoken to Mme Feuillère, but I should doubt whether this is an accurate picture of her. After the first night of *Partage de Midi* at the St. James's, the French Ambassador and Mme Massigli gave a party for the company. Mme Renaud and M. Barrault were genially available to everyone. They smiled, they nodded, they mingled among the other guests, they were ready to engage anybody in conversation, either in fluent French or gallant English.

Mme Feuillère, on the other hand, was tired and aloof. She sat in a distant corner of the great saloon at the Embassy, barricaded by a table, and anyone who wished to speak to her stood in a slowly moving queue whose members she received with cold, indifferent dignity. Only once, when John Gielgud reached the place of introduction, did she show any sign of pleasure. Then, briefly, a wan smile came to her face.

M. Kemp says she is secretive; she hides from the sunlight; there are few anecdotes about her. Consequently, little is known of her marriage, except the plain fact that it was not a success. Pierre Feuillère and his wife Edwige set out on the road to fame, but only the lady arrived. Feuillère had culture, a love of literature, and taste, but he fell further and further behind his brilliant wife. He felt humiliated, and they were divorced, but he allowed her to keep the name to which she had brought celebrity and he had not. Like many young men between the wars, he was haunted by the thought of suicide, which became more insistent as the years went by, and in 1940 he did in fact take his life.

It is obvious that Mme Feuillère's career has not been an easy, nor always a happy one. Great as has been her success both on screen and stage, she has passed through experiences that either deepen or destroy. What they have contributed to her art and personality I cannot say, because I do not know enough about them. But they have left her an actress of extraordinary power and majestic sadness. Her voice is miraculously soft, and comforting, and sensuous, and caressing, and warm; in swathed Edwardian costumes she glides about the stage with the utmost grace. Apparently she can induce tears to stand in her eyes, and make them glitter like stars, at will. She is at all times in command of her performance, and throughout *Partage de Midi* she did not once sit down in her rocking-chair on the deck, however emotional the crisis, without unobtrusively sliding one hand down to steady it. She uttered words as simple as 'How hot it is' with such languor, with such a sense of voluptuous suffocation, that the air of the theatre seemed heavy with heat. She has gaiety too, a sadder gaiety than that with which Mme Renaud had enchanted us a few nights before in Marivaux's *Les Fausses Confidences*. Into the gaiety of both these actresses pain can enter. But whereas with Mme Renaud one knows the pain will soon pass, and sun-

G

shine return, with Mme Feuillère the pain is always there, though the rippling laughter sometimes hides it.

There is a kind of religion that is passion and agony, a rending of the spirit, and a dividing asunder of the bones and marrow. This is the religion of desperate questioning and high emotion and mystic exaltation; and we get something of it in *Partage de Midi*. That other kind of religion, of the quiet, steadfast gaze, that is a stay and a refuge, that casts out fear in a perfect confidence in the goodness of God, that eschews emotion, and is restful and refreshing, has no part at all in M. Claudel's play, but it is fundamental to *A Sleep of Prisoners* (St. Thomas's Church, Regent Street, May, 1951). This work of Mr. Fry's, and Peter Ustinov's *The Love of Four Colonels*, were the only new British plays of outstanding merit produced during the Festival of Britain.

There is an incident in *Partage de Midi*, in the second act, in which Mesa deliberately sends de Ciz to his death by suggesting to him, with a deceptive air of off-hand dissuasion, an appointment in some disease-ridden colony. I have already mentioned this incident, but not pointed out the most curious thing about it, which surely is that M. Claudel apparently regards it as hardly worthy of notice. Mesa's sin is that he is an egoist; murder is not reckoned up in his account at all. Mr. Fry has a keener sense of the sanctity of human life. Indeed the first time I saw *A Sleep of Prisoners* this notion of the sanctity of human life seemed to me its chief quality. Mr. Fry appeared to be horrified at the thought of death artificially induced, whether by murder or by war. On a memorable occasion during the rebellion of the American colonies Edmund Burke in the House of Commons said, 'The proposition is peace'. Not peace at some unspecified date in the future, not peace with all the objects of war gained, not peace with honour, but peace unqualified, peace absolute, peace now. Mr. Fry seemed also to be saying the proposition is peace.

His play is a dreamed dream. His four soldiers in a bombed church in enemy territory one after the other fall asleep, and confused memories of the Old Testament return to them. Cain again slays Abel, David mourns for Absalom, Abraham is ready to offer up Isaac, and Shadrach, Meshach, and Abednego walk unharmed through the burning, fiery furnace.

I am not going to say that every line, nor even every incident in

Mr. Fry's play, was crystal clear. A critic in Oxford was laughed at somewhat for supposing that the miracle of the fiery furnace was really the story of Jonah and the whale. It seems to have been a conclusion too quickly jumped at from one of the soldiers exclaiming,

> Fish, fish, fish in the sea, you flash
> Through your clouds of water like the war in heaven,

and again,

> God, have mercy
> On our sick shoals, darting and dying.

In all conscience, it was a sufficiently unintelligent guess, but Mr. Fry must himself accept some responsibility for the confusion. He is an allusive author, and his audience often has to take long jumps from his words to his meaning. Audiences being what they are, it was risky of Mr. Fry to mention fish in connexion with the Old Testament if he did not wish us to think of the biggest thing in the ocean, even if, pedantry ruling, it is not a fish at all.

But though many passages in *A Sleep of Prisoners* remained obscure, despite the miracles of clarification that Michael Mac-Owan achieved as director, there were features in it most encouraging to those who entertain high hopes of Mr. Fry as a dramatist. In it Mr. Fry remembers that a play is to be seen as well as heard; he who has always satisfied the ear, now satisfied the eye as well. I do not mean by the provision of sumptuous spectacle, by the parade of elaborate scenery, by the display of beautiful women. I mean that in *A Sleep of Prisoners*, Mr. Fry, for the first time in his work so far as I can recall, used sight as well as hearing to advance his story and to produce dramatic effect. When Cain slew Abel, for example, the body of the watching Adam strained and struggled to hold back the murderer's hand in an action that threw him, held by invisible bonds, into the likeness of a man on a cross. Without one word being spoken, we realised that for Mr. Fry, every time a man is killed, our Lord is crucified again, and the effect was purely visual.

The play does not contain much of the highly charged imagery characteristic of Mr. Fry; in its place there is often a new and dramatic economy. When Joab lurches back with the body of the slain and defeated Absalom in his arms, David anxiously asks,

> Joab, is that you? Joab, is that you?
> What are you bringing back?

and Joab replies, with succinct and frightening irony,

> The victory.

That, to Mr. Fry, is what victory is, a corpse. 'Are you sure it is victory, Joab?' says David.

> Are you ever sure it's the victory?
> So many times you've come back, Joab,
> With something else.

I do not see that victory can logically be maintained always and to all sections of the world community to be thus barren of profit. To the world as a whole, yes; the earth is poorer than it was when the series of modern wars started in 1914. But there are sectional benefits almost invariably. It can hardly be denied that the position of Russia was stronger five years after the war of 1939–45 ended than it was five years before it began; it is doubtful whether, but for two devastating conflicts, the United States would loom so large in world affairs as it does today; even in Britain, incontestably an over-all loser, there have been gainers, for the recent wars have given an immense impetus to the welfare of the working classes. The price that has been paid, at any rate in Britain and in Russia, in lives lost and in wealth dissipated, has been enormous. But the corpse, to those who can despoil it, is attired in rich trappings.

Mr. Fry, however, is not advancing an argument, but expressing a feeling. And in the end his feeling is positive, not negative. The last emphasis of *A Sleep of Prisoners* is not on the uselessness, nor even the wickedness, of war, but on the actual goodness and power of God. In confidence and quietness shall be thy strength.

> Good has no fear;
> Good is itself, what ever comes.
> It grows, and makes, and bravely
> Persuades, beyond all tilt of wrong:
> Stronger than anger, wiser than strategy,
> Enough to subdue cities and men
> If we believe it with a long courage of truth.

There is the heart of the play, a heart that beats strong and true.

To this quiet confidence the theatre has brought us from the anguished questioning of *Sayonara*. It has perhaps brought us further than life.

The four actors in *A Sleep of Prisoners* were Denholm Elliott, Hugh Pryse, Leonard White, and Stanley Baker. They rightly subordinated themselves to the play, and gave performances of sincerity and understanding.

Chapter Four

THE INVOLVED THEATRE

I HAVE written of *Le Diable et le Bon Dieu* as if it were a religious play, or at least as if it raised certain religious problems. But it is also a political play, and on this aspect of it Sartre himself dwells with emphasis. In the sixteenth century, he says, men were poised between rival systems of religion, and today they are poised between the U.S.S.R. and the United States. Presumably there is significance in the fact that his hero decides to get on without help from either side.

M. Sartre is the principal European exponent of *Le Théâtre Engagé*, the theatre mixed up in politics and the problems of the day, which I have called, at the head of this chapter, the involved theatre. I have had to make this inadequate translation because in current English there is no phrase corresponding to *le théâtre engagé*, just as there was no word for Socialism in Anglo-Saxon or for atom bomb in Latin, neither of these things then existing. The English theatre has kept itself remarkably aloof from political considerations since the war, even more than some foreign observers think.

When Mrs. Aimée Stuart's *Lace on Her Petticoat* (London, Ambassadors, December, 1950: New York, October, 1951) was produced in the United States, for example, that brilliant and perverse critic, George Jean Nathan, whom I always read with admiration and apoplexy, seemed to think that the play had some observations to make on the subject of social snobbery; whilst John Gassner more heavy-footedly felt that it ought to appeal to America's democratic sympathies. If these are the standards of the involved theatre, it would be hard to deny to the most romantic novelette about the marriage of a mill girl to a duke some degree of social significance. In London, however, *Lace on Her Petticoat* was taken rather less seriously. This story of the friendship between a poor little girl and a rich little girl in a Scottish village of sixty or seventy years ago was produced just before the Christmas holidays; and in the small Ambassadors theatre it furnished a pleasant enough seasonable entertainment to many young people temporarily released from the grind of boarding-school. But I am afraid that its claims to be considered a social document escaped our attention.

In western Europe a certain intellectual standard has to be attained before a play can be held an example of the involved theatre: a proviso that, in England, at any rate, immediately makes an immense slaughter amongst the prospective candidates.

The fact is that we have already had our involved theatre. It was written by Shaw, Galsworthy, Houghton and the other dramatists of the Manchester school in days when, as Mme Dussane has remarked, the Parisian theatre was given over chiefly to frivolous entertainment. Even so it must be admitted that conditions in England are not so favourable to the production of politically conscious drama as they are in France. There are, it is true, theatrical organisations in London which are extremely aware of the incidence of political theories. No one can accuse the lively and tendentious Unity Theatre of political indifference. That, from this particular point of view, is the trouble with it. The Unity Theatre is an example of politics using the drama, whilst *le théâtre engagé* is the drama using politics.

In London and New York the men of the theatre and the men of affairs belong to different coteries. Occasionally they meet, on such occasions as the receptions that the French Ambassador and his wife, M. and Mme Massigli, give when a company of his countrymen visits London. At such times leading actors and Secretaries of State come together in the same room; but they do not have much to say to each other. Business men, players, and politicians can be seen dining or lunching at the Caprice or the Ivy, but, as the boarding-house advertisements say, they have separate tables. The result is that the statesmen do not talk about the theatre, and the actors and dramatists do not talk about politics. The two worlds cold-shoulder each other.

It is not so in Paris. People of the theatre, politics, fashion, and literature are there mixed up in glorious confusion, all mutually interested in each other's preoccupations and problems. They can be seen in certain cafés, at the Pléiade concerts, and at the British

Embassy, talking animatedly, the whole lot of them, about U.N.R.R.A., U.N.O., the Goncourt award, and why Maurice Chevalier took off his trousers at the Variétés. All these questions interest all these people all the time. That is the way to make politics theatrical, and the theatre political.

This consciousness of political questions was, of course, greatly accentuated during the war. In London our life was settled for us by external regulations, and these regulations were never personal. We had not to decide how much our conscience would permit us to eat: the question was resolved for us by the authorities, who also laid out the part we were to play during air-raids. It was in fact possible for us to fulfil our duties during the war with a certain absence of mind, and to concentrate our attention and thought on the many aspects of existence that remained fundamentally unchanged.

In Paris, between 1940 and 1944, between the time when France surrendered and the time when barricades were thrown up at the point where the Boulevard St. Michel meets the Quai des Grands Augustins, this detachment, this serenity, were not possible. Before the war, and even during the winter of 1939–40, there had, in some quarters, been perhaps too much of it. On New Year's Day, 1940, for example, General Gamelin, who was in supreme command of the French army then at war with Germany, is said to have sent this message to friends who had given his family their Christmas greetings: 'My wife, who is too busy to reply herself, asks me to thank you for your good wishes, and very sincerely to send you ours for the New Year.' But a few months later it was not possible even for a general to separate himself from the war quite as completely as that.

For four years in Paris the streets were filled with grey-green uniforms. The most attractive goods in the shops were bought by German soldiers to be sent back into Berlin or Hamburg. Forty brothels were placed at their disposal. The Occupying Power controlled the newspapers. The German soldiers were indeed everywhere. They prowled the streets at night, where one of them, Ernst Junger, was accosted by an ugly but business-like cocotte with the sensible words, 'Don't pay any attention to the face. It's the work that counts.' The antique shops and the book boxes on the Left Bank were not free from them.

Row on row, they filled the best parts of the house at the *générales* of the Comédie-Française.

Every Frenchman had to make up his own mind what his relations with these ubiquitous invaders would be. It was a personal matter not to be resolved by official instructions. There were some men of letters who decided for fraternisation. One of these, the poet Robert Brassillach, was condemned to death after the Liberation, and shot in February, 1946, to the still great grief of his friends. Another is said to have been reprieved at the last moment by the intervention of an Allied Ambassador. Still others took appalling risks by sheltering men for whom the Germans were seeking. Others again—and of these Sartre was one—published clandestine attacks upon the invaders. Over these there hung the perpetual threat of torture and of death. In those four years 29,600 French men and women were shot for secret resistance, many of them in Paris.

It is not surprising therefore that a great deal of modern French drama is taken up with problems arising out of this kind of political, personal, and intellectual atmosphere. But the war, which increased its incidence, imposed conditions on it. The German censorship in Paris was not always clear-sighted, but it obviously would not have permitted the performance of plays directly attacking the Occupation. The criticism always had to be veiled, and the meaning partly concealed. This did not weaken the drama. On the contrary, it strengthened it, for the direct statement is often less effective than the oblique suggestion.

In London we have not had the opportunity of seeing many of these plays. The Group Theatre, however, on Sunday evening, November 25, 1951, produced one of the most famous of them, Sartre's *The Flies*, at the New Theatre. We have several Sunday societies in London, some of them, like the Repertory Players, of well-established repute. The object of most of these societies is to discover new plays of merit not too far out of the usual rut to make them suitable for commercial production later. There is nothing wrong in this, but it means that the Sunday societies in the main are merely an extension of the ordinary West End theatre. They supplement and support the West End theatre, but they do not, as the Stage Society used to do, widen its range by presenting pieces of merit of an uncommercial nature. That, however, is a service that the Group Theatre seems inclined to render, and it is a service of a most valuable kind.

The chairman of the Group Theatre is Alan Jarvis, and it has a board of directors that includes T. S. Eliot, John Lehmann, Herbert Reed, Graham Greene, John Piper, and Rupert Doone. But these men can do nothing unless the Group Theatre obtains the large and loyal public membership that its work deserves.

The level of classical scholarship in England at the old universities is probably higher than it is anywhere else in the world, just as, among the general public, the amount of classical knowledge is about as low as in any civilised country. Ben Jonson, who wrote classical plays, was in London eclipsed by Shakespeare, whose inspiration was mainly national. But the greatest and most popular dramatists of France, Racine and Molière, established a classical tradition among the theatregoing public that endures in Paris to this day. Without the slightest self-consciousness, a modern French dramatist can retell an old classical story, and rely on the meaning of all his variations on it being clear to every member of the audience.

This circumstance was, of course, particularly useful when it became necessary for the drama to proceed by implication instead of by direct assertion, for a play that was really about the German Occupation could be presented as the rehandling of an ancient myth. There was nothing odd in this. If English dramatists began resuscitating Aeschylus and Menander, there might be cause for suspicion, but in France dramatists had been rewriting the classics for generations as a matter of common form. On the face of things, there was no more reason for the German censorship to question the motives of Sartre's *The Flies* than there was for it to suspect Obey's *Lucrece* or Giraudoux's *Amphitryon 38*, both of them written when the German armies were still at home.

The reason that Sartre chose to tell again the story of how Electra and Orestes avenged the murder of their father Agamemnon by his wife Clytemnestra and her lover Aegistheus, and were subsequently tormented by the Furies, was partly political, and partly philosophic. The politics belong to Electra, for she has, first, a cry of defiance and then an act of rebellion, both of which echoed with a sombre encouragement and magnificence in the hearts of the Parisian audiences who saw the play when it was

produced by the late Charles Dullin at the Théâtre Sarah Bernhardt in 1942.

The cry of defiance came in the first act, when Clytemnestra
demanded of Electra that she should come to the great feast of the
dead over which the murderer Aegistheus was to preside. 'You
may say to the king', replied Electra, 'that I shall not appear at the
feast', and these few words of refusal stood as symbols of that
spirit of resistance which in 1942 had not yet begun to translate
itself into action. Even the theatre in which the play was presented could not then be called by its real name. In the public edi-
tions of the play this is still, years after the end of the war, recorded
to have been created at the Théâtre de la Cité, for the racial theories
of the Nazis were offended by the name of Bernhardt. The defiance in *The Flies*, then, was not actual, for the Parisian public
was still dominated by the invaders; but it was like a small light
at the end of a long tunnel, beckoning, at an immense distance,
onwards.

It is clear that the circumstances of its production gave to *The
Flies* in the Paris of 1942 a meaning and an excitement which it
could not expect to have in London ten years later. During the
first act at the New Theatre a strong effort of the historical imagination was necessary before the play could be injected with life.
Electra's refusal, one knew, must have sounded with a brazen
clangour in Paris in the days of the fall of Singapore; but in
London one could hear only a faint echo, boldly though Miss
Yvonne Mitchell delivered it; and it was mildly confusing to find
Jupiter and Clytemnestra in costumes that might have been taken
out of the British Museum, talking to Orestes' tutor clad in green
plus-fours. Only at one point, and momentarily, in the first act,
did the play in London have direct dramatic force of its own. This
was the entrance of Clytemnestra round one of the pillars of
Aegistheus' palace. Soon afterwards she said to Electra, 'Be
quiet. Anyone in the world can spit in my face and call me
criminal and prostitute. But no one has the right to judge my
remorse', to which Electra replies, 'You see, that is the rule of the
game. People implore you to condemn them. But be careful
to judge them only on the faults they admit: the others are nobody's business, and it is bad taste to discover them.'

Then came these words of Clytemnestra's, 'Fifteen years ago,

I was the most beautiful woman in Greece. Look at my face now, and judge how much I have suffered.'

It was to this speech that Miss Mary Hinton keyed her entrance as Clytemnestra. She came round the pillar slowly, a regal figure, yet oppressed by the weight of a deadly sin. Her dress made her, from shoulder to foot, a blaze of scarlet, and through the hard lines of her face could be seen the beauty that had once been there. For a second the house caught its breath, and then the play went on as before.

The second act had a more continuous excitement. The moaning, groaning crowds in front of the tomb, dressed in the shapeless black of French peasants, wringing their hands as the priest intoned his ceremonial oratory by the side of a hideous stone deity, were excellently drilled by the producer, Mr. Doone. Electra's decision, at the last moment, to attend the feast, and her arrival, dancing, instead of in grief, and in a transparent white dress instead of in respectful black, horrifying Aegistheus, and rousing the crowd to impious defiance as they saw that heaven did not loose a thunderbolt against her, heightened the tension still further; and a true theatrical climax came when Electra's triumph was crushed at its summit, as the horrible god sensationally lifted his hand, and the crowd fell on its face, whimpering in terror. Thereafter the murder of Aegistheus and Clytemnestra did not add much to the excitement, though it was a well-pleased audience that was ready for the third act.

It was in the third act that M. Sartre's philosophy of freedom, of man's complete lack of responsibility to anything or any theory but himself, a philosophy that had been hanging around ever since the beginning of the play, now broke with overwhelming force. This act marks the division between Electra and Orestes; it is the defeat of the one, and the triumph of the other. The Furies, in the shape of giant flies, with loathsome wings and coloured bulging eyes, creep round the two murderers, avid to suck their blood. Electra is sorry for her crime; she shrinks in horror from her brother; she cries to Jupiter in terror, wildly promising to be his slave and possession, to kiss his feet and his knees, if only he will save her from the flies. 'I repent, Jupiter,' she screams, 'I repent', and rushes in panic from the stage.

But Orestes does not repent. It was because Aegistheus had not been able to bear with an easy conscience his murder of Agamemnon, that his crime had wandered round the walls of the city, like a dog that has lost his master. 'But, men of Argos,' cries Orestes, 'understand that *my* crime is mine alone; I boast of it in the face of the sun, it is my reason for living and my pride'. The laws of morality, the proscription of murder cannot harm the man who refuses to believe in them. Orestes is entirely and absolutely free. He walks from the stage untouched, and untouchable.

In the struggle between slavery and freedom, M. Sartre is on the side of freedom. But it is a freedom that to many will seem hardly less undesirable than slavery. It is, as I have said, a freedom that is uncurbed by any of the considerations of religion and morality that the western world has found necessary for its preservation in the past. But it is also a freedom for which the case is in *The Flies*, after the first act, presented with fire and intellectual acumen. The production was elaborate and impressive, though Mr. David King-Wood might have made more of the rhetoric of Orestes.

The Flies was produced in the France of Pétain and Laval; and Pétain and Laval, though they are called merely The Marshal and the Prime Minister, were the leading characters in Peter Ustinov's *The Moment of Truth* (London, Adelphi, November, 1951). This was a play of very high pretensions; it was symbolic, and it aspired to the condition of tragedy. Like the great tragedies of the past, it dealt with the fortunes of men of lofty station and vast responsibility, at moments, moreover, of intense crisis.

Now, obviously, to judge a tragedy merely as a melodrama would be to do the author a grave injustice. Nevertheless, I think that practically every great tragedy is capable of being enjoyed as a melodrama first. Tragedy, we know, purges the soul with pity and terror; Aristotle says so, and what Aristotle says must naturally be true. Nevertheless, hundreds and thousands of good honest folk, men and women with no nonsense about them, have enjoyed *Oedipus* and *Hamlet* and *Macbeth* without having the slightest suspicion that anything drastic was being done to their souls. They have enjoyed these plays as rattling good stories, dripping with blood and murder, worthy of being set side by side with Dick Barton or Maria Marten and the Red Barn.

I am not being in the least disrespectful, therefore, to *The Moment of Truth*, nor at all forgetting the position of Mr. Ustinov as one of the few young English writers of today capable of developing into a major dramatist, when I point out that, on the ground of melodrama, this play was extremely successful. Tragedies that cannot stand as good stories collapse under the weight of their own verbosity. A tragedy must have more than a good story, of course; but without a good story it turns into a solemn yawn.

The making of *The Moment of Truth* as a melodrama was the Prime Minister. When the world of Paris is falling round him, this Prime Minister is a Sir Percy Blakeney in reverse. The great point about Sir Percy, as I remember him, was his lounging insolence; and the great point about Mr. Ustinov's Prime Minister was his insolent gaiety. Sir Percy was not frightened by the yelling revolutionaries; the Prime Minister was unafraid of the conquering Germans. The object of Sir Percy's courage was the saving of his friends; the object of the Prime Minister's courage was the surrender of France. Morally, therefore, the distance between them was considerable, but theatrically they were brothers under their skins. They both offered the rousing spectacle of men going into mortal danger as lightheartedly as to a ball.

The Prime Minister's big scene came in the second act. His country is defeated; the invader is in the city; one of his ministers has fled abroad in order to carry on resistance from beyond the seas; the Foreign Minister is still at hand, counselling continued fighting, but with a shaking voice and trembling knees. The Prime Minister is resolved on surrender; it is the only way, he thinks, to save useless bloodshed. It was at this point that he received in audience the Victor, to find out the terms of surrender that the Victor would accept. Such, at any rate, was the Victor's notion of what was going to happen. He was not a foolish man, this Victor, though a little stiff and formal. He was not easily disconcerted; he kept his head. But the Prime Minister did not care if he lost his; and this gave him an immense advantage. He had a splendid recklessness with which the Victor, strong, serious-minded man that he was, could not compete. The Victor had apparently all the cards in his hand, and the Prime Minister but a Yarborough. Nevertheless, when the hand was played out, it was the Prime Minister who made all the tricks. He made them with such bravura and gay apparent carelessness that on the first night the audience responded as to the call of a trumpet.

Charles Goldner played the Prime Minister, and played him very well, if not always audibly. Some of the words in his long speeches, uttered at enormous speed, got here and there into each other's way, but Mr. Goldner had the right spirit, and it was the spirit that mattered. He had the proper nonchalance, the essential glittering insolence.

Mr. Ustinov set his play in the Council Chamber of a Democratic Republic. He was no more precise than that. France was not mentioned, nor Paris, nor the Germans; we were never told the Prime Minister's name, nor the Marshal's. Yet the parallel with the events of 1940 was obvious, and it did not take the first night audience long to guess that the Prime Minister was to some extent modelled on Pierre Laval. I must admit it came to me somewhat as a surprise that Laval's character should suggest such buccaneering courage.

I had the curiosity after seeing the play to look up the account of Laval's trial given by Jean Galtier-Boissière in his lively and deliberately indiscreet diary, *Mon Journal dans la Drôle de Paix*. Among M. Boissière's many qualities exuberance is more noticeable than accuracy; perhaps it is because of this that his pictures have a certain bold attractiveness. The bearing of Pierre Laval in M. Galtier-Boissière's pages is remarkably similar to that of the Prime Minister's in Ustinov's play. There is the same gaiety, the same insolence, the same shamelessness, the same refusal to be downhearted. Right to the end of his trial after the war Laval thought he had a chance of turning the opinion of his judges. All the time he defended himself without the least indication of regret or feeling of disgrace, and was never at a loss for some lighthearted verbal impertinence. It wasn't he, he asserted, it was Weygand, who created the Legion of French Volunteers. 'When soldiers make war', he said, 'they don't always win, but when they meddle with politics, it is a catastrophe.' He dwelt with relish on his efforts to avoid the war. 'In the same year 1935', he rattled off, 'I saw Mussolini first: three days later the Pope: a few weeks later still, Stalin: on my return from Moscow, Goering. Is it possible to meet a greater variety of people? And if I'd known the address of the Devil, I'd have visited him as well.'

At this point a distinction must be made. I have said that *The Moment of Truth* is successful as melodrama. A more accurate way of stating the matter would be to say that there is a very good melodrama in it. In tragedy, however, the melodramatic story and the tragic story are the same, viewed on different planes. In *Oedipus Rex*, it is the excellent detective tale of the king who investigated a crime and found himself to be the criminal that is, on another plane, the tragedy of the insensately brave, the splendidly obstinate hero who, having put his hand to the plough, would not draw it off though the heavens fell about him. But in *The Moment of Truth* the melodrama and the tragedy were separate, the one being the story of The Prime Minister, and the other that of The Marshal. This was the play's weakness, for the fate of the Marshal, far from moving the audience as tragedy, did not even hold its attention as an exciting tale.

Mr. Ustinov chose a symbolic title; and there is perhaps more symbolism in it than he intended. He is an amateur of the bull ring, and has seen the modern masters, the young Aparicio and Litri, more than once. The moment of truth is the end of the conflict, when the matador, having finished his sport with the bull, delivers the death blow. 'At this moment', says M. A. Lafront in *La Corrida*, 'prudence is permitted only if the animal is crafty. . . . But if the bull is straightforward, has no malevolent intentions, then to the nobility of the animal the man must reply with equal loyalty. Up till now he has been allowed to carry on the fight in his own way, the spectators have not shown themselves unduly particular about the means he has employed, nobody has bothered even if he has not kept his feet still . . . But from now on the matador must not depart a hair's breadth from the austere rule. The honesty of the fight demands that, at this instant which Spaniards call 'the moment of truth,' chances should be equalised. Observance of this condition is the sole justification for the weakening of the bull by the picadors, a weakening that would have no meaning if the matador were authorised . . . to get rid of his adversary in any manner he pleased.'

Now, there was a time when the moment of truth was the crown and culmination of the whole bull fight. This was so until the beginning of the war of 1914–18. It kept in the top rank of matadors men who had no other merit besides that of being fine killers. Then, however, came Juan Belmonte, one of those extraordinary men who have no qualification for their job except genius. Just as Thomas Hardy broke the elementary rules of good writing, just as Irving lacked the first graces of an actor, so Belmonte was physically insignificant and feeble. And out of this insignificance and weakness he built a method of bull fighting which has revolutionised the art of the corrida. Some people say that the bull fight today is in a condition of decadence. Whether this is so or not—and it is also possible to maintain that it is now at one of the peaks of its achievement—the modern corrida is the creation of Juan Belmonte.

Belmonte, during the active period of his career, which lasted, with varying intervals of retirement, from 1912 to 1935, fought in 750 corridas, and killed 1,550 bulls. Yet, in the moment of truth, he was never particularly good. He lacked both strength and agility. But he had extraordinarily long arms, and it was on these arms that he erected the technique which has changed bull-fighting from a tragedy into a plastic art, from a battle into a sort of ballet. Before Belmonte the bull fight was a wild struggle, with animal and man dashing hither and thither, the matador often finishing with his clothes torn, his tie floating in the wind, but in the last moment rising on an inspiration, gruesome and majestic, of avenging death.

For this kind of fight Belmonte had no talent. But he had the gift which has been said to be nine-tenths of acting, repose. He could stand stockstill while the infuriated bull charged so close that the horns grazed his chest; and by a series of interconnected passes of the muleta, without moving his heels, he could dominate the animal so that it weaved round him a sort of mesmerised dance. The capacity to do this, to control the bull so that it is absolutely within the matador's power, is today the mark of the master bullfighter. This control, naturally, is easier to achieve with a small bull than with one of great weight and strength. In consequence, of late years, bulls have been bred of lesser weight than was usual before Belmonte.

The important thing, from our point of view, is that 'the moment of truth' is no longer the crux of the bull fight. It is not the way the bull is killed that is any more, after Belmonte, the aesthetic justification of the corrida: it is the way the bull is made to behave whilst he is still alive. Unhappily, in *The Moment of Truth*, it was the death of the Marshal on which Mr. Ustinov

H

lavished all his dramatic care. The Marshal is called in by the Prime Minister to act as a figure head to the state in its acceptance of defeat. He has been the greatest general of his time (which I do not think that Pétain had ever been), but now, in extreme old age, he is doddering and senile, playing childishly with toy soldiers. That very forceful actor, Eric Portman, was wheeled on to the stage in a chair, and had little to do but whimper in senile disintegration. In writing the play Mr. Ustinov had in mind not only a parallel with the corrida, but also with *Lear*, and he bungled the second parallel as he altered the emphasis of the first. Lear is mad, but the Marshal was only feeble-minded, and the difference between feeble-mindedness and madness is the difference between a crushed reed and an earthquake. Lear, at his worst moments, had flashes of undiminished grandeur, and his rage was terrible. The Marshal only slobbered in purposeless petulance, and his futile anger was the painful ill-temper of a half-witted child. Not until the end of the play, when, a prisoner condemned in perpetuity to national disgrace, he held in his arms the body of his dead daughter (one of whose names was Cordelia), did mental lucidity come to him. Then he realised how he had been duped: this was his moment of truth. The waiting for it had been distressing and even when it arrived it was not particularly moving.

Nevertheless, only a man of talent and poetic imagination could have written *The Moment of Truth*. But Mr. Ustinov's abilities, his whimsicality, his theatrical invention, his sprawling opulence of vitality, were better displayed in *The Love of Four Colonels* (London, Wyndham's, May, 1951). This was a mixture of play, vaudeville, fairy story, pantomime, and farce that proved very popular with intelligent audiences. The four colonels were the French, English, Russian, and American representatives on the Control Commission in some part of Europe. They were plagued by a bad fairy and protected by a good, and there was a great deal of hullabulloo about visiting a fairy castle and waking up a sleeping beauty. This device was remarkable chiefly for giving the author the opportunity of writing four little inset plays showing how the sleeping beauty was awakened by the various colonels according to Mr. Ustinov's reading of the inner springs of their national character. The stolid, matter-of-fact Englishman, for example, appeared, not in a realistic playlet of clipped monosyllables, but in a robust Elizabethan, blank verse melodrama: for Englishmen at heart are poets, even though they are ashamed of it. The boisterous, shouting American became a nonconformist parson reforming a whore in a Far West mining town, which seems a fairly accurate representation of the United States' attitude towards the rest of the world. This part of the play was brilliantly written, much better than the sham-Elizabethan section. Colin Gordon gave an excellently dry performance of the Englishman, Moira Lister was admirable as the Sleeping Beauty, and Mr. Ustinov himself played the wicked fairy with abounding energy and frank delight in the exuberance of his own invention.

Somewhat earlier in 1951 than *The Moment of Truth*, another young author and actor, John Whiting, gave us a play, *Saint's Day* (London, Arts, September, 1951), in which extreme old age also played an important part. I have already noted that during 1951 the Arts Theatre, which is much the most efficient of our private club theatres, had run a £700 prize competition designed to find a new play of merit. One of the conditions was that this new play should have some 'contemporary significance'. This was a puzzling qualification. Every good play has significance, whether aesthetic or otherwise, and this significance must be contemporary, or we should not perceive it. The words therefore mean nothing. Nevertheless, it was felt that to the judges of the competition— Christopher Fry, Alec Clunes, and Peter Ustinov—who presumably had joined them together, they conveyed some meaning not strictly contained in them. The general assumption was that these gentlemen were asking for a play that had a direct bearing on our current social and political problems: that is, for a specimen of the involved theatre. This, however, did not prevent nearly a thousand aspiring playwrights from submitting their work, and I believe that thirty or forty of these survived the preliminary investigations, and came in for serious consideration by the three judges. Eventually three plays were chosen to undergo the ordeal of production, the first of them being *Poor Judas* (Arts, July, 1951).

The choice of this play was ominous. It was understood that one of the objects of the competition was to find new writers. But the author of *Poor Judas* was Enid Bagnold, an experienced novelist and dramatist, a fact which suggested that new writers of quality had not shown themselves in very large numbers. The second disturbing fact was that *Poor Judas* was not even a new play, since it had been produced in the north of England a few years before. When this old play by a familiar writer turned out to be a bad play as well, it became clear that the competition had run into difficulties.

The first act of *Poor Judas* was quite good. The place was a house in Dieppe, the time the outbreak of the last war. Two men were writing, one, very old (Jules Pasdeloup Calas, played by Ernest Jay), engaged on a monumental history of treason: the other, younger, (Edward Mission Walker, played by Robert Harris), his secretary. Calas had been a great writer and pamphleteer, but he was now too old to do anything but amass materials and sketch out ideas: it was Walker's job to put them into a coherent work. The German armies drew nearer and nearer, and Walker packed his things to cross the Channel. Calas would not accompany him, but he gave up all his notes and manuscripts, and it was understood that Walker would make them into a book, and sign it with Calas's name. There was an excitement about this scene, a feeling of tension and approaching doom, that was quite promising.

But the rest of the play was a pomposity drained of life and reality. Walker did not write the history of treachery, and years later Calas came over to England, discovered that he had been tricked, banged his stick on the table till it rattled, and had a fit. I really cannot see what all his anger was about; I cannot feel that there is any desperate crime in one man's failing to write another man's book, nor do I see that this problem of vicarious authorship is of much general significance. The conception and nature of treachery is indeed a matter of considerable moment in the twentieth century, when social changes have brought about many modifications of traditional loyalties. But the symbol of it with which Miss Bagnold provided us was extremely perfunctory, and her dialogue seemed to have come out of a literary essay by a painstaking member of the Upper Fifth.

The second of the three selected plays was C. E. Webber's *Right Side Up* (London, Arts, August, 1951). Where *Poor Judas* had seemed pedestrian and plodding, *Right Side Up* struck most people as carrying pretentious simplicity to the point of silliness.

The hero lived in a tree, and washed in the cloakroom of Charing Cross Railway station. In order to clear his brain, he was in the habit of standing on his head, in which position he could understand everything and see through everybody. He was brought home one night by a prostitute, who had some difficulty in believing his story of living in a tree: her life had not been such as to encourage credulity, and who can blame her? She was involved with gangsters, who sought the young man's life. He was vulnerable enough on his feet, but when standing on his head they had no chance with him. Mr. Webber presumably was trying to portray one of those divine fools who are wiser than the subtle of this world; he had some notion in his head that the universe is paradoxical and topsy-turvy; and odd recollections of the Fall of Man kept cropping up in his dialogue. But he showed no talent for the style of writing the play needed; not once did he hit on the inevitable simple phrase that would have lighted up our darkness. Some of the situations in which the young man faced his persecutors with what ought to have been a cheerful innocent courage might, with better writing, have been exciting; but they were all ruined by the dialogue's ineptitude.

By now the idea was abroad that the Arts competition had been a failure, and the curtain did not rise on *Saint's Day* in any spirit of optimism. As I have said, its central character, played by Michael Hordern, was a very old man. He had a patriarchal white beard, and occasionally he roared and ranted in remembered flashes of his Apocalyptic youth and middle-age, when his revolutionary poems and pamphlets had been ignored and derided. Often, however, he lapsed into senility, and whimpered like a beaten and half-witted child. This was his eightieth birthday, and he was expecting from London a distinguished literary critic, who was to take him back with him to some celebratory luncheon given by a company of admirers who had tardily recognised his past greatness.

This decaying genius lived in a strange and remote household, with a white-faced daughter who had married an artist, a mere boy much younger than herself. They had no money; they had little food; and they seemed to be beleaguered by the inhabitants of their village, who apparently regarded them with loathing. The girl was brooding and mystical; the artist worried because she

would not pose for him nude. Then the critic arrived, a slick
and neat young man to whom John Byron gave an agreeable alert
assurance in sharp contrast with the shaggy beard and the dim
mouldering frescoes that set the atmosphere of the dark and
crumbling cottage. Thereafter the play was a wild melodrama
clouded by Ibsenite symbolism. Three marauding soldiers terror-
ised the village after the stuttering parson, in an episode I have
already mentioned, released them from imprisonment. The
bright critic fired a gun that shot the girl, who was standing behind a closed door, thereby furnishing her husband with a model
that could no longer object when her clothes were taken off; and
the play ended with the critic, now manifestly mad, advising
everyone to commit suicide.

This play was sharply, angrily criticised by my colleagues;
and I spoke ill of it myself. We were, however, dissatisfied with
it for different reasons. The objection commonly made to it was
that it was obscure. Yet through its mist and fog a meaning did
hugely loom, the more impressive perhaps for not being explicitly stated. The world is doomed to disaster and bloodshed unless
it learns to listen to its poets and prophets: and it shows no sign
whatever of so learning to listen. This at least was part, or so it
seemed to me, of Mr. Whiting's message; some of his scenes,
especially that of the terrified parson, were vigorously written;
and at all times he showed a considerable mastery of rhetoric.
But because the play had not the simplicity of a nursery rhyme, it
was on all hands condemned.

During 1950 and 1951 the French dramatic critic, Paul Léautaud, had a long series of literary and biographical discussions on
the Paris radio with the young poet, Robert Mallet. There is a
passage in them that is relevant to this question of obscurity which
was raised by *Saint's Day*. In the fifth interview the subject was
Léautaud's *Poètes d'Aujourd'hui*: *Morceaux Choisis*, which was
originally published about fifty years ago, and has since been
many times reissued. Talking of the Romantic poets, and especially of Alfred de Vigny, Léautaud remarked that they broke all
the rules of the French language.

PAUL LÉAUTAUD: When Vigny writes 'appuyée aux branches incertaines' it isn't the branches that are doubtful.

ROBERT MALLET: The phrase is quite clear, 'les branches incertaines'.

P.L.: It is their solidity that is doubtful.

R.M.: You know very well what the words mean. You say you don't understand them, but you do, all the same.

P.L.: I say that it is bad French. There. I refuse to understand. It is the firmness of the branches, it is their resistance for leaning against that is doubtful, but they are not doubtful, they are there.

R.M.: We say: a doubtful statement.

P.L.: Yes, but we do not say; leaning one's arms on doubtful branches! The branches are there, immovable.

R.M.: They aren't immovable if the wind shakes them . . . But I think we had better not go on like this. We are now in the full flood of Romanticism. We have referred to Verlaine, and I should like you to say something more about him . . .

P.L.: Yes, and how pure is his language! You know the poems dedicated to his wife. The language of them is perfect. Not only is Verlaine's language perfect, but its exactness is absolute, marvellous.

R.M.: You recognise in him the power to cast a spell?

P.L.: I recognise in him what I say, not what you say. Besides, he has some very moving things. And it really is the atmosphere, the poetry, the vagueness, the impreciseness, yes . . .

R.M.: Yet you like precise things even in poetry, since you count it a fault in 'branches incertaines' that it is imprecise.

P.L.: Not at all. The fault I find is that the phrase is inexact. The branches aren't doubtful; they are there.

R.M.: I am sorry for having brought the matter up again.

As a literary critic, M. Léautaud stresses linguistic accuracy too much for English tastes. But the view he is expressing is sound. When writing of the shadowy and impalpable, exactitude of expression is as desirable as in ordering the week's groceries. It is in travelling over difficult and unknown country that accurate maps and instruments are most requisite. Mr. Whiting did not provide such maps and instruments, and that certainly was a fault in him. But they are not easy to come by. Getting plans of Hackney is not at all the same thing as obtaining those of the suburbs of Persepolis. Must we never go further than Bishopsgate?

I daresay we should be more content if we did not. To stick to the old roads, to comfort ourselves with the old consolations and beliefs, to argue that revolution ceased with the Declaration of

Independence, and that the mind has no secrets that were not known to Henry James and his brother William is a pretty good recipe for happiness. Only it is one that now we cannot take. Freud and Picasso have made us restless; there are more things in the depths of the unconscious than are dreamed of in manuals of logic. The young dramatist of today who is really abreast of his time sees neither in himself nor in the world round him the bright certainties of personality and politics that seemed so sure and shining in the 1920s. By impulsive forces that bear down on him as unceasingly as the atmosphere, he is started out on explorations into rough, unknown country; and the exploration will continue even if it turns out to be an exploration into nightmare. The escape will come by breaking through on to the other side, not by refusing the challenge. If the first reports of these explorations to reach us in the theatre—Kafka's? Whiting's?—are confusing and confused, it is exasperating to both audiences and critics. Possibly the reports are ill-founded, garbled, or badly drawn up; possibly the explorer has officiously taken on a job too big for him. But it is to be remembered that he has gone out into mysterious and dangerous country, an enterprise showing both presumption and courage. There is at present a stronger case for suspending judgment than for issuing denunciations.

I cannot claim that I suspended judgment on Mr. Whiting's play. I said that it was the best of the three that had been submitted to us, but that none of them was worth the £700, which ought to have been funded for the widows of dramatic critics. Mr. Ustinov, Mr. Clunes, and Mr. Fry did not suspend judgment either. Immediately the first reviews appeared, they handed Mr. Whiting the prize. A little later they published a statement declaring their faith in the play, which seemed unnecessary, since they had already backed their opinion with money. Somewhat later still Peter Brook and John Gielgud announced their confidence in Mr. Whiting's talents.

Henry Wallace called the twentieth century the 'century of the common man'. But Mr. Whiting's difficulty seemed to be that for him the common man does not exist. I do not know whether he saw R. C. Sherriff's *Home at Seven* (London, Wyndham's, March, 1950), but he had plenty of opportunity to do so, for the play ran for nearly a year. If he did, Sir Ralph Richardson's performance in it of David Preston must have shown him the living, untransfigured, undistorted thing that was missing from *Saint's Day*. David Preston was a bank clerk who came home at his usual hour one evening, and found his wife in a state of intense anxiety. For twenty-four hours he had been missing from home and from his work. The day was not Tuesday, as he thought, but Wednesday. Yet Preston himself knew nothing whatever about the lost day and night. This complete lapse of memory was in itself sufficiently disturbing, without any other symptoms or attendant circumstances, but it became downright alarming when sound reasons presented themselves for supposing that, during the extra time he had been away from home, Preston had committed a murder of which all recollection had now departed from him.

Mr. Sherriff had, I think, conceived his play as a melodrama. He stood outside his story and manipulated its ending according to considerations not really aesthetically relevant. When David Preston went upstairs at the end of the third act convinced that he was a murderer there was nothing in the substance of the play to indicate whether he would blow his brains out or come down again and hear his wife's releasing explanation. It was a mere toss of a coin whether the play should finish in disaster or happiness. As a matter of fact, I believe, the play on various occasions had different endings. In its preliminary run at Brighton it ended with the pistol shot, but in London Preston refrained from suicide, and all was well.

This is not the way to fashion a masterpiece. A good play has an interior logic whose conclusions are not to be whimsically set aside. But *Home at Seven*, though in story not more than an an agreeable evening's entertainment, had in David Preston a character of great merit, and in Sir Ralph's performance something of real and quiet and perceptive beauty. Scott lamented that, although he could do the big stuff as well as any man living, he lacked Jane Austen's touch that made commonplace people and things interesting. Kipling has noted the same quality, the quality that enabled Jane Austen to make irresistibly fascinating a novel in which some incident such as a man riding up to London to get his hair cut would count as a rare and exciting event. Sir Ralph also makes the ordinary man interesting, but not quite in Jane Austen's way. For Miss Austen was satirical; there was a sly gleam in her eye; she saw the forked radish more readily than the son of God. There is in Richardson more of Wordsworth than of Miss Austen, of the Wordsworth who saw the qualities of beauty and goodness interfused through all the universe, in the light of setting suns and in the mind of man. Sir Ralph gave us a David Preston who was puzzled and bewildered, distressed as his own doubts grew stronger inside him, but who always was thinking of his wife rather than himself. The man's quietness and integrity and goodness shone with a steady and heartwarming glow, yet all the time he remained a quite ordinary, a quite commonplace being. But there were no commonplace people in Mr. Whiting's *Saint's Day*. That, rather than its obscurity, was what was wrong with it.

Mr. Whiting at present seems incapable of meeting an ordinary man walking down Regent Street, and seeing him as an ordinary man walking down Regent Street. If he has ever done such an ordinary thing as catch the Brighton Belle, I am sure the train looked to him as though it had been designed by Emett, all bubukles and spindly chimneys. He sees the world only under the aspect of the grotesque. The unimaginative gentleman in Wordsworth to whom a yellow primrose was only a yellow primrose has often been derided; but if Mr. Whiting could now and again assume his prosaic outlook he would greatly improve as a dramatist. For, not to put too fine a point upon it, all the characters in *Saint's Day* were mad; and where madness is universal it loses its significance. In a world where everybody was the same height, there would be neither tall ones nor small ones. We lost interest in Mr. Whiting's extraordinary characters because he gave us no yardstick to measure them by.

I understand that *Saint's Day* was an early play of Mr. Whiting's and that the previously produced *A Penny for a Song* (London: Haymarket: March, 1951) was actually written later. In this play as in the other, Mr. Whiting's world was peopled entirely by creatures outrageous and outlandish. But there was a distinct difference in mood. The characters of *Saint's Day* were grotesque; those of *A Penny for a Song* eccentrics. The first set were frightening, the second lovable. The world of *Saint's Day* was mad and doomed and desperate; the world of *A Penny for a Song*, though equally devoid of reason, was gay and bright and gloriously coloured.

The scene was a Dorset garden in the year 1804, when Britain hourly expected the French to invade, led by Bonaparte in person. No preparations had been made by the Government to repel such hostile forces as should appear. This slackness greatly disturbed one public spirited gentleman, Sir Timothy Bellboys, who resolved to take upon his own shoulders the defence of the entire kingdom. To this end he devised a scheme of extraordinary subtlety, which involved a combination of theatrical costumes and French phrase books. For Sir Timothy was convinced that, if he could only learn enough French in time, he could baffle the opposing forces by dressing up as Napoleon, appearing in front of them, and ordering them to re-embark for France.

Sir Timothy was a charming character: a true and civic-minded patriot, single-minded, and copious in invention, capable of dealing with every situation as it arose by methods of striking originality. Alan Webb played him with the proper zeal and conviction. Sir Timothy was surrounded by men and women in the Whiting fashion, as remarkable as himself. There was, for example, his brother, as mild and gentle a creature as ever lived, yet who had a consuming passion for setting things on fire. There was his brother's wife, whose mild heart was loudly contradicted by her deep voice and Amazonian appearance. A blinded soldier wandered in on the play from a pilgrimage to the Holy Land; he was walking to London to ask the King to stop the war, and was accompanied by a grave, wide-eyed child in a huge hat. All these people abounded richly in their strange but endearing idiosyncrasies, and were watched by a stranger from London who had come down to the country to rest from the bustle of the metropolis.

The stranger from London: Mr. Whiting appears to be very fond of visitors from London: as of soldiers who break in on curious households: and of beleaguered citadels, like the England threatened by the French in *A Penny for a Song*, and the old poet's cottage attacked by the villagers in *Saint's Day*. But this stranger in *A Penny for a Song* was saner than the homicidal critic in *Saint's Day*. He was a quiet, meditative, sardonic observer, a welcome pointer towards Mr. Whiting's future capacity to see ordinary things ordinarily, without of course losing his faculty for recognising the extraordinary practically everywhere.

Mr. Ustinov and Mr. Whiting are both young dramatists, though Mr. Ustinov's talents have been familiar to us for some time. It is a commonplace that the drama of the future rests upon the shoulders of writers who have not yet reached their maturity. M. Salacrou says in one of those stimulating essays which he adds to his published plays, that there can be no really healthy theatre unless the young men are treading on the heels of the middle-aged and the old. This is true of France; it is depressingly true of Britain. Depressingly, because here the young men are harder to find. The young men themselves, of course, and the young women, say they are not found because no one looks for them. But this is hard to square with the facts. We have just seen the search made by the Arts Theatre Club, and its unsatisfactory results: whilst larger managements, like H. M. Tennent and Henry Sherek, have an excellent record in respect of young and untried dramatists. It was Mr. Sherek who put on *Desert Rats*, the first play by Colin Morris, whose *Reluctant Heroes* (London: Whitehall; October, 1950) had a run of over two years. It was Mr. Sherek again who presented Peter Watling's first play, *Rain on the Just*; and it was he who took the risk of bringing T. S. Eliot, with *The Cocktail Party*, into the rough life of the commercial theatre.

The attitude towards young writers of the Tennent organisation is equally enlightened and adventurous. *A Penny for a Song* was a Tennent presentation in which an entirely unknown author was given London's most gracious theatre, the Haymarket, and the dazzling services of Peter Brook as producer. This firm had enormous commercial successes with *Seagulls over Sorrento* and *Waters of the Moon*. I shall consider these plays later; at the moment it is sufficient to say that their authors, Hugh Hastings and N. C. Hunter, had hardly been heard of at the time that Tennents put their plays into production. And it was Tennents who accepted Mr. Watling's second play to reach the West End, *Indian Summer* (London: Criterion, December, 1951).

In my opinion, therefore, it cannot be said that the best London managements are not willing to take considerable risks with the works of new young authors, and to present them with every advantage of company, direction, and scenery. Can the same generosity be discerned in the principal London critics? *Seagulls over Sorrento* and *Waters of the Moon* had notices in which their theatrical merits were generously recognised, and Denis Cannan's first London play, *Captain Carvallo*, was sympathetically received. But few critics warmed to the virtues of *A Penny for a Song*, and *Saint's Day* was attacked with more savagery than was necessary. *Indian Summer* also was to my mind treated with incomprehensible and unconscionable contempt.

During the period with which this book deals two plays were presented in London which were met with justified derision. The first of these, *Storks Don't Talk* (London: Comedy, July, 1951) was an ignoble farce about a young man who wished to prove himself illegitimate; the second, *Mary Had a Little . . .* (London; Strand: November, 1951), dealt with a young girl who was hypnotised into asking every man she met to give her a baby. Of the two, *Mary Had a Little . . .* was the better; it had one or two situations which, but for the play's lamentable striving after impropriety, might have been not unfunny. Nevertheless, both entertainments deserved the hoots and catcalls with which the gallery punctuated their performance, and the boos that greeted the final curtain-fall.

Naturally, these plays received extremely bad notices the next morning and at the week-end. I read most, or all, of the reviews, and I do not believe there was a single one that found anything in either production to praise or commend. It is common enough for a play to get a good press or a bad press. Opinion usually crystallises sufficiently for the author and players to know whether the critics, on the whole, think that they have done well or ill. But almost invariably there are dissenting judgments from the preponderant verdict, for the London critics differ from each other widely both in taste and standards.

There was an example of this after the production of *Peter Pan* (London: Scala: December, 1951), with Joan Greenwood in the title role, and of *Cinderella* (London: December, 1951). *The Times* had this to say of the first: 'The revival this year is one of those half-successes it is perhaps fairer to judge on points. Point one is against it, and unfortunately this is an important point, Peter Pan himself. There seems no earthly reason why Miss Joan Greenwood should not do the part perfectly. Indeed, when she first comes on, we believe she is going to. But in her care not to come the leading lady over the part, she only contrives to slip into the background. It is not all modesty, perhaps, not altogether voluntary; for when she does seek to dominate us she fails in authority for the simple reason that even in the front rows it is not always possible to make out her words—something which a little care and determination would very soon rectify, and then we might well have a first-rate Peter.' The relenting spirit in the last sentence is charming, but this cannot be regarded as other than a harsh notice: Miss Greenwood is largely inaudible, and her performance is insignificant.

In the *News-Chronicle* Alan Dent, a Scotsman, and like most Scotsmen not generally easy to please, took a very different view of Miss Greenwood's Peter. 'Joan Greenwood', he wrote, 'is an unusually "fey" and graceful Peter in the first half of this year's revival and an extraordinarily moving one in the second half. She is, in fact, quite the most satisfying Peter since the unforgettable Jean Forbes-Robertson . . . The new Peter Pan flies away with the play, as any really good Peter must.'

There was a similar refreshing individuality of opinion about the *Cinderella* production. Miss Elizabeth Franks began quite enthusiastically. 'For good, gaudy, and nearly straightforward pantomime Bertram Montague's *Cinderella* wins the holly and the mistletoe; and Christine Norden—who started as a crooner and then moved into films—tops both these careers as principal boy. Cherry Lind is a suitably wistful Cinders, and Derek Roy an impudent Buttons, who entirely bowls over the younger members of the audience.'

The Times, on the other hand, did not appear to have enjoyed *Cinderella*. 'Cinderella,' it remarked, 'most romantic of fairy tale heroines, imposes special obligations on those privileged to tell her story; and the obligations in this instance are lightly, even perfunctorily, honoured . . . The story is in the hands of the principals, and none of them can be accepted without reservation. Prince Charming has many songs to sing, but Miss Christine Norden appears to find the high notes an embarrassment. Miss Cherry Lind has a charming voice, but her Cinderella is a sadly self-pitying creature. Mr. Derek Roy has the brilliant eyes of a ventriloquist's dummy, but he gets very little out of the part of Buttons.'

There are those who will regard this difference between critics as a criticism of criticism itself. They are wrong. There are all sorts of valid reasons why critics may differ in the judgment they pass on a theatrical entertainment. Criticism is not an exact science. Writing a review of a play is not like solving a mathematical problem: there is no single answer that is right, whilst all the others are wrong. A theatrical performance is not a pure entity in itself, but an amalgamation of entities. It is a synthesis of the work of the director, the author, and the players. Now, a bad play may be cleverly produced and only moderately acted. On the performance of such a play, three critics, the first of whom is most interested in writing, the second in acting, and the third in the problems of production, may give quite differing verdicts, all of which can be defended by a relatively valid aesthetic of the theatre.

Nor, in the majority of cases, can any unanimity of opinion be expected about the value of the play itself, questions of acting and direction being excluded. Dramatic criticism is an art; and at the foundation of an art is the artist's own personal feeling, style, nature, and conviction. There are no two critics in whom these things are alike; because of this necessarily criticisms differ. Ivor Brown, for example, whose books on words are among the most entertaining of our time, attaches great importance to the splendours, subtleties, and various pleasures of verbal expression; and so does J. C. Trewin. My colleague on *The Sunday Times*, J. W. Lambert, likes a play to have style and grace. A. V. Cookman, of *The Times*, insists on sound, logical construction. I was brought up in the provincial theatre of Martin-Harvey and Matheson Lang, and a play that has one or two emotional moments, or an actor or actress with a moving or an exciting voice has a comparatively easy task in giving me pleasure. These differences in taste and judgment and response are comparatively superficial; but in themselves they are sufficient to lead to wide divergences of opinion.

I emphasize this point in order to show how rarely complete unanimity of verdict is to be expected. It was found, however, with *Storks Don't Talk* and *Mary Had a Little* . . . because these were plays in which it was unusually difficult to discover merit of any kind. It happened also, but much more surprisingly, with

Mr. Watling's *Indian Summer*. Mr. Watling is a young dramatist whose first play, *Rain on the Just*, had been critically accepted as showing outstanding promise: *Indian Summer* had a company that included such admired players as Jane Baxter and Robert Flemyng, and it was presented by an organisation whose name has never been connected with anything mean or unworthy. Yet my colleagues massacred this play. It was dismissed as a dull, poor-spirited, monotonous study of failure, and the hero was considered to be a conceited weakling in whose problems no one could be expected to take an interest. I believe that T. C. Worsley of the *New Statesman*, and myself were the only London critics who could be persuaded to discern in it any merit whatever.

I say 'could be persuaded', because in my case persuasion was necessary. *Indian Summer* early built up in my mind a prejudice against it that only two admirable scenes later in the evening, and what I took to be the value of its central conception, succeeded in removing. I think it is desirable to say, in view of its extraordinarily severe reception, that, after initial misgivings, I was both impressed and moved by it.

Its general purport was curiously misunderstood. It was supposed to be a story of failure, whereas actually it was nothing of the kind. It was a study of a problem that, since the war, has become of considerable social importance, the reception back into civil life of men who have been for several years in the armed forces. Such reception is not always easy, either to society or to the men themselves. Tales of housebreaking and violence, of assault and murder in the daily newspapers attest its difficulty.

Mr. Watling's hero, Sam Hartley, was not of the kind to break out into physical excess. He had no inclination to be a spiv; he was not one of the cosh boys: his bark was very bitter, but his bite remained metaphorical. Nevertheless, he made a poor job of becoming a civilian again. He was in the service of a film company, and on its behalf went to theatrical first nights to report on plays that might make suitable cinema material. This is a respectable and even honourable occupation, but to Sam Hartley it was an ill-paid bore. It seemed a poor thing after the excitements of the African campaign, in which he had distinguished himself for courage and enterprise. He lived in a household whose members were continually complaining of the state of modern

England, of its restrictions, of its drabness, its dreary approaches to social equality, and to these maundering laments he added his own bitter sarcastic dissatisfactions.

This part of the play irritated and then wearied me. Few things are so theatrically trying as weak-kneed, whimpering, self-pitying grumbling. A little of it may be amusing, or accepted for the sake of character development; but, through the mouths of Sam Hartley, his mother-in-law Muriel Petersham, and his wife's sister, Priscilla Lane-Roberts, Mr. Watling gave it to us in such prodigious quantities that, during the whole of the first act of the play, and the greater part of the second, our stifled souls cried in vain for mercy. Things got to such a pitch that every time Margaret Halstan, as Mrs. Petersham, came on the stage, my heart dried up inside me.

Then a crisis occurred. After some particularly flagrant neglect of duty, Sam Hartley was sacked. The dismissal came over the telephone one morning, before he was properly up and dressed. Just before this, he had walked over to a mirror, and recited ironically to himself the record of his career: boyhood at a small public school, a good second in Mods at one of the dimmer Oxford colleges (that is how Mr. Watling puts it, but he must be a Cambridge man. There were no dim Oxford colleges in my time), a poor second in Greats, a good war record, and during the peace nothing worth talking of. It was at this point, for the first time, that I began to be interested in *Indian Summer*. For it was at this point that Sam Hartley began to stand for something more than himself.

I will not say that he is a universal figure, but he is very widespread. His youth, his good second in Mods, had encouraged hopes that maturer life, except for one brief interlude in the army, had not fulfilled. Most men have moderate expectations for themselves; they are satisfied if, at the end of the day, in Stevenson's phrase, they have managed to preserve a few rags of honour, and have kept a roof over their heads. The Sam Hartleys are not like that. They had looked for fairer prospects, and they take the clouding of the bright sunrise hard. They are reluctant to realise that you cannot drive the mill with the water that is past, or with the water in the next river. They will not acknowledge that they can be satisfied with their own little stream. They will not diminish gracefully into the stature of the common man.

I

Their only hope, of course, lies in perceiving that so to diminish has about it a grandeur of its own. To recognize that you are not as clever as you thought you were, that you are in fact quite an ordinary fellow, and not the distinguished creature of your early dreams—to do this without groaning and without loss of contentment calls for a not despicable amount of courage. What Mr. Watling showed us was not a failure, but a man who, though he learned this lesson hard, did learn it in the end. There were moments when the process of learning was very moving.

In the second act, the scene in which Hartley pulled himself together, and took the telephone call of his dismissal instead of leaving it to his wife, brief though it was, began to stir the pulses; and the final episode of the conversation between these two, in which Hartley for the first time faced the sorry spectacle that he presented to the world, refrained from shoving the responsibility for it elsewhere, and yet contrived not to be utterly despairing, was gallant and tender and true.

The play was directed by John Gielgud, who did not succeed in getting out of Miss Halstan and Nora Nicholson performances that concealed the tiresomeness of the parts Mr. Watling had written for them. Betty Ann Davies was much praised as Hartley's fascinating sister-in-law. For myself, I found her too arch, too determinedly playful. Clive Morton, as a professional soldier not overcumbered with brains, but nevertheless practically the only character on the stage with a job and the resolution to do it, was excellent, as he invariably is within a limited range. Miss Baxter is always a thoroughly healthy, open-air girl; she meddles neither with psychoses nor poetry. As Kate Hartley, Hartley's sensible, conscientious, and courageous wife, she was admirable, and in the last scene her understanding and sympathy became very moving. There remains Mr. Flemyng as Sam Hartley.

In discussing Mr. Flemyng's performance, it is useful to recall the distinction made between the *acteur* and the *comédien* by M. Gilles Quéant in *Théâtre de France*. The *acteur*, says M. Quéant, imposes himself on his part, the *comédien* becomes it. The *comédien* has range and variety, the *acteur* is always himself.

M. Quéant then introduces another distinction. The adjectives one applies to the *acteur* are 'extraordinary, astonishing, or extremely bad'; but of the *comédien* one says that he is 'perfect, remarkable, or intelligent.' Charles Dullin used to say of Sarah Bernhardt—'she was often very bad, worse than bad . . . But . . . there were evenings when she twisted your guts and turned the world upside down.' The other sort of player was Réjane: 'she was always perfect', always intelligent. Réjane was a *comédien*, Bernhardt an *acteur*, the *Monstre sacré*.

Now, one of the features of the English stage today is the intellectual power of its chief players. I doubt if there has ever been a period in British history when its greatest actors were so anxious to appear in plays of high literary value. Men like Olivier,. Gielgud, and Guinness are not content, as Irving, for example, was content, to secure a personal triumph in pieces of no literary merit. They are men of education and taste, and this has brought the English stage great and obvious advantages. It has resulted, for example, in the fostering of the genius of Christopher Fry. But all advantages are bought at a price, and this is no exception. The judgment that Olivier and Gielgud bring to bear on their choice of plays they bring also to bear on their own performances. They see them in relation to the whole effect. They consider them as constituent parts of a complicated picture. They do not think that the chance blaze of their own genius is sufficient counterweight to a ramshackle production of something in itself worthless. It is true that at the beginning of his career Sir Laurence had the makings of a *monstre sacré*. He could, fifteen years ago, be unimaginably bad or transcendently good. Every performance of his was a gamble. Now he is a safe bet, but the stakes are not as high as they were in the days he played his first Hamlet for the Old Vic. Only in Donald Wolfit does something of the spirit of the *monstre sacré* still linger.

In this sense of erratic inequality of performance, English players therefore are not, in the main, *acteurs*. But in the sense first mentioned, that of either being themselves or of impersonating others, my own opinion is that they can still be divided into *acteurs* and *comédiens*. The animal power and the dry wit that are part of Olivier always enter into his performances, as does Gielgud's high nervous tension into his; these men are decidedly *acteurs*, though M. Quénet, impressed, as are most Frenchmen, by the differences between his Hotspur and his Richard III, regards

Olivier as a *comédien*. I once looked on Sir Ralph Richardson purely as an *acteur*, as a player who used to artistic ends his natural qualities of kindness and humanity. But his performance as Doctor Sloper in *The Heiress*, a performance of extraordinarily precise and clinical cruelty, showed him to be a *comédien* also. Mr. Alec Guinness, too, is decidedly a *comédien*.

Mr. Flemyng, on the other hand, is an *acteur*. I do not mean that he has the divine and infuriating egotism of the *monstre sacré*, for that, as I have said, is almost extinct on the London stage. But he is even further removed from the nature of the *comédien* as this is somewhat cruelly described in Diderot's *Paradox*. The stage player, according to Diderot, can exactly reproduce the character of other people simply because he has no character of his own. He can fill himself with the personality of his part because his own personality is a vacuum. This, of course, is a ludicrously savage description of those high qualities of intelligence and observation, of imitation and study, that go to make a Guinness or a Réjane.

Mr. Flemyng, however, is not a player of this kind. He does not slip easily into the skin of another character than his own. I have already spoken of his difficulties with Edward Chamberlayne in *The Cocktail Party*, where he gave a very moving performance, but endowed his part with an integrity that Mr. Eliot had not written into it. Mr. Flemyng is not a smooth and supple player. Even his hair perpetually seems to be stiffly standing to attention. It was said of Sir Laurence in his early days that his speech could not be fitted into the rhythm of poetry. There is a jerkiness, too, about Mr. Flemyng's delivery, though it is becoming less marked as the years go by. If these are faults, it is to be remembered that faults have never yet in themselves proved fatal to the exposition of high talents. Gielgud, as Mr. Alan Dent remarks, walks as if he had a silken scarf tied round his knees. Irving's voice squeaked. Hardy split his infinitives.

Mr. Flemyng's voice is very stirring, not as a trumpet, but as a cello is stirring. It is troubled in great depths of suffering, but the anguish in it is restrained. It has in it some of the notes of the nightingale, of the old, deep-sunken pain of Arnold's tawny-throated. I can never listen to it unmoved. The moment before Richardson or Olivier comes on the stage I am always in a state of excitement, and I invariably await the appearance of Mr.

Flemyng with the same pleasurable tension. I found his performance in *Indian Summer* extremely moving.

A play by Andrew Rosenthal, *Third Person* (Arts Theatre, October, 1951; Criterion, January, 1952) followed *Indian Summer*. Oddly enough, it dealt with the same problem of the readmission into civil life of the demobilised soldier, but at a more glittering and sophisticated level. The scene was in the East Sixties of New York, at Christmas, 1947, in a room in the house of Hank Moreland, a youngish American business man. The tiny Arts Theatre stage put up a wonderful show of wealth, of cut glass, chromium, and silks and velvets; and the dialogue put up a similar show of epigrams and cynicism. In the army, Hank Moreland had acquired a young friend, Kip Ames, played by Denholm Elliott. He had brought him home to stay for a few weeks, and he had stayed for a couple of years. He was, in fact, resolved never to leave. Moreland had a young child, and Kip Ames was delightful with children, but beneath his dangerous charm he was determined to keep Moreland, and Moreland's riches, for himself, even if it meant driving Moreland's wife, Jean, out of the house. Moreland had another friend, of many years' standing, one Felix Callender, who understood the nature of Kip Ames's hold on Moreland, and was flippantly, but exceedingly, jealous.

In spite of its fling of sophisticated repartee, *Third Person* was discreetly written; so discreetly indeed that Hank Moreland was able, in Roger Livesey's guileless performance, to remain ignorant of the quality of the emotions that were bedevilling his household. These manifested themselves most clearly in the tense hostility between Kip Ames and Callender, an almost feminine rivalry that put a remarkable tension into the theatrical atmosphere. But the best parts of the play occurred in Ursula Jeans' performance as the wife, more puzzled perhaps than distressed, not doubting the fundamental goodness of her husband, but justly suspicious of Ames and Callender. As in *The Cocktail Party*, Miss Jeans listened beautifully, with a hurt, silent serenity not, I think, to be seen in any other actress.

Though *Third Person* was smoothly written, I cannot believe that it had as much significance as the struggling and faulty *Indian Summer*. The world is full of ex-soldiers who, like Sam Hartley, feel that their post-war job does not fully exploit their talents.

But Kip Ames and Hank Moreland are special cases without much relevance to the general problems of demobilisation. The claims of *Third Person* to be a part of the involved drama were more plausible than real.

At the same time it was quite a good little play, and, as being American, was doubly welcome. For one of the least satisfactory features of the post-war theatrical world has been the decline, perhaps temporary, of the American drama. Until the first world war the attitude of America towards European art was respectful and imitative. As late as Henry James, American authors desired to write as close to European models as they could. But between 1918 and 1939 the respective positions of the Old and the New Worlds were greatly changed. America began to loom as large on the literary and dramatic horizons as she did on the political and financial. In their own spheres Wall Street and the growing American navy did not exert a greater influence than did Hemingway and O'Neill in theirs. Alongside the English dramatic world of drawing rooms and epigrams there was set up, in many a London theatre, another world of hoboes and saloons and gangsters and roaring newspaper offices brought across the Atlantic in the works of O'Neill, Kaufman, Odets, and Rice, Steinbeck and Ardrey. Crude and often coarse, with no sense of nuance or grace, it was nevertheless a world that had real values of its own, of which the chief were directness of attack and overwhelming vitality.

This great energy of the American theatre continued through the second world war. Between the assault on Pearl Harbour and the bomb on Nagasaki, Broadway enjoyed one of its golden periods of financial prosperity. Ward Morehouse, in *Matinée Tomorrow*, says: 'During the wild splurge nearly every night was New Year's Eve in the Broadway area. Theatres, bars, and restaurants were jammed; so were snack counters and the supper clubs. There was a stampede upon the restaurants, and at 5.30 p.m. thousands were standing in slow-moving dinnertime queues. Hotels sold out nightly; guests slept on cots in parlours and in ballrooms and in chairs in the lobbies. Mid-town Manhattan presented the strange spectacle of playgoers swarming to the stage plays in shirtsleeves. Coatless war workers, without ties, who had seen but few plays in their lives—or perhaps none at all—

stepped up to the ticket windows with wads of money. House treasurers became accustomed to changing fifty-dollar bills, and without their patrons knowing, or caring, anything about the play they were going to see.'

Whether or not this was a good foundation for the time being on which to build, it has not proved enduring. The wild splurge has ended; the worker, with or without his coat, no longer comes up to the box office with fifty-dollar bills. Theatrical activity, which in London and Paris is as great as ever, is in New York merely a fraction of what it used to be in the 1920's. Paris is only half the size of New York, but it has twice as many theatres in regular production. During the twenties Broadway put on 200 new shows a year. On the night of December 27, 1927, for example, no fewer than eleven plays were presented for the first time. Now there are only sixty or seventy a season.

This is partly due to the increasing competition of the television and the cinemas, and partly to the rising cost of production. *The Children's Hour* before the war cost $8,000 to present; today the production expenses of a straight play are about $60,000. But another reason seems to be that the supply of good new plays is drying up. America still plays a great part in the international theatre, but at the moment her importance is almost entirely due to her supremacy in monster musicals. When *Oklahoma!* came to Drury Lane early in 1947 it was a revelation in gaiety, sentiment, dancing, and discipline. *Carousel* (London, Drury Lane, May, 1950) and *South Pacific* (London, Drury Lane, November, 1951) had not the freshness of *Oklahoma!* but their music was immensely superior to that of practically all modern British musical plays.

In the realm of significant straight drama, however, America has lost the lead to France. Yet there are grounds for believing that this may be only a temporary phenomenon, due to social changes which for the moment are unfavourable to the production of important new plays. The great upsurge of American drama between 1920 and 1945 was due to a tremendous pride in America on the part of American authors and public. America had suddenly emerged as a great power, as the greatest of great powers, and her typical figures, her big business men in their shiny cars, her workmen in their overalls on the assembly line, her farmers and ranchers ceased to seem rough and upstart in comparison with the aristocratic civilisation of Europe, but on the contrary became the triumphant exponents of a new, rich, and self-confident democratic way of life. Plays like *Life with Father* and Thornton Wilder's *Our Town* were products of an emotional patriotism that felt itself happy and secure. Even the plays that were critical of certain aspects of America, like Maxwell Anderson's *Winterset* and John Steinbeck's *Of Mice and Men*, had no sense of there being a better civilisation elsewhere. They were criticisms from strength, not weakness. American pride and self-confidence between the wars resembled in some ways, though not of course in all, the sweep and splendour of the Elizabethans, and, like the first Elizabethan age, resulted in an outburst of vigorous creative activity.

A great deal of this pride was based on the conviction that America was a revolutionary and progressive country. Until the outbreak of war in 1939 the average American assumed as a matter of course that his country was the leader in social change. He never forgot that America was founded in rebellion, and that the Declaration of Independence was a revolutionary document. These things meant an enormous amount to him; he felt himself to be in the vanguard of social development.

Since 1945 America has had to face the fact, the disconcerting fact, that revolution has taken the wrong turning. It no longer works for free enterprise and the American way of life. The revolutionary flag has passed back from the New World to the Old, and America is not yet accustomed to having lost it. It sees itself with difficulty as the world's foremost conservative. It has become uncertain of itself, and of its mission in the world. When its own view of right could be identified with the revolutionary trends in society, America was happy, confident, and creative; now that this situation has completely passed away, it is ill at ease.

But there is no reason why America should not be able to adjust itself to this development, and be as forceful in its new role of the world's crusted Tory as it was in the old one of the young sansculotte. When the adjustment has taken place, American creativeness in the drama will once again challenge that of the leading countries of Western Europe.

Meanwhile, in the period covered by this book, the significant

American contribution to the British stage has been confined to two plays, Arthur Miller's *Death of a Salesman* and Tennessee Williams's *A Streetcar Named Desire*. The first of these was produced at the Phoenix Theatre in July, 1949, with Paul Muni and Kathleen Alexander at the head of the cast, and ran for six months.

It was a play that questioned the very foundation of American social morality. No figure is more typical of American life, or of American ideals, than the travelling salesman, the man who sells more and more goods for more and more money, able at the end of the year to express his advancement in life in exact statistics of dollars and cents. Willy Loman saw himself as a brash, hearty fellow, roaring round the countryside in a twenty horse-power car, at intervals loudly congratulating himself on being a husband, a father, and an American, slapping women on the bottom, swapping stories, getting bigger and bigger orders, noisy, good-natured, generous and coarse, the sort of man whom many observers, forgetting Harvard, and Lee, the Century club, Henry James, and the South, would accept unhesitatingly as the characteristic democratic American hero. Mr. Miller took this man, and showed that, far from being the masterful creature he thought himself, he was weak, pitiful, and sad; that his boasted triumphs were vulgar illusions; and that the end of him, and by implication, of the American way of life, was bitterness, disappointment, and death.

The play was beautifully and movingly written, eloquent, yet perfectly within the common American idiom. The last scene, when Loman's wife Linda, and his two sons, Happy and Biff, and his friend Charley, stood round his grave, and wondered how he should have come to take his life, was exquisitely touching and tenderly wise.

LINDA: I can't understand it. At this time especially. First time in thirty-five years we were just about free and clear. He only needed a little salary. He was even finished with the dentist.

CHARLEY: No man needs only a little salary.

LINDA: I can't understand it.

BIFF: There were a lot of nice days. When he'd come home from a trip; or on Sundays, making the stoop; finishing the cellar; putting on the new porch; when he built the extra bathroom; and put up the garage. You know something, Charley, there's more of him in that front stoop than in all the sales he ever made.

CHARLEY: Yeah. He was a happy man with a batch of cement.

BIFF: He had the wrong dreams. All, all, wrong.

HAPPY: *almost ready to fight Biff.* Don't say that!

BIFF: He never knew who he was.

CHARLEY, *stopping Happy's movement and reply.* *To Biff*: Nobody dast blame this man. You don't understand: Willy was a salesman. And for a salesman, there is no rock bottom to the life. He don't put a bolt to a nut, he don't tell you the law, or give you medicine. He's a man way out there in the blue, riding on a smile and a shoeshine. And when they start not smiling back—that's an earthquake. And then you get yourself a couple of spots on your hat, and you're finished. Nobody dast blame this man. A salesman is got to dream, boy. It comes with the territory.

The tenderness of this, and the rhythm seem to me exceedingly moving and true; and I have never heard in an American play anything wiser, better said, or better worth saying, than Charley's 'No man needs only a little salary'. In America, no more than anywhere else, can man live by bread alone. But in America, a country so favoured by nature, and so rich in resources and energy of character, it is a lesson peculiarly hard to learn.

The glittering Mr. Nathan took a much higher view of *Death of a Salesman*, when it was produced at the Morosco Theatre in New York in February, 1949, than he does of such theatrical phenomena, for example, as the acting of Miss Eva Le Gallienne, or Keith Winter's *The Rats of Norway*, or of the Oliviers in Shakespeare and Shaw. But he faulted it on the ground of its ordinary speech, in which he saw no true tragic grandeur. 'The average man's, the common man's, tragedy, save it be laid over and lifted above itself with the deceptive jewels of English speech, can be no more in the temple of dramatic art than the pathetic picture of a lovable idiot lifting his small voice against the hurricane of the world.' It seems to me that the voice Mr. Miller lifts up against the world's hurricane, in the words of Charley that I have just quoted, is by no means a small one; and that not many dramatists have written speeches that drive harder at the heart, or are more memorable, than those of Linda near the end of the first act, when she is trying to stand up for her cowed and beaten husband against his unsympathetic children;

LINDA: I don't say he's a great man. Willy Loman never made a lot of money. His name was never in the paper. He's not the finest character that ever lived. But he's a human being, and a terrible thing is happening to him, So attention must be paid. He's not to be allowed to fall into his grave like an old dog. Attention, attention must finally be paid to such a person. You called him crazy—

BIFF: I didn't mean:

LINDA: No, a lot of people think he's lost his—balance. But you don't have to be very smart to know what his trouble is. The man is exhausted.

HAPPY: Sure!

LINDA. A small man can be just as exhausted as a great man.

The flat, grave, grieved voice in which Mildred Dunnock in New York brought out these words touched depths of sadness, and reached heights of loyalty, that passed beyond royal and purple speech. I cannot agree with Mr. Nathan that the play, for any purpose, and at any level, was inadequately written.

Whatever argument there might be about the merits of Mr Miller's writing, the excellence of Elia Kazan's direction of the play both in New York and in London was hardly questioned at all. It could not be. The stress that the American theatre places upon skilful direction is something that immediately strikes every visitor to Broadway. George Freedley, in his *History of the Theatre*, says that two 'main forces influenced the American theatre early in the present century. One took the form of a developing national drama and the other was a vital standard of play production in all its aspects . . . It is only when you have both that a great theatre exists.'

Mr. Freedley's statement that these two forces are needed before a theatre can have the stamp of greatness is questionable. It will already have become clear that I consider the French theatre of today the most important in the western world, but it certainly has not 'a vital standard of play production'. The theatres of Irving, of Garrick, and of Kean were all great in the sense that they gave to their spectators true theatrical experiences in an extremely heightened form, but they neither had producers in the modern meaning of the term, nor were they the product of 'a developing national drama'.

But that America has at the present moment a very high

standard of play production is something that cannot be doubted. The conditions on Broadway throw the director into high relief. The cinema takes up a great deal of the time and attention of British players, but it leaves them free for stage work on a scale unknown in the United States. Denham is only twelve or fifteen miles from the West End, and an actor who goes there to make a film is within easy range of the London theatres. But the American actor who lives in Hollywood rapidly loses all connexion with Broadway, and that instinctive sympathy with and understanding of the theatre that comes only of close and constant proximity. Consequently, whilst English players continue to appear in the West End with some regularity, the leading Americans tend to make only sporadic appearances on the stage. They therefore need someone to drill and organise them more than do their English or French counterparts. They have to recover the 'feel' of the stage which English and French players, owing to differing circumstances, do not find it so easy to lose. And the man who aids them in this recovery is the director.

Sometimes, however, one has the impression that the process followed by the director is one, not so much of helping, as of bulldozing. It is odd that in America, a country which on the whole seems to have a considerably developed sense of the free and easy, the stage should exhale such an air of discipline and even of tyranny. A characteristically produced American play has the inexorability of fine machinery. Its precision, efficiency, and co-ordinated movement are things to marvel at. The danger, of course, as Raymond Rouleau remarked when he went to New York to direct Colette's *Gigi*, is that in this superbly developed mechanism there is no room for spontaneity. But despite this, on occasion the results can be impressive.

They were impressive in *Death of a Salesman*. I have already spoken of a moving passage in Miss Dunnock's performance. I thought it the best thing in the play. But American critics were impressed most of all by Lee J. Cobb's Willy Loman. This was an interpretation of really extraordinary life and energy. Mr. Cobb went through the play like a typhoon, and yet one felt that every movement, every intonation of what seemed like a human storm was exactly calculated and rigidly controlled. This display of organised abandon must have been an extreme strain on the actor, and indeed Mr. Cobb had to relinquish his part after about a hundred and thirty performances.

But that there are limits to the power of the director, even when he is manipulating American players, who do not as a rule appear to have the independence of spirit which makes, for example, an actor like Pierre Brasseur resent what he is liable to consider the interference of the *metteur en scène*, was shown when *Death of a Salesman* came to London. Though Miss Kathleen Alexander, who took the part of Linda Loman at the Phoenix Theatre, is far more physically resplendent than Miss Dunnock, Mr. Kazan got from her exactly the same muted performance, and many of the other players (most of them imported from America) reproduced the New York interpretation. But Paul Muni's Willy Loman had no resemblance at all to Mr. Cobb's. Mr. Cobb's Loman was a man rejoicing in his enormous vitality, and quite unaware of his essential uselessness, the realization of which came upon him at the end as a shattering and incomprehensible paradox. Mr. Muni's performance, on the other hand, was that of a sad little chap beaten from the start, pushed around by life and his fellows, pathetically incompetent, touching and exasperating by turns. Mr. Cobb took the play along with splendid drive, but hardly ever unsealed the springs of pity. Mr. Muni was frequently moving, but occasionally became a bore.

Mr. Muni's weariness, melancholy, and defeatism are to be found also in the work of America's leading contemporary dramatist, Tennessee Williams. Mr. Williams speaks for the South, a defeated country, whose institutions values, and civilisation have been overwhelmed by the vigorous Philistinism of the North. The South, in Mr. Williams's plays, particularly in *A Streetcar Named Desire* (London, Aldwych, October, 1949), is a degenerate and desperate Europe.

Demoralised, devitalised, and disintegrating, it clings, blindly and drunkenly, to those standards and ideals which the energetic and confident North in its heart despises. In the hot, poker-playing slums of New Orleans, Blanche du Bois still cherished a love for poetry, an admiration for fine manners, still responded to chance acts of kindness and sympathy. To the robustly Puritan and wholesome North, the descendants of the Pilgrim Fathers, and of the men who fixed a scarlet A on the bodices of fallen girls, such tastes are suspicious; they are of no value on the ticker tapes of Wall Street; they are probably associated with a loose moral life. They are so associated, too, in the mind of Mr. Williams, who apparently believes that America is a country in which it is no longer possible to combine culture with decency. To him the battle has been lost; the healthy hosts of barbarians have routed the feeble forces of the sensitive and civilised, to whom there now remains no comfort but drink and debauchery. This may be taken as yet another censure upon culture, but that is not how Mr. Williams intends it. His heart is filled with pity, sometimes beautiful and sometimes mawkish, that love of tenderness and grace should have been brought to such a sorry pass, and he lifts his voice in a lamentation devoid of hope.

Blanche du Bois is a schoolmistress who has been betrayed by the weakness of her own nature, and also by her longing for gentleness and love, into disreputable associations that result in her being driven out of her home town, and taking refuge with her younger married sister in a heat-oppressed tenement in New Orleans. Her frail chances of happiness are ruined by the discovery of her past, and the play ends with her being taken off to a mental home. The play is brutal and raucous as well as sad and often beautiful, and it aroused one of those stupid controversies that from time to time make Britain ridiculous. None of the bodies officially connected in London with the preservation of decency protested, so far as I know, against such plays as *Mary Had a Little* . . . or *Storks Don't Talk*. It may be said in their defence that protest was unnecessary, since both plays rapidly failed, and were taken off. But another farce, almost as offensive as these—*The Dish Ran Away*—had more than a hundred performances in the West End without any protest being made. Yet Mr. Williams's work, which is a matter of artistic importance, was greeted with an absurd howl of execration from ill-advised moralists, and Vivien Leigh, whose performance of Blanche du Bois was sensitive, touching, and extraordinarily lovely, was subjected to a virulence of criticism that would have broken the spirit of a less gallant lady.

There are, of course, Americans who, unlike Mr. Williams, rejoice in the rough barbarism of the north. At the Alvin Theatre in New York thousands upon thousands of them were moved to raucous laughter and simple tears by Thomas Heggen's *Mister Roberts* (New York, Alvin Theatre, February, 1948; London, Coliseum, July, 1950). This play in America ran for more than two years, and it won intense admiration, not only from hicks and hoboes, but from a critic of such fineness of mind and taste as John Mason Brown. It is a phenomenon that baffles me. Nearly two hundred actors, bare-chested, dripping with sweat, on the most meticulously accurate representation of a ship I have seen on the stage, spent the evening, either peering through telescopes at a girl taking a shower bath, or planning imbecile practical jokes at the expense of the ship's captain, or behaving like hooligans when they went ashore on leave, or becoming embarrassingly mawkish over a gallant lieutenant. If *Mister Roberts* had been written by a Russian, I should have regarded it as another libel on the American people; but apparently American theatre-goers received it as a just and not unpleasing portrait, which I suppose shows that a country, like an individual, is not really aware of its own best or worst features.

Chapter Five

THE OLD AND THE NEW

IN recent years the English theatre has offered the gratifying
spectacle of the best players in the best plays. It is unbelievable
that an Irving of today would consent to act in a modern *Bells*.
His gorge would rise at the thought: his pride would be offended,
and his literary taste outraged. An Olivier, a Gielgud, or a Richardson is presumably not indifferent to the opportunity of display-
ing himself in a part that exercises his peculiar qualities; but if such
a part occurs in a shoddy play there is nothing in the history of the
London theatre in the last ten years which suggests that any of
these actors would agree to appear in it. As I say, it is gratifying
that the best players should act in the best plays. But it is not so
pleasing that the best plays should often turn out to be old ones.

In fact, the main feature of the English stage during the period
under review is the number, importance, and excellence of its
revivals. The Old Vic has ranged from the teeming, bawdy
rumbustiousness of Ben Jonson's *Bartholomew Fair* to the controlled classicism of *Electra*. Anthony Quayle at Stratford, with
the help of players like John Gielgud and Michael Redgrave, has,
for the moment at any rate, raised the Memorial theatre to the
rank of one of the world's really important play-houses. Mr.
Gielgud, in a production directed by Peter Brook, achieved a run
of 211 performances for *The Winter's Tale*, without making any
unworthy concessions in the attempt to win popular approval.
The Oliviers presented Shaw's *Caesar and Cleopatra* on alternate
nights with Shakespeare's *Antony and Cleopatra*, and the result
showed affinities between the genius of the two authors that must
have been equally disconcerting to Shaw's enemies and to Shaw
himself. Whilst Alec Guinness offered us a *Hamlet* (London,
New Theatre, May, 1951) which started one of the big theatrical
controversies of recent years.

After a disastrous first night my colleagues and I agreed that Mr.

Guinness's Hamlet was very bad. One critic called it the worst Hamlet he had ever seen, though he was probably referring to the production as a whole rather than to Mr. Guinness's own performance. This production had several idiosyncrasies. Thus, Hamlet wore a tiny Imperial beard. Now Mr. Guinness is not a big man, and this absurd decoration gave him the air of a precocious child aping the appearance of his elders. Rosencrantz (or perhaps it was Guildenstern) had a black patch over his eye. This was intended to suggest the piratical nature of these two gentlemen, but the effect was to make it look as if one of them had tripped up in the wings. The production's elaborate lighting scheme went hopelessly wrong. Scenes that are usually played in a relatively bright light were enveloped in darkness, whilst the Ghost of Hamlet's father positively blazed with illumination.

It may be thought that professional critics ought to be able to make allowances for first night mishaps, and in general this is true enough. But the difficulty of this *Hamlet* was that it set out to be an unconventional interpretation. Mr. Guinness in an interview given to the *Stage* had warned us that his performance would illustrate the darker aspects of Hamlet's character. He said that he had learned much of evil in the last few years, and that this would contribute to his interpretation of the part. He suggested that many people would dislike his performance. We therefore went to the New Theatre prepared for unusual things; and when unusual things happened we were never certain whether, though they looked like accidents, they might not be parts of some obscure master-plan.

Further, though here I enter more or less on realms of speculation, I believe that Mr. Guinness himself was disconcerted during the performance, and that by things which the most perceptive critic could not be expected to understand. He delivered one of the great soliloquies standing near the footlights on an empty stage. On the backcloth was painted a vast sky, with, on the horizon, a galleon bearing all her sails spread. Half way through the soliloquy, this galleon began to bob up and down upon the waves, and Mr. Guinness, catching sight of it out of the corner of his eye, for a minute flash of time seemed surprised. I have been told that the idea of making this ship wobble was a last-minute inspiration that occurred to someone backstage after Mr. Guinness had begun

K

his speech. It had never wobbled at rehearsals. Mr. Guinness did not know it was going to wobble at the first performance. If this is a true account of the incident—and I am assured that it is—it seems reasonable enough that on the opening night Mr. Guinness was not at his best.

He had said beforehand that public and critics might not like his interpretation of the play, and in this he was right. But all the same I think he was taken aback by the virulence by the opposition. It would require superhuman self-control to remain unmoved by such notices as were written on this *Hamlet*. Though there was some booing from the gallery at the first night, subsequent audiences were impressed and touched by Mr. Guinness's performance. It is said that on some occasions he came forward at the end, and observed to the small but cheering house, 'You are applauding what one critic calls the worst Hamlet he has ever seen.' His bitterness was comprehensible, and he was not to be placated. When a second notice appeared in one newspaper, much more favourable than the first, all he is recorded to have said is, 'It's a bit late, isn't it?'

The play opened on a Thursday evening, and the next night I had to be in Pitlochry, five hundred miles away. This *Hamlet* therefore was one of the few important productions of which I have written a notice immediately after the fall of the curtain. A Sunday critic generally has the opportunity for careful thought, if, that is, we suppose him capable of such a thing. But of this *Hamlet* I had to write with speed. I put my notice through the letter-box of *The Sunday Times* three hours after the end of the performance, and set off by road for Scotland at three o'clock on Friday morning, May 18. I drove all through the night and the next day and reached Pitlochry at dusk on Friday evening. It was not until Saturday that I read anything my colleagues had written on the production, or saw that they and I were agreed in our judgment on what had been offered to us that Thursday night.

My own view of the matter was expressed in the title of my article, which was the single word 'Disaster.' I recalled that Dickens had had his *Hard Times*, Hardy his *Laodicean*, and Napoleon his Waterloo, and I implied that Guinness's Hamlet came into the same category. Indeed, I said that it was a mark of genius to fail in a big way on occasion, and that the cropper Mr. Guinness had come was monumental, and I proceeded to give my reasons for being of this opinion.

After the publication of this article I received a sufficiently large number of letters from people who had seen a performance later than the first, and who seemed to have been greatly moved by their experience, to wonder whether I ought not to see the play a second time. Accordingly I went again one Thursday afternoon three weeks after the play opened, and I found it difficult to believe that I was seeing the same actor in the same play.

There were several superficial changes. The ship no longer bobbed up and down on cardboard waves; the black patch had gone; and Guinness had shaved off his beard. This last alteration was the only one among these three of considerable importance; the clean-shaven Guinness had more dignity and ease than the bearded. But what was enormously important was that Mr. Guinness, free from the distractions of that miserable first night, was now giving a performance that truly embodied his mind's thought.

He was dressed sombrely, and the whole production, with scenery by Mariano Andreu, had a dark and heavy air befitting Guinness's conception of Hamlet's character. Mr. Guinness had no notion of the Hamlet who was the glass of fashion and the mould of form, or of the Hamlet whose spiritual perception at the end enabled him to say 'The readiness is all.' His Hamlet had closer affinities with the suggestions thrown out by Dr. Akenside to George Steevens, 'that the conduct of Hamlet was every way unnatural and indefensible, unless he were to be regarded as a young man whose intellects were in some degree impaired by his own misfortunes; by the death of his father, the loss of expected sovereignty, and a sense of shame resulting from the hasty and incestuous marriage of his mother.'

This was the kind of Hamlet that Mr. Guinness presented. It might almost have developed out of Steevens's remark that Hamlet had hitherto been mistakenly 'regarded as a hero not undeserving the pity of the audience,' in spite of the fact that 'Shakespeare has taken the pains to point out the immoral tendency of his character'. What Shakespeare is here alleged to have pointed out with care Mr. Guinness underlined with relish. His

Hamlet was a man whose mind had been overthrown by his experiences, and in its overthrow revealed dreadful, indeed, unmentionable things, but which occasionally caught rare and radiant visions of the nobility it once had been. It was a coherent conception, disturbing, but with some flashes of notable beauty and pathos.

The fate of this *Hamlet* was unhappy. It ran only for six weeks, and a projected visit to the United States was, after the first night notices, abandoned. But *The Winter's Tale*, one of Shakespeare's most absurd and ill-constructed plays, a sad effort to graft the darkness of *Othello* on to the pastoralism of *As You Like It*, filled the Phoenix Theatre from June, 1951, to January, 1952, with a company that included John Gielgud, Diana Wynyard (standing in the last act, a tinted statue, miraculously still), and Flora Robson.

This production was part of the splendid recovery which the genius of Mr. Gielgud has continued to make during the years covered in this book. This recovery is one of the finest things that has happened to the English theatre. The theatre has, in Mr. Gielgud, a servant who is utterly devoted to it, and no more fortunate circumstance can occur than that he should meet with steady and complete success, for the drama flourishes in the prosperity of its best friends.

Towards the end of the war, and for some time afterwards, the trend of theatrical events went against Mr. Gielgud. During the war, James Agate had been able to dedicate a theatre book to him as 'Our Leading Player'. Nearly twenty years of distinguished work on the London stage had given Mr. Gielgud an undisputed claim to this title. He had used his position to great and unselfish ends. He delighted to appear, not in pieces that provided opportunities for bravura personal display, but in classics whose uniform perfection of performance prevented any one actor from shining above the rest. Thus, in the last days of the war, he was acting at the Haymarket Theatre in a series of productions of *The Circle*, *Love for Love*, *The Duchess of Malfi*, and *A Midsummer Night's Dream*, which, for high excellence of conception and execution, may never be equalled again. But it is to be doubted whether Mr. Gielgud's part in any of these plays was such as to enable him to raise his reputation as an actor. Mr. Gielgud has always wished to draw attention to the play rather than to himself, which is noble but risky. There is no actor in the world who can afford to ignore the personal publicity of high-sounding parts.

At this moment, defying Nature, there shot into the centre of the theatrical sky, two veritable suns. Laurence Olivier and Ralph Richardson were released from the armed forces in order to re-establish the Old Vic, somewhat shaken by the war. Their success was astounding, unparalleled, and deserved. In a series of tremendous performances, tragic, comic, and melodramatic, they isolated the Old Vic, and themselves with it, in the brilliant spotlight of the world's admiration. For the first time for ten years Mr. Gielgud's position as the country's most celebrated actor was challenged, and then lost.

During part of the time, Mr. Gielgud was away from his kingdom, touring in Burma for S.E.A.C. When he came back to England he realised what had happened, and the necessity for finding plays which, besides being good in themselves, would illustrate effectively his own exceptional talents. He was not, for some time, successful. His Raskolnikoff, in *Crime and Punishment*, at the New Theatre in 1946, was not a failure, but it was not a triumph. A visit to the United States was only partially satisfactory. Moreover, about this time, Mr. Gielgud came to an end of the parts which, from his youth onwards, he had wanted to play. Some of his greatest London performances, in Shakespeare and Chekhov, he had first sketched out, in the nineteen twenties, at the old Oxford Playhouse in the Woodstock Road. But the finished, enriched portraits of his Richard II, his Vershinin, his Hamlet, he had now given to London, and for the moment there were no others which he felt the need of playing. During this period of indecision he put on St. John Hankin's *The Return of the Prodigal*. It met with neither critical nor popular approval.

All this time Mr. Gielgud does not seem for a moment to have contemplated lowering his artistic standards in order to find a bravura part. He was more anxious than he had been for several years to find such a part; indeed, he recognised that it was necessary for him to do so; but he insisted that it should be in a play of high quality. The manuscript of Christopher Fry's *The Lady's Not for Burning* came into his hands. This play had been successfully presented by Alec Clunes at the private Arts Theatre whilst

Mr. Gielgud was in America. Mr. Gielgud at once perceived its merits from reading the text, and, in a mood of excitement and hope, conceived the project of bringing it to the public stage. It was a daring enterprise. Mr. Fry was unknown to the general public, and his style of writing both original and difficult. But the play had incontestable literary virtue, and the part of Thomas Mendip, the dusty soldier of fortune who tried to save a woman suspected of witchcraft from burning, at least approximated to the current requirements of Mr. Gielgud's career, in that it was both theatrically impressive and finely written. The play was presented at the Globe Theatre on May 11, 1949, and was received very warmly by the first night audience. After that, there was a short period of doubt before it became an established success. But in a brief while it was evident, that, with *The Lady's Not for Burning*, Mr. Gielgud had begun the exciting recovery which culminated in *Much Ado About Nothing* (London, Phoenix Theatre, January, 1952).

The Lady's Not for Burning had to be withdrawn after a nine months' run because Gielgud had previously engaged himself to appear at Stratford-on-Avon in the Memorial Theatre during the summer of 1950. I shall at a later stage speak of the work done by the Memorial Theatre under the really momentous management of Anthony Quayle. Here it is sufficient to note that Mr. Gielgud, though in a revival of *Lear* his own performance at the first night did not seem as electrical as it had done elsewhere on some previous occasions, continued with a firm tread his upward march. He was a lean, ague-racked Cassius in *Julius Caesar*, a part he has since played on the screen, and an Angelo in *Measure for Measure* remarkable for his suggestions of a nature originally good but now tormentedly evil. At the end of the Stratford season, after which he went to America for several months, Mr. Gielgud had not lost any of the ground re-won in *The Lady's Not for Burning*.

On returning to England, he appeared at the Phoenix in *The Winter's Tale*. I fear I am not the critic for this play. I saw many beauties in Peter Brook's production and in Gielgud's performance as Leontes. Mr. Gielgud struck twelve all at once. He opened the play on the very flood-tide of Leontes's jealousy; without any time for preparation or for building up effects he launched into

the thunderous heart of the matter. This was very fine. Miss
Robson was a common-sense Paulina who brought some downright and welcome humour into the play. George Rose's Auto-
lycus was fruity and genial. Miss Wynyard was a prodigy of
ravishing stillness as the statue in the last act. Christopher Fry's
incidental music was charming. And so I could go on, adding
delight to delight, without in the least concealing that I was not
delighted. Everyone else, however, was, and the play had what
must have been for it a record run. Mr. Gielgud in particular
was highly praised by my colleagues, and warmly commended
by the public. I did not like it myself, but this was another step
upward.

In January, 1952, the first big production of the new year,
came *Much Ado About Nothing*. From the very beginning, sitting
in the sun-kissed garden that Mariano Andreu had designed for
Leonato's home in Messina, it was obvious that Beatrice was going
to be one of Diana Wynyard's best parts. Lovely, intelligent, and
witty, Miss Wynyard sped Beatrice's arrows gaily to their mark;
and her mischievous happiness being based on thoughtfulness,
she was able, hidden in the arbour, to overhear the tale of Benedick's supposed passion with a sudden and altogether beautiful
gravity.

Mr. Gielgud did not begin quite so well as Miss Wynyard. I
thought that in the early scenes he shouted too much; Benedick's
jests, instead of being tossed lightly into the air, were positively
hurled at the audience; and when he listened to the unlikely story
of Leonato, Claudio, and Don Pedro that Beatrice was in love
with him, he started, not as one whose heart has been punctured,
but as if a needle had unexpectedly been inserted into his skin.
Thereafter, however, all was perfection; and at one point perfection of a thrilling and difficult kind.

The church scene in *Much Ado About Nothing* is one of the best
things in middling serious drama that Shakespeare ever wrote.
But it is not easy to play. What makes it difficult is the presence
of the audience. Claudio has insulted Hero, Beatrice's cousin,
at her marriage service; there has been a great commotion in the
church, and the wronged woman has fainted. She is carried off,
and Benedick and Beatrice are left alone. The period of their
raillery and sarcasm is over, and shadows have crept across the

sun. They have in a few short sentences, shy and broken, to admit their love for each other, and then Beatrice has suddenly to traverse this affection with her sharp cry, 'Kill Claudio', which Benedick repudiates instantly, with 'Not for the wide world.'

My introduction to *Much Ado About Nothing* was by way of the radio. It was a Sunday afternoon performance nearly twenty years ago, with Henry Ainley as Benedick and Marie Ney as Beatrice. Those two exciting words, 'Kill Claudio', leapt out of the wireless set like a flashing dagger, and they enormously impressed me. Later, when I saw Renée Ascherson and Robert Donat play this scene on the stage, I was surprised to find that the audience laughed a little nervous laugh. I was still surprised when exactly the same thing happened at Stratford in 1949 in the production in which the principal players were Miss Wynyard and Mr. Quayle. It happened again in 1950 at Stratford, with Miss Peggy Ashcroft and Mr. Gielgud, but by this time I was used to it. I had in fact been informed by then that, whenever this scene was played, the theatre audience, unable to make the sudden transition of mood which Shakespeare demanded of it, always, invariably laughed in instinctive, automatic self-defence. But at the first night of *Much Ado About Nothing* at the Phoenix there was no laugh. Miss Wynyard and Mr. Gielgud played the scene, right up to and through the tremendous but difficult line, in an absolute silence in the house, As soon as the curtain fell, John Barber, who was sitting only a couple of seats away, turned to me and exclaimed excitedly, 'They didn't laugh. They didn't laugh.' He was one of the few people in the audience who knew how great the triumph of the players had been.

Half the credit was due to the two players; and half to Mr. Gielgud alone as producer. Mr. Gielgud had been producer at Stratford in 1949 and again in 1950; but neither with Mr. Quayle nor with himself had he then discovered the way to defeat that disconcerting laugh. This scene is invariably played in an ascending scale. The words 'Kill Claudio' are built up to as a climax; and as a climax they prove too sudden and too sharp for safety. Approached in this way, they induce another disadvantage. They make the rest of the scene, and in particular Benedick's final words, 'As you hear of me, so think of me. Go, comfort your cousin: I must say she is dead, and so farewell', seem flat and tame. At one period of theatrical history, when leading players were more histrionic and less scrupulous than they are today, this was felt so strongly that Beatrice used to repeat:

Benedick, kill Claudio!

and Benedick replied, 'As sure as I'm alive I will!' Laurence Irving, in his biography of his grandfather, relates that this was how Irving himself concluded the scene.

Mr. Gielgud's method of approaching the problem presented by the anticipated laugh, solved this difficulty also. Miss Wynyard and he took the scene, not towards a climax, but towards a falling close. They spoke their few words of love to each other, in the solemn shadows of the church, in a tone almost of awe, as if they were afraid to break the holy silence with words only of carnal import. They knew that they were greatly changed from their former irresponsible selves, and the knowledge made them strangely still and quiet. Into this mood all the words that either spoke fitted in an unbroken harmony, so that the scene did not snap in two at Beatrice's murderous entreaty, but moved on beyond it to its grave and peaceful ending, which Mr. Gielgud uttered softly, as he left the stage, with Beatrice gazing after him, a solitary figure in the vast house of God.

The rest of the company was worthy of its principals. Paul Scofield made Don Pedro a figure highly fantasticated but restful, witty, dry, and urbane, moving with slow and careful grace. His youthful dignity gratified the eye more than his rather thin voice did the ear; but that often happens with Mr. Scofield. It is something to which he will have to pay attention. Sir Lewis Casson played Leonato with real feeling, and Robert Hardy spoke Claudio's verse with pleasant zest and music. Only Dorothy Tutin as Hero was disappointing. Possibly she was miscast. She has a roving eye and a provocative face, and holds great store in the piquant and saucy. These are not precisely the qualities that the chaste and misjudged Hero requires, and this may have been the reason why Miss Tutin did not discover any way of playing her that escaped the inane.

I have already noted that *Much Ado About Nothing* had been produced first of all at the Stratford-on-Avon Festival. It was one of Stratford's best productions, but there were many others worthy of being mentioned alongside it. Between 1947 and 1952 the Stratford Memorial Theatre became the first Shakespeare theatre in the world, displacing the Old Vic from the position it had occupied for many years, a position which the performances of Sir Laurence Olivier and Sir Ralph Richardson at the end of the war seemed to ensure to it for ever. But the moment that the Old Vic began to decline, Stratford moved masterfully forward.

The first steps were taken under the direction of Sir Barry Jackson, who brought to the front the shining talents of Paul Scofield. Sir Barry's achievements in the world of the theatre in the last forty years, both in Birmingham and in London, have been of the highest value to the drama, and it seemed that he was going to make his career at Stratford a splendid epilogue to what he had done in these other places. But Shakespeare today is apparently a fecund source of disagreement; whenever he is touched, quarrels arise. The Old Vic Governors got rid of Olivier and Richardson at the summit of their powers and popularity; later Donald Wolfit rid himself of the Old Vic Governors; and in the meanwhile, the directors of the Old Vic School—Messrs. George Devine, Michel St. Denis, and Glen Byam Shaw—broke off from the Director and the Administrator of the Old Vic. Nor did things, immediately after the war, go more smoothly at Stratford. At a time when critics and public alike were congratulating the Memorial Theatre on its considerable artistic advance, it was announced that the services of Sir Barry Jackson were no longer desired by the Theatre Governors.

This strange decision might easily have wrecked the theatre, but it did not. Sir Barry was succeeded by Anthony Quayle, whose management of the Memorial Theatre has been one of the high features of the post-war dramatic scene. Mr. Quayle is an actor, an actor of considerable talent who sometimes awards himself leading parts, even when he has in his company players of greater fame than he. He takes these parts well; his Falstaff in both sections of *Henry IV*, though liberally stuffed and garnished, was more than a mere assemblage of skilfully concealed cushions. Nevertheless, the management of a company by an actor who is not, in the accepted sense of the term, precisely an actor-manager, must present difficulties. But if it does, Mr. Quayle has triumphed over them. Actors of fame tell me that Mr. Quayle is a wonderful man to work for and under; he can produce in his company a spirit of happy co-operation. This is not the only way to a successful production, for the theatre has room for tyrants if the tyrants have genius. But it is a good way, all the same. When John Beaufort, dramatic critic of *The Christian Science Monitor*, one of the best dramatic critics in the United States, and therefore in the world, came to England during the Festival of Britain, the two things in the British theatre that most impressed him were the performance of Sir Ralph Richardson in *Three Sisters*, and the productions at Stratford of the cycle of Shakespearean histories from *Richard II* to *Henry V* that Mr. Quayle presented during the spring and summer of 1951.

This cycle of Histories was an exciting, a memorable experience. To see remorse for the murder of Richard II eating into the hearts of his Lancastrian successors, poisoning the sleep of Henry IV, souring the triumph even of his resplendent son, was a pleasure, an illumination rather, rarely afforded in the theatre. *Richard II*, *Henry IV*, *Parts* 1 and 2, and *Henry V* are often played separately. Maurice Evans, John Gielgud, and Alec Guinness have played the first; Robert Atkins, Olivier and Richardson have appeared in revivals of the second and third; and both Alec Clunes and Ivor Novello have acted *Henry V*. Excellent as these plays can be when presented in isolation, fine as are some of the performances that have been given in them, they are only single branches of a mutilated tree. But in 1951 Mr. Quayle gave us the whole tree in its magnificence and majesty: and in doing so provided good reason for modifying the view that Shakespeare dashed down his plays in reckless inspiration, caring only for the immediate moment, and thinking nothing of what had gone before, or was to follow after.

Richard perhaps gains most from this presentation of the entire cycle: not in performance, but in retrospect and continuing influence. He is not a candle ruthlessly snuffed out, as in a performance of a single play he appears to be. In death he wields an ineradicable power greater than he had in life, and the pillows of none of his successors are free from his pitiful, tormenting ghost. Mr. Michael Redgrave made him a figure of irresponsible gaiety, of petulance and superficial glitter, visibly deteriorating as the play progressed. Thus, by suggesting that Richard had been a better man before the play opened than he is when seen before our eyes, he was the first actor I have encountered in the part who managed to offer a hint of a Richard who in his youth had been able to settle Wat Tyler's rebellion.

The plays were given a permanent setting by Tania Mosei-witsch. A steep and treacherous staircase ran up one side of the stage, to a balcony overlooking a space in the centre which was used indiscriminately for battles, the interior of Mistress Quickly's inn, Shallow's Gloucestershire garden, the watchfires of Agin-court, and John of Gaunt's death chamber. The advantages of this setting were, of course, a great saving in expense, and an equal gain in swiftness of transition from scene to scene. Some poetic effect might also have been expected from the contrast between the permanence of the set and the fleetingness of the men and women acting their little turbulent unhappy lives upon it. I do not think, however, that any such effect was obtained, and as the plays progressed one felt increasingly that the dark, enclosed atmosphere of stairs and balcony was inimical to any feeling of green grass or the open air.

With the beginning of *Henry IV, Part* 1, the merits of the con-tinuing cycle became fully apparent. The Bolingbroke we had left at the high point of glory, dealing with rebellion with confi-dent, victorious hand, now appeared, though still in the strength of middle age, bowed by revolt, and conscience-harried. To see *Richard II* alone is not to know the sequel of murder; to see *Henry IV* alone is to be plunged into expiation without experience of the crime. To see one after the other more than doubles the pleasure of either, by adding to both a sense of grand yet terrible inexor-ability. Mr. Harry Andrews, who played the Duke of Hereford both as Bolingbroke and as Henry IV, rose to the best opportunity his seasons at Stratford had yet afforded him, and gave perform-ances of authority and feeling.

During the season there were other things that caught the eye: Michael Gwynn's presentation of the Duke of York in *Richard II* as a garrulous old fool, a performance that added humour to a play not rich in that commodity; Mr. Redgrave's immensely spirited Hotspur in the first part of *Henry IV*, a notable essay in the Newcastle accent, a shrewd blow for the provinces at the court of kings; Mr. Loudon Sainthill's bewitched and blasted island set for *The Tempest* (Memorial Theatre, Stratford-on-Avon, June, 1951); Mr. Hugh Griffith's resonant delivery of John o' Gaunt's dying speech, and the comic solemnity this actor gave to Glendower's magic pretensions in *Henry IV*; and, of course, Mr. Quayle's Falstaff. From the entire season, however, there was one thing that stood out: the performance by Richard Burton, in the two parts of *Henry IV* and in *Henry V*, of the Prince Hal who became King Henry.

I had seen Mr. Burton before, as the young Humphrey Devize in *The Lady's Not for Burning*. He had made me laugh indulgently at Humphrey's kindly simplicity, but he had a heavy air, almost of sullenness, about which I did not altogether make up my mind. Perhaps it would be true to say that, in *The Lady's Not for Burning*, I had not admired Mr. Burton as much as some of my colleagues had done.

Either I had not noticed that Mr. Burton was listed in the Stratford company for 1951, or I had forgotten to link his name with the cast of Mr. Fry's play. Anyway, when the first part of *Henry IV* began, I had no expectation of seeing the Humphrey Devize of *The Lady's Not for Burning* appear as Prince Hal; and this Prince Hal made on me the impact of a memorable actor and a notable stage personality some time before I recognised him as the Richard Burton I had seen two years earlier. It was, of course, only a matter of seconds before the recognition came. Nevertheless, the thing is as I have said. I had decided that this Prince Hal was a considerable actor before I saw that he was Richard Burton.

Since it all happened in the space of seconds, my initial respect for this Prince Hal can hardly have been because of his perform-ance of the part. He had scarcely got this performance started before I felt that the Stratford audience that night was in the presence of no ordinary player. Those learned in matters of the bull ring tell me that it was not necessary to see Manolete, who was killed at Linares in 1947, actually fighting in order to realise that he was an artist. Sacheverell Sitwell says 'No matador walked into the bull ring as did Manolete . . . He was of the order of a Chaliapin or a Nijinsky. "No tragedian ever trod the stage, nor gladiator ever entered the arena, with more grace and manly dignity."' Grace and manly dignity are perhaps largely a matter of opinion. Grace I should say that Mr. Burton certainly does not possess, nor does his figure instantly suggest the adjective digni-fied. It shows rather a stocky, stolid strength; he has a breadth of shoulder that makes him seem hardly above the middle height, though I believe he insists that he is as tall as Olivier. Yet he has a presence on the stage as immediately impressive, without his doing anything to justify the impression, as Mr. Sitwell says was Manolete's, even before he began to fight.

I have said that the idea of playing the English historical plays in sequence aids and enriches then; it must be added that the know-ledge that the victor of Agincourt will follow two nights later on the roysterer of Gadshill imposes difficulties on the actor who, whilst playing the joyous tavern-haunter must keep in mind the valiant and self-justifying king. Mr. Burton solved this problem by simply not playing the light-hearted libertine, the friend of street wenches and disreputable old men, at all. It was a very solemn face that he took to Mistress Quickly's ale house; and when he smiled, as he occasionally did, quite wonderfully, it was more the smile of a saint who for a moment has forgotten the sorrows of this world than of a happy, reckless, carefree youth rejoicing in its pleasures.

Perhaps the Europe of the fourteenth and fifteenth centuries, with its battles, its executions, its butcheries and bloodshed had affinities with the spirit of the corrida today; and again the com-parison with Manolete suggests itself. Of late years bull fights, which Mr. Sitwell admits he can neither resist nor condone, have provoked a great deal of literary activity. It has become the fashion to write of them, not in terms of a cruel and savage sport, but as if they were the manifestation of an exalted art, or even of religious ecstasy. It is now not sufficient to regard Juan Belmonte as a brave and revolutionary matador: he has become the incarna-tion of the spirit of pathos, a wistful Barrie of blood and sand, as Chicuelo is the spirit of grace, Bienvenida of joy, and Manolete himself of mysticism.

The extent to which this man Manuel Rodriguez Sanchez, usually known as Manolete, tall, thin, melancholy, with the ascetic face which no smile ever lit up, has imposed himself on the imagination even of those who, like Mr. Sitwell and myself, never saw him, is prodigious. The prose of French and Spanish writers, when they come to talk of Manolete, moves with a passionate solemnity, a subdued, religious excitement. It is impossible not to be moved by the awe of the writer of the pamphlet, of which no copy can now be found, that was issued soon after he was killed at the age of thirty. 'August the twenty-fifth, the Feast of St. Augustine. A *corrida de toros* in the square of Linares. At eight o'clock in the evening, in the café of the Lion d'Or, the meeting place of aficionados, in the rue d'Alcalá, Saavedra, the great expert in bullfighting pictures, brings us the first news: "Manolete has received a great wound . . . His condition is very serious". Then, the whole night, till the dimness of the dawn, we stayed there, waiting for the telephone, anxiously expecting news, which came from various sources, and which we persuaded ourselves was exaggerated either by emotion or excitement . . . We had already heard enough not to be surprised at anything, and we refused to believe the most sensational stories . . . But this time, no, Manolete was about to die, Manolete was dead.' '*Mais cette fois, non, Manolete va mourir, Manolete est mort.*' The echo could not be more sombre if a god had been struck down.

It is in fact in hieratic language and symbol that the style of Manolete has been most often described. 'He received the charge of the bull in the most absolute stillness . . . The thread of his golden tassels ripped by its horns, Manolette, motionless, straight as a cypress, sometimes with his eyes fixed on the sky, as if lost in a mystical ecstasy, would fight with the pure gestures of an officiating priest.' So says Pavo Tolosa; and between this mystical temper of Manolete and the performance of Mr. Burton as Prince Hal I cannot help finding resemblances. A few days after the first performance I remarked on the strange power of Mr. Burton's eyes. They seemed, I said, not quite of the earth; they too, clear and tranquil, were often lifted to the skies. In *The Sunday Times*, speaking of the character of Prince Hal, I wrote, 'This Prince prefers taverns to palaces, and bawds to statecraft. He enjoys brawling, he likes the company of loose women, he revels in youthful disgraces. Of this enjoyment and liking and revelling, Mr. Richard Burton . . . conveyed nothing. Through the gaiety and noise and lechery in which he chose to move he carried a quiet face whose repose was a constant, dumb rebuke. This face . . . is occasionally lit by a small smile of thoughtful radiance, and its eyes seem not quite of the earth. Mr. Burton looked like a man who had had a private vision of the Holy Grail, and was as determined to say nothing about it as he was incapable of forgetting it . . . An actor, it cannot be too often repeated, is not merely an embodiment of other men's ideas. He has a flame of his own to light, and to get it going he sometimes burns the paper his author has written on. Instead of a light-hearted rapscallion, Mr. Burton offers a young knight keeping a long vigil in the cathedral of his own mind. The knighthood is authentic, the vigil upheld by interior exaltation.' These are the kinds of terms in which those who saw him discuss Manolete.

But the great strength of Mr. Burton as an actor lies in his stillness. Whilst the stage swirls and sways with the lively, feverish activity of the other characters, he, oftener than not, is an absolute point of rest. Yet every eye in the audience is riveted upon him. He has an interior force, so that he is doing everything when he appears to be doing nothing. The emergence of Mr. Burton as a leading actor was, as I have said, the single most exciting thing about the 1951 Stratford Festival.

I wish there were anything in the recent history of the Old Vic about which I could be equally enthusiastic. Olivier and Richardson, in the middle 1940s, raised this ancient and honourable theatre to a dangerous elevation. They put it upon an Everest peak of dramatic achievement, which is only another way of saying that they placed it in a position from which a move in any direction means descent. Descent is always a painful experience, and every mountaineer knows that coming down a hill is more dangerous than going up, particularly if the climbers cut the rope that holds them together. It was in the autumn season of 1950, after its prolonged sojourn in the agreeable and fashionable exile of the New Theatre in St. Martin's Lane, that the Old Vic organisation, amid general rejoicing, returned to its traditional home in the Waterloo Road; and before a year had passed the rope was severed.

The Old Vic, besides being a producing entity, also has a school, and it is desirable that both sections of the organisation should work together in harmony. In the first half of 1951 it became plain that this was not going to happen, and a time came rapidly when three eminent figures connected with the teaching and training side of the Old Vic's activity resigned. Hugh Hunt was then Director of the Old Vic, and he hurriedly telephoned Tyrone Guthrie to ask him if he would help in the crisis that had supervened. Mr. Guthrie was in Liverpool, organising that city's contribution to the dramatic side of the Festival of Britain in the provinces. Mr. Guthrie replied that he would do so, provided he were given unhampered powers. Mr. Hunt agreed to Mr. Guthrie's conditions, and he and Mr. Guthrie then together set about tackling the Old Vic problem.

One of Mr. Guthrie's first actions was to engage Mr. Donald Wolfit as the leading player for the 1951–52 season. He also devised a scheme for having two Old Vic companies, playing in London and the provinces alternately. It was curious that for the second of these companies Mr. Guthrie did not appoint a front-line principal player. Thus it happened that, whilst the 1951–52 season opened with a terrific hurly-burly production of Marlowe's *Tamburlaine*, led masterfully by Mr. Wolfit, the second company, presenting *Othello*, had in the chief part a relatively unknown actor of the name of Douglas Campbell. At the end of October, the *Tamburlaine* company, and Mr. Wolfit with it, departed from London into the outer places of the provinces, whilst the Old Vic stage was occupied by a production that had no star. Mr. Campbell proved to have a pleasing personality, and, though light in tone and too much given to smiling, he worked up a satisfactory semblance of passion in the later stages of Othello's distress. But he did not reveal himself as an actor of unusual promise, and it seemed tactless to banish Mr. Wolfit into the country to make way for him. Just before Christmas, 1951, Mr. Wolfit returned to London with a most charming performance in *The Clandestine Marriage*. After four weeks at the Old Vic he was supposed to go back to the provinces, but he preferred to resign from the company instead. Thus, by the end of 1951, the Old Vic had no leading player of national repute. At this time Mr. Guthrie put on a production of *A Midsummer Night's Dream* that was singularly drab and dull for a director justly renowned for his daring and inventive genius.

Between 1949 and 1952 there were, it goes without saying, many delightful and even impressive things to be seen at the Old Vic, or in Old Vic productions at the New Theatre. Michael

L

Redgrave gave a performance of Hamlet remarkable for the spiritual serenity into which this grief-stricken Prince emerged; Roger Livesey offered a refreshingly and genially agile Sir Toby Belch in a generally undistinguished *Twelfth Night*, and a pleasingly gay Falstaff in *The Merry Wives of Windsor*; *Tamburlaine* was quite outstanding for its truly Elizabethan savagery and tumult, its captive kings harnessed like horses to the chariots of their conquerors, and its hung slaves transfixed by arrows; its sadism was far more effective than anything in the $2\frac{1}{2}$ million pound M.-G.-M. *Quo Vadis'*; whilst Mr. Lambert tells me that Alec Clunes's *Henry V* (which I did not see myself) was very fine. Nevertheless, one's prevailing memory of the Old Vic during this period is of a lack of distinction. It would be rash as well as ungenerous to suggest that this want of distinction will continue. It is a thing that can vanish overnight.

It would be equally unfortunate to give the impression that all the unsatisfactory revivals of important plays seen in London during this period were associated with the Old Vic. We have already recorded the failure of Mr. Guinness's *Hamlet*. If this was the greatest theatrical disappointment that I shall have cause to refer to in this book, the next was the Tennent production of Chekhov's *Three Sisters*. This production is a striking proof that in art it is impossible to guarantee success. Tennents took immense care over this revival. The principal London managements laboured considerably during 1951 to see that the metropolitan stage should be worthy of the Festival of Britain, and *Three Sisters* (London, Aldwych, May, 1951) was the play chosen to inaugurate their efforts. The opening of the Festival, theatrically, could not have been entrusted to a better management. Tennents have great financial resources, and control many theatres; they can call on the services of a high proportion of the best actors and directors in Britain. What is even more important is that their policy is in the hands of a young man of extraordinary talent. The nickname of Hugh Beaumont—Binkie—often crops up in the lyrics of small, intimate, satirical revues like the *Sweet and Low* series at the Ambassadors; but I doubt if the general public realises that Mr. Beaumont is one of the greatest of impresarios: that his influence on the modern English theatre rivals that of Laurence Olivier or John Gielgud. In his selection of entertainments for the many houses that Tennents operate his taste ranges extremely widely; he keeps his eyes on America as firmly as on France, or on the rising or established authors of Britain; nor do young and unknown dramatists escape his vigilant and beneficent but exacting attention. He presents a quite untried writer like John Whiting with the same care and munificence as he lavishes on, for example, Terence Rattigan; and he understands the demands of tragedy as well as those of the gayest comedy, or the lightest intelligent revue. I can praise Mr. Beaumont the more unreservedly, perhaps, in that he is one of the few leading figures in the London theatre to whom I have never even spoken.

For *Three Sisters* a most distinguished company was gathered together. The sisters themselves were Celia Johnson, Margaret Leighton, and Renée Ascherson, Vershinin was played by Ralph Richardson, and Masha's husband by Walter Hudd. The director was Peter Ashmore. Sometime in April, 1951, I ran into Richardson in the drawing room of the Athenaeum, and suggested to him, not very seriously, that there were too many stars in *Three Sisters*. There are not enough, he replied; in Chekhov, every part should be played by a star. Neither of us, of course, intended what we said to be taken literally. I merely meant that stars tend to concentrate attention upon their own part, whilst in Chekhov it is the whole impression that matters. Sir Ralph's meaning, naturally, was that in Chekhov every part, even the least considerable, is of such importance to the whole impression that it deserves the lavishing on it of the highest talent. In the upshot, none of the eminent players in the company at the Aldwych over-emphasised their personal importance; they all loyally subordinated themselves to the play and to the author. At the first night there was none of the misfortunes and mishaps that dogged *Hamlet*; yet the production could only be called partially a success. It ran for half a year, but it is not in terms of popularity or finance that I am speaking. Until the last act, it was all the way through a hair's breadth off-key. Only a second of time, only the slightest displacement of light will change a glorious sunset into a leaden muddle of cloud. A sunset either is perfect or it is nothing. It is the same with Chekhov. Victory or (not Westminster Abbey), but Kensal Green. In the first three acts it was Kensal Green, but in the fourth victory's wings could be heard. Miss Leighton's overwhelming grief at the officers' departure, her white, tear-stained face, her quivering mouth as she sat in the sunshine on the verandah whilst her husband, in a kindly verbosity, prattled on to give her time to recover were extremely moving.

Nevertheless, recent years have not been very fortunate for Chekhov. Miss Irene Hentschel, one of our best producers, gave us a *Seagull* (London: Lyric, Hammersmith, Oct., 1949; St. James's November, 1949) which did not quite capture the elusive Chekhovian atmosphere, though a lesser Chekhov, *Ivanov*, was revived at the Arts (April, 1950) with some success. Less satisfactory revivals than this last were Hugh Walpole's *The Old Ladies* (London, Lyric, Hammersmith, October. 1950), in which Miss Mary Clare failed to find the glitter of decayed poetry in the horrible Agatha Payne; *Macbeth* (June, 1950), the hundredth production at the Arts Theatre under the direction of Alec Clunes, but notable for no other reason; an overfarced production (London, Saville, February, 1950) of Pinero's *The Schoolmistress*, which had previously been seen at the Arts in a quieter and better presentation; and perhaps *The Second Mrs. Tanqueray* (London, Haymarket, September, 1950). Miss Eileen Herlie played Paula Tanqueray in this revival. Few considerable actresses have been more overpraised in some of her parts, notably in *The Eagle Has Two Heads*, than Miss Herlie, but on this occasion she came in for more criticism than she deserved. She was accused of making Paula too cold, and of giving her too little charm. These are precisely the accusations that were originally brought against Mrs. Patrick Campbell, though they have now been forgotten except by browsers in old newspaper files. The truth is that Pinero gave Paula Tanqueray only a small degree of womanliness, and the actress should not be too much blamed for not finding in her qualities which the author omitted. That fine actor, the late Leslie Banks, manfully did his best for Aubrey Tanqueray, but made him so solemn a fellow that one wondered how he could ever have wandered far enough from the church vestry to meet such a woman as Paula, let alone have the idea of marrying her. As Cayley Drummle, Ronald Ward brought the only genuine emotion that the performance contained. Mr. Ward is a most uneven actor. On a bad night his timing can be so inaccurate that the

audience is in an agony of apprehension that he has forgotten his
lines. But when all goes well with him, his lightness of touch, his
capacity to suggest kindness of heart and sympathy beneath a
flippant exterior, can be, as they were in *The Second Mrs. Tanqueray*, extremely charming. The production was decorated sump-
tously by Cecil Beaton.

Far more successful than *The Second Mrs. Tanqueray* revival was
that of *Man and Superman* by John Clements and Kay Hammond.
This came to the New Theatre early in 1951, had to be moved
at the height of its popularity to the Princes Theatre in order to
make way for Guinness's *Hamlet*, and ran till close to the end of the
year. Miss Hammond is the only actress I have ever seen who has
managed to make Anne Whitefield attractive. Shaw's notions
of what constitute sexual charm in a woman are not those of other
men, and this cold-blooded liar and hypocrite is a singularly
repulsive creature. There is nothing in her character or wit to
explain how she could possibly enslave Octavius Robinson, let
alone John Tanner. The famous comparison with the boa-
constrictor is nonsense. One of the easiest things in the world
is to avoid boa-constrictors. South America is full of men who have
done so. But Miss Hammond's Anne was quite a different proposition. She was utterly ravishing. Her languishing eyes, her pout-
ing lips, her drawling voice, her half smile of sly fun would have
run away with any man's heart. Miss Hammond in fact did with
Anne Whitefield what Miss Herlie failed to do with Paula Tanqueray. She supplied, in enormous quantities, the charm the author
had missed out. Mr. Clements' John Tanner was of a calibre
worthy of capture by this enchanting, predatory, and irresistible
woman. He delivered Shaw's rhetoric magnificently, with immense fire and spirit, even when, as on the first night, he was
handicapped by a broken ankle.

I can hardly speak in these terms of the revival of Noel Coward's
Fallen Angels (London: Ambassadors: December, 1949). In this
play appeared these two admirable comediennes, Hermione
Baddeley and Hermione Gingold, neither of whom sets store
on charm of any kind, sexual or otherwise. Twenty-five years
ago, Tallulah Bankhead and Edna Best acted in this play, and the
scene in which they made themselves tipsy whilst waiting for
a former lover to turn up again caused a good deal of scandal.

Miss Best and Miss Bankhead were personable young ladies, but it is among the glories of the Misses Baddeley and Gingold that they claim to be none of these things in their stage characters. They will outface any of the gargoyles on Notre Dame; they teeter and hiccup, and explore the grotesque in its most recondite aspects. They therefore burlesqued the drunken scene instead of seeking in it for piquancy; and the spectacle of these two mature and deliberately outrageous harridans awaiting the return of love with gallons of whisky was a most entertaining sight to connoisseurs of incongruous emotions.

Quite another matter was Sir Laurence Olivier's revival of Shaw's *Caesar and Cleopatra* and Shakespeare's *Antony and Cleopatra* (London: St. James's, May, 1951). This was the big theatrical event of the Festival of Britain. It was awaited with the most breathless expectation, and received with the highest enthusiasm. Sir Laurence always presents his productions like a prince of the Medici: in an age of austerity he spends money on his plays as though he picked the stuff up in the gutter. He demands the finest scenery and the most renowned actors; he rehearses till his artistic soul is satisfied, even if the stage hands are not released till the early hours of the morning, and Trade Union overtime has to be paid three hundred per cent. This is very remarkable. The Anglo-Saxon peoples live in a world of high average well-being, and it would be foolish to deny the greatness of this achievement. But it is an achievement that exacts a diminution of standards in other respects. The biggest things are now beyond humanity's reach. Houses as magnificent as Chatsworth will never be built again. Even the best dinners will not be as long as they used to be, nor the cooking attain such refinements of curious excellence. This applies as much to the United States as to Great Britain. A great fuss was made over the spectacular scenes in Metro-Goldwyn-Mayer's *Quo Vadis*, a film made in 1951. But actually, in scale and impressiveness these scenes were less striking than those in *Intolerance*, which dates from the middle of the first World War. Everywhere the world is having to shorten its reach, to be satisfied with something less than has been achieved in the past. But Sir Laurence Olivier, when it comes to theatrical production, refuses to recognise this. For him the world is still in its splendid, confident morning, and he behaves professionally as if we were living in a golden age. He accepts no limitations, knows no bounds to excellence, to prodigality, to scale and magnitude of effort.

The most enormous superlatives should, therefore, be brought out for Sir Laurence's two Festival productions, which were played throughout the summer of 1951 on alternate nights; and many of my colleagues supplied them. Roger Furse designed some splendid scenery, a colossal Sphinx between whose paws the kittenish Cleopatra of Shaw's play was discovered on the rising of the curtain; and a very fine arrangement of Roman pillars leaping superbly out of the burning desert sands for most of the other scenes of both dramas. In *Caesar and Cleopatra* Robert Helpmann was an excellent Apollodorus, and he took a flying leap into the sea off the African battlements that will be long remembered. It was a miracle of grace, strength, and sensationalism. Some other performances were less good. Norman Wooland's Enobarbus, for example, spoke many of the loveliest lines in the play in a voice so gruff that it was deprived of all beauty.

But both *Caesar and Cleopatra* and *Antony and Cleopatra* are plays that depend for the most part on their two principal actors. Neither magnificence of scenery, nor skill of direction, nor lavish costumes, nor illustrious presentation of minor parts can make up for lack of greatness in the title roles. As Cleopatra in Shakespeare's drama Miss Vivien Leigh deeply moved my colleague Ivor Brown, who recorded the effect upon him of Miss Leigh's performance in noble and memorable words. Miss Leigh spoke with a cold, clear beauty, never spoiling the music of her superb lines; and throughout both plays she looked exquisitely lovely. But I did not think her Cleopatra in its tragic phases a performance as outstanding as, for example, her Sabina in *The Skin of Our Teeth*. All that part of Cleopatra which is enchantress Miss Leigh managed with enviable ease. That she could set Antony on fire, no one in the audience was ever in doubt; but that she could blaze herself was never evident. She provoked fire but did not answer it. She aroused passion, but did not respond to it. She raised the conflagration, but did not herself perish in it.

Sir Laurence's Caesar was much admired; and it was admirable. There was a time when Sir Laurence was all fire and frenzy. When he was a young man his abandonment to passion on the

stage was by some thought to be a reprehensible example of over-
acting, whilst the surge and swell of it swept others off their feet.
I was one of these last. The bitterness of his disillusion, the sad
disintegration of his ideals as the young schoolmaster in *The Rats
of Norway*, for example, his resigned, hopeless recitation of
Allingham's *Four Ducks on a Pond*, with its heartrending evoca-
tion of a simple happiness vanished beyond recovery, is one of the
most powerfully moving things I have known in the theatre.
But the years pass by, the natural strength diminishes, and I suppose that fire and élan decline. Olivier is still a young man, but
he has taken to himself the cares and also the interests of maturity.
He has assumed the management of an important West End
theatre; he directs his own productions; he is responsible as an
employer for the livelihood of a large number of players; he has
become a big business man as well as an artist. Other qualities
are required of him as well as the quick response to emotion:
shrewdness, foresight, literary and financial judgment. So it
happened that his Caesar in Shaw was better than his Antony in
Shakespeare. In his present phase of development he compasses
the wise man who has never known passion better than the ageing
roué who is being ruined by it. It is a strange stage to have been
reached by the least restrained of the brilliant young actors of the
1930s, a curious commentary on the uninevitability even of
character.

There still remain for consideration many important West End
productions, besides the plays presented at the Club theatres.
The New Torch Theatre in Knightsbridge, the New Boltons
Theatre (for a long while under the intelligent management of
Peter Cotes), the Embassy Theatre at Hampstead, and the New
Lindsey in Notting Hill Gate each offered productions during
the period under review at the rate of one a month, or even one
a fortnight. At the New Boltons there were several performances of outstanding merit by Joan Miller, who has lately
been affecting roles of a macabre character, but in general none of
these theatres succeeded in getting many pieces of real value.
The way of the Club theatre in these days is hard. The West End
managements are astute and enterprising; they are ready to look
for talent in unexpected places, and it is becoming more and more

difficult for a private theatre to discover a neglected genius.

Of the West End productions not yet noticed, *Seagulls Over Sorrento* (London: Apollo, June, 1950): *The Little Hut* (London, Lyric, August, 1950): *To Dorothy, a Son* (London, Savoy, later Garrick, November, 1950): *Gay's the Word* (London, Saville, February, 1951): *Waters of the Moon* (London, Haymarket, May, 1951): *Relative Values* (London, Savoy, November, 1951) and *South Pacific* (London, Drury Lane, November, 1951) were overwhelming popular successes. Most of them ran for more than a year, and at the first nights of all of them except *The Little Hut* there were scenes of considerable enthusiasm.

The Little Hut began shakily, but after a few weeks settled into sturdy prosperity. It is André Roussin's most popular play in his own country, where despite frequent changes of cast it filled the Nouveautés for more than 1,300 nights. I saw the Paris production in August, 1950, and thought shabby the stage setting of the desert island on which two shipwrecked friends share a wife with such satisfactory results to the husband and torments of jealousy to the intrusive lover. In a brilliant review of the London presentation Jack Lambert wrote eloquently of Oliver Messel's London designs, where bloomed the breadfruit, 'the bizarre banana, the all-purpose coconut, and pumpkins fit for Cinderella.' There was none of this glitter and lusciousness upon the drab Parisian stage, nor did Mlle. Jacqueline Porel wear anything to rival the dazzling clothes that, in London, Miss Joan Tetzel managed to salvage from the wreck.

Mr. Lambert began his review with a quotation from Shelley. 'Many a green isle needs must be, in the deep wide sea of misery', he wrote, and added that 'the cloud-cuckoo-land where this sun-baked frolic bubbles away the time is one of them.' This opening, I subsequently learned, gave particular pleasure to M. Roussin. Many people have told M. Roussin that his plays are witty. What delighted him was Mr. Lambert's perception that they are allied in spirit to poetry. And, of course, he was right to be delighted. M. Roussin's desire to be praised for poetry rather than wit has nothing to do, of course, with the comedian's traditional ambition to play Hamlet. The proper characters for the comedian to play are the great comic characters; but, provided that a comedy has the requisite theatrical qualities to enable it to hold the stage, it is in proportion to its poetic spirit that it has enduring value. This is a truth hidden only from the lesser realists: the greater among them have known it as well as did Shakespeare himself. Why otherwise are the plays of Ibsen saturated with symbolism? Why does the wild duck fly through them, why are there vine leaves in the hair, but for this reason, that a play's greatness depends upon the degree, no matter how naturalistic it may be in form, to which its spirit transcends the superficial imitation of life, and starts the imagination thrillingly wandering in realms not bounded by the railway guide and P.A.Y.E.?

I think myself that there are other plays by M. Roussin which are more genuinely poetic than *The Little Hut*. One of them is *Bobosse*, in which, under the title of *Figure of Fun* (London, Aldwych, 1951), John Mills gave an excellent performance.

Figure of Fun, cunningly adapted by Arthur Macrae, was constructed with considerable ingenuity, and could be enjoyed on all sorts of levels. First of all, it had an interesting story. Freddie, an actor, was appearing in a play in which his fiancée deserted him at the same time that his wife left him in his real, private life. Merely as an anecdote it was pleasant to see how M. Roussin presented the impact of Freddie's home upon his career. Secondly, it was enjoyable on the plane of wit, for M. Roussin's fancy was never livelier than in this play, nor did he ever create a more diverting character than the radio interviewer whose ordinary conversation was a passion of stuttering but whose professional performances on the air were miracles of swift, smooth speech. *Figure of Fun*, too, had its comment to make upon Diderot's famous paradox of the actor, which maintains that the great actor can imitate anyone only because in himself he is nothing. He is a chameleon, with no colour but what he derives from his surroundings. He is a vessel which can hold anything, merely because it is itself empty. Was this the explanation of Freddie? Had he no character but that of the part which his author had given him? The best of it is that you can argue either way, that Freddie acted in his play because his character turned him towards such parts, or that such parts gave him his character. Lastly, underlying the piece was a philosophy, a highly unfashionable philosophy, but which nevertheless an eccentric dramatist should, if he so wishes, be allowed to express. M. Roussin takes the view, unusual in the best modern drama, that life is worth living. If one were to give M. Roussin a sharp knife and a roast turkey, I should not be at all surprised if he used the knife in order to carve the turkey, instead of to do the philosophically conventional thing, which would, of course, be to cut his own throat. *Figure of Fun*, then, was a happy play; it blandly, as if it were the most ordinary thing in the world, assured us that the romantic view of life is right, that erring wives often return home, that marriages can frequently be contented, and that there is even a strong probability that the sun will rise tomorrow.

I believe that Roussin's own favourite among his plays is *Nina*, in which Elvire Popesco played for more than 400 performances at the Bouffes-Parisiens in 1949 and 1950. It was taken in translation to America in 1951, with Gloria Swanson in Mlle. Popesco's part of a middle-aged woman whose lover is beginning to tire of her. Miss Swanson soon tired of her, too, and during the preliminary run of the piece in Philadelphia, freely expressed her opinion that there was nothing in the character worth playing. Miss Swanson probably did find nothing in Nina, for in New York the play ran for only a week. Mme. Popesco, however, either searched more diligently, or had better eyesight than Miss Swanson, for when I saw the play in Biarritz in August, 1951, it was not notably lacking in either comic or philosophic content. Robert Vattier, of whom I have already spoken as a member of André Barsacq's company, gave a performance of the mild little husband that was extraordinarily rich in a sense both of fundamental self-satisfaction and of open-eyed admiration of the fascination of Nina's conquering and handsome lover. Mme. Popesco is one of those actresses who, like our own Cicely Courtneidge, is the life and soul, the beginning and the ending, of any play in which she appears. It is only a text strong in its own integrity and power that can stand up to the exuberant attack of such an apparatus of energy as Mme. Popesco. Normally from an actress like her one does not expect either subtlety or pathos. It is enough that she blows like a great and genial wind through the theatre, clearing away the dust from one's mind and spirit. Yet at the end of *Nina*, Mme. Popesco was very moving; in the twink-

ling of an eye she changed from the mood of farce to that of
poetry, when she came to deliver one of the best speeches in
modern light drama that I am acquainted with.

Gérard, her lover, has told her that he is leaving her: he will
go as far away as Mexico, and she, in a sudden and quiet sorrow,
says to him: 'Almost all women know as I do that they have not
the husband they need, and nearly all those who have a lover
know that they are not happy. And almost all men know both
in their homes and in their liaisons that they have missed the truth.
We are like everybody else, my dear, trying to come to terms with
love and happiness and marriage and liberty. You are like all men
who think in their bed at night without speaking. And I am like
all women who pretend to be asleep. What do you imagine they
are thinking of, those men who don't speak and those women who
seem asleep? What are they thinking of, as they lie silent side by
side? Of happiness? No, my dear, they think of all the things
they will never do! . . . They think even of murder! of flight! of
divorce! of liberty! Every one of them thinks of leaving for
Mexico. They think of their unhappiness, and their solitude and
of ways of getting out of them. Every one of them! Every one
of them thinks of Mexico! And none of them ever goes!'

There are not many passages in modern English comedies in which
the author's imagination rises above the particular circumstances of
his story, and, as in this speech in *Nina*, reaches universality. It
would be absurd to expect such a thing from, for example, pieces
like *Ten Men and a Miss*, a farce about a pretty girl marooned in an
army camp in the desert, which ran for a brief while at the Aldwych in 1951; or from the Robertson Hare and Arthur Riscoe
comedy, *Will Any Gentleman?* in which the innocuously pompous
Mr. Hare developed, under stage hypnotism, all kinds of daring
and dashing qualities which were greatly to the taste of audiences
at the Strand for many months during 1950. The sole aim of
plays like these was laughter. *Will Any Gentleman?* achieved
laughter, and *Ten Men and a Miss* did not. Neither of them had
anything to do with poetry.

Noel Coward's *Relative Values* (Savoy, November, 1951) was
more ambitious than these. It came at a critical point in Mr.
Coward's career. Mr. Coward has won amazing and dazzling
success; he has borne this success with modesty, self-respect, and

coolness. These are things that the world finds hard to forgive There are always people ready and even anxious to note any faltering in the master's stride. Coward's musical, *Ace of Clubs* (Cambridge, 1950), though it contained one of his best satirical lyrics— *Juvenile Delinquents*—was a clumsily contrived melodrama about a sailor who unwisely wandered into a doubtful night clubs; its music, pleasant and tuneful, obviously did not spring from genius at the white heat of inspiration; and at the end of the evening it was booed from the gallery. The importance of booing can easily be exaggerated. Some of the greatest authors—Henry James, for example—have been booed. Some of the stage's greatest successes, including *The Belle of New York*, have been booed at their first performance; Mr. Coward himself was booed many years ago at the first night of *Sirocco*. Nevertheless, though booing does not mean as much as is sometimes thought, it is not an agreeable thing; and all Mr. Coward's friends, as well as, I think I may say, the critics whose respect he has won both as a man and as an author, earnestly wished that in *Relative Values* he would give us something that could be legitimately hailed as a success.

That is exactly what he did. His story of a foolish young earl who fell in love with, and wished to marry, a Hollywood actress was not particularly striking. But in the centre of this story he put one of the best and most amusing characters he had ever created, the earl's mother, a lady who, whilst refusing to admit to any snobbish ideas about misalliances and differences in social status, was nevertheless determined that the marriage should not take place. Gladys Cooper played this part with assured mastery from beginning to end. She looked a great lady, and easily persuaded us that she was a great wit. From the moment of her first entry the cheers and enthusiasm at the end of the evening could be foreseen; and the curtain did eventually come down on one of the biggest ovations that even Mr. Coward has ever received. But here, as is usual with Mr. Coward, the values were satirical and not poetic.

Lesley Storm's *The Day's Mischief* (Duke of York's, 1951) was neither poetic nor satirical. It was, however, better than the great majority of original English plays presented since the middle of 1949. It had a very good first night, it was attentively listened to and warmly received, and more people than myself were surprised when it received only sufficient public support to keep it running for a month or six weeks. The trouble with it, I think, was that the target Miss Storm hit was not the one she was aiming at. She intended a well-made play, and wrote a play very vulnerable to rational criticism but containing two good sketches of character.

Her hero was a schoolmaster with whom one of his pupils was in love. This girl, the daughter of a local journalist, disappeared one night, and the schoolmaster was suspected of having murdered her. The first thing that raised doubts in the audience's mind was the schoolmaster's home. The softly shaded lamps of his drawing room, the thick cushions and opulent couches, the freshly decorated walls suggested an income far beyond what the Burnham Scale considers adequate for assistant masters. Thus was sown, as soon as the curtain went up, the first seed of disbelief. This seed came to enormous flowering, when, towards the end of the play, the girl, after three days' absence during which her mother had nearly gone out of her mind with anxiety, and the teacher had lost his job and was in danger of being put on trial for murder, calmly walked in, and announced that she had been on a visit to London, a visit about which it had not occurred to her hitherto to breathe a word to anyone.

I suspect that Miss Storm's intention had been to tell an interesting and plausible tale; and she failed to do because her heroine's behaviour was so recklessly thoughtless as to be incredible. But into this impossible story she introduced two excellent and well observed characters, the schoolmaster and the journalist. Both were men of integrity, both respected each other, and their difficult relationship was admirably handled, not less by the actors, Ian Hunter and Walter Fitzgerald, than by the authoress. But these studies of character, it seems, were not accepted by the public as satisfactory recompense for an ill-told story.

Thirteen major productions remain, and to each one of them I shall apply this test of poetry that M. Roussin passes. I shall ask whether the author ever uses any situation at which his play has arrived to introduce some unexpected yet natural phrase which suddenly illuminates our deepest experiences and longings. I am not demanding poetry in the ordinary sense. I am not in this connexion joining myself to the plea often eloquently and convincingly made by Ivor Brown and J. C. Trewin for a return of the drama to the big drums of verse. I am not thinking of the great set pieces, some of which I have quoted with admiration, with which Christopher Fry is wont to decorate his plays. What I am asking for is independent of the power of words as magic and incantation in themselves. The sort of thing I am thinking of may be undistinguished in phrase and rhythm. But in the first place it rises firmly out of the dramatic situation; and in the second it transcends that situation so that, in an unexpected flash, it reveals the very horizons of humanity.

The thirteen plays, then, are as follows. *Seagulls Over Sorrento* (Apollo, June, 1950); *Before the Party* (St. Martin's, October, 1949); *Bonaventure* (Vaudeville, December, 1949); *The Way Things Go* (Phoenix, March, 1950); *Mr. Gillie* (Garrick, March, 1950); *Background* (Westminster, May, 1950); *Captain Carvallo* (St. James's, August, 1950); *To Dorothy, a Son* (Savoy, later Garrick, November, 1950); *Who Is Sylvia?* (Criterion, October, 1950); *The Happy Time* (St. James's, January, 1951); *Red Letter Day* (Garrick, February, 1952); *Waters of the Moon*; (Haymarket, April, 1951); and *The Deep Blue Sea* (Duchess, March, 1952).

Not much perhaps need be said of *Seagulls Over Sorrento*. After its first night I remarked of this naval farce by Hugh Hastings that it was the first hundred per cent., A1, copper-bottomed smash hit of the 1950 spring season. One is sometimes wrong about first night receptions (I have already admitted being deceived by the warmth which greeted *The Day's Mischief*), but on this occasion I had no reason later to revise my forecast. The play immediately hit the taste of the public, and ran with immense popularity for many, many months. Justly so, for it was very amusing. Nigel Stock, Bernard Lee, and Ronald Shiner appeared as three lower deck sailors who volunteered for service on a dangerous mission somewhere off the coast of Scotland. The theme, however, was not heroism, but the joint hostility of these three men to those set in petty authority over them, and their friendship with each other. For the greater, and the successful, part of the evening this theme was treated farcically, with Cockney jokes, and impudent defiance of superior orders. Mr. Hastings had occasional moments of seriousness, during which the judicious playgoer worked out his income tax returns, or looked the other way, or, in the manner best suiting his own fashion, took his mind off what was happening on the stage. For Mr. Hastings's style, racy while concerned with rough humour, became stilted and self-conscious when aspiring to be impressive. The letter which the best educated of the seamen left behind to be read after his death was acutely embarrassing, and its grammar doubtful. Nowhere in the play was there any of that poetry of which I have been speaking.

Before the Party was a much more serious play than *Seagulls Over Sorrento*. Its origin indeed lay in one of the masters of the modern age of writing, but one of those masters from whom the spirit of poetry is most remote. It was adapted by Rodney Ackland from a short story by Somerset Maugham. Mr. Maugham does not seem to have great powers of invention, for most of his tales are suggested by incidents he has encountered in his travels in various parts of the world. But if he is not an inventor, he is a great organiser, and what life leaves untidy and incomplete he finishes off in a neat bundle, smartly tied to some humorously depreciative label. The clever, satirical, depreciatory spirit is generally too clear-sighted and sharp for the mystery of poetry, which dreams vaguely, and attains its ends by means hardly susceptible of logical analysis.

Mr. Ackland, however, is of a different temper from Maugham. His own plays, beginning with *After October*, are written in the manner of Chekhov. Where the salt of Maugham is in the neat management of incident, and the sardonic judgment he never fails to pass upon his characters, the typical merit of Ackland lies in the creation of a brooding, indefinable, but pervading atmosphere. Mr. Ackland does not always create this atmosphere very well. He has the tastes, but not the talents of Chekhov. But if he were able to do all he sets out to do, it is like Chekhov that he would write. Maugham, on the other hand, is closer to Pope.

The combination of these two writers, then, was unexpected. It was as unlikely as an adaptation by Jane Austen of a novel by Walter Scott. When two incompatibles meet, the result is often a useless and inconclusive struggle. In this case, the result was better than that, for the younger man and lesser talent (though the more poetic) gave way to the older and greater. In other words,

Mr. Ackland entirely submitted himself to the temper of Mr. Maugham, and did so, in my opinion, with remarkable skill and success. The heroine of this play, on the eve of her wedding, announced to her stuffy and conventional family that her first husband had been a hopeless drunkard, and that she had murdered him. It was at this point that Maugham ended his story, but in the theatre it took us only to the end of the first act of a two-act play.

What followed was Mr. Ackland's invention, and how could one give it higher praise than to say, as one must, that the invention was perfectly in the spirit of such facts as Mr. Maugham had given? The heroine's second husband was a personable and attractive young man, as tall and clear-eyed as Roderick Lovell could make him. What could be more in the sardonic manner of Mr. Maugham than to suggest, as Mr. Ackland did, in half a dozen touches, that he also was marked out as a drunkard, destined to be the subject of a second murder? This had the acid Maugham flavour. It left one with the authentic laugh-on-the-wrong-side-of-one's-face. At least, it would have done, had it not all been a little too subtle. The hints that Mr. Ackland dropped were easily to be picked up by an attentive audience. English audiences, however, as authors ought to know, cannot reasonably be expected to be attentive. They have too many other things of greater significance to do. They have to keep their cigarettes lighted. They have to munch their choc-ices. And the intervals are too short for them properly to complete their important work in the bar. Hence a certain amount of woolly-wittedness in any theatre auditorium. Hence too the failure of the first night audience to recognise that the heroine's second husband was a horse of the same colour as the first. But Constance Cummings' fine performance as the unfortunate but resourceful heroine was easily appreciated.

Bonaventure gave to Fay Compton the unusual part of a nun who was also a detective. A girl artist convicted of murder was brought to a convent in East Anglia, and immediately after her arrival this convent was cut off by floods from the rest of the world. Had *Bonaventure* been a film I can easily imagine that photography might have given it some poetic quality. The convent, sole relic of civilisation, cut off by the rising waters from all intercourse with

M

the rest of humanity, could have been a fine and moving pictorial symbol of the isolation of the human spirit. Dorothy Sayers, in *The Nine Tailors*, obtained something of this spirit in her descriptions of the ice-bound Fenlands. Description, however, is out of place in modern naturalistic drama; is not that said to be one of the reasons why M. Salacrou prefers the drama to the novel? Anyhow, Charlotte Hastings, in what I believe was her first play, conveyed nothing of this feeling of isolation. *Bonaventure* had to stand purely as a detective tale, and the detection in it was neither credible nor clever. As the condemned artist Mary Kerridge gave a performance of tense nerves with no variety or depth in it, and even Miss Compton's lovely voice could make little of the nun's elementary investigations, which were uneasily based on a conviction of the girl's innocence, suspicion of the convent doctor, and a bundle of newspaper cuttings. The applause at the end was curious. *Bonaventure* came after several plays had been booed. There was no question of booing here. The clapping and cheering were remarkably prompt, loud, and continuous. One looked round instinctively for a cheer-leader.

In March, 1950, Frederick Lonsdale, in *The Way Things Go*, offered us one of his witty little pieces about the impoverished aristocracy. The family of the Duke of Bristol was exceedingly anxious that one of the younger sons should rehabilitate the family fortunes by marrying a young American heiress. The son himself had scruples; the young lady had not; and the big scene of the play came when, with Glynis John's pert charm and insistent voice, she got him marooned in a cottage as isolated as Miss Hastings's convent, and tried to seduce him. This was bringing Shaw's theory of the predatory female into the realm of the shocker, and somehow it did not look very well there. The audience was mildly interested rather than scandalised, and the play, in spite of many witty lines, did not have a long run.

A better thing was James Bridie's *Mr. Gillie*. Beneath the realistic surface of this play there was an insight into fundamentals. In writing *Mr. Gillie* Bridie was troubled by the same sort of unease that led Galsworthy to write one of his most moving short stories, that of the bootmaker whose trade grew less and less, but who continued until the end, in spite of increasing poverty and hardship, to make good boots. Was this man a success or a failure? Is it a bootmaker's business to make good boots, or to keep his family's head above water? The question is not to be answered lightly. To make good boots is no doubt a proud boast for a craftsman; but the craftsman is not the whole man, who has his duty to perform as father and husband as well as artist.

There is no doubt where Bridie's sympathies lay. He took a more arguable case still than Galsworthy's bootmaker, who was at least a clever man of his hands. Bridie's hero was not even very good at his job. He was a teacher, and the only pupils of his who made much noise in the world did so in the flashy surroundings of barrow boys and spivs. But whether Mr. Gillie taught to much purpose or not, he taught with his whole heart and mind and soul. Of all modern dramatists Bridie wrote with the most passion and idiosyncrasy, was most the master of the suddenly poetic phrase. At his best this power could raise him to great heights of theatrical impressiveness, as in the dazzling performance that Dame Edith Evans gave in his *Daphne Laureola,* and the deep and disturbed and reckless love that Peter Finch movingly portrayed in the same play.

But even in *Daphne Laureola* Bridie's defects of craftsmanship were apparent: his inability to conceive a story that would drive hard and true from the beginning to the end, his fondness for mythological parallels full of dramatic confusion, his frequent failure of fictional invention. These were apparent in *Mr. Gillie,* which began portentously with two celestial beings, one at each side of the stage, arguing the case of the hero's success or failure, and thus weighting the story with an importance it would have been better to leave implicit. Nor was one sure that Alastair Sim was altogether the right actor for Mr. Gillie. Mr. Sim has given several fine performances in Bridie plays, plays that have called for the exercise of intellectual subtlety more than for the manifestation of simple moral goodness, Mr. Gillie was a good man before he was a clever one, and this was a difficulty Mr. Sim never quite got over.

Soon after *Mr. Gillie* came W. Chetham Strode's *Background.* If Bridie was a feeble craftsman with flashes of genius and spirit, Mr. Chetham Strode is a conscientious and capable workman undisturbed by flashes of any kind. Mr. Chetham Strode could never, I think, write the brilliant drunken speeches of Lady Pitt in

M*

Daphne Laureola, but I doubt if he would ever let a play come to pieces in his hands as Bridie did—and not on that occasion only—in the third act of *The Anatomist*. Chetham Strode is the social commentator of the British stage. He is our one dramatist who can be relied on to write about things that matter. When the National Health Service was uppermost in people's thoughts, he wrote a play on the National Health Service. When there was a National report on opening the Public Schools to the children of the poor, he wrote a play about opening the Public Schools to the children of the poor. It is a pity that he often gives the impression of writing about these things, not because they matter to him, but because he thinks that they matter, or ought to matter, to other people.

Background, too, was about a serious social problem. What is, asked Mr. Chetham Strode, the effect on children if their parents get divorced? Very bad, he replied, putting his reply into a rather more melodramatic form than usual. One of the children in the play, in fact, got involved with a gun in an incident whose violence was somewhat at odds with the sober discussion of the rest of the entertainment. For myself, I never once felt that the husband and wife had been in love with each other, and I failed to respond to the fact that Mr. Chetham Strode told me they now loved each other no longer.

So far our English dramatists have not come very well out of the implicit comparison with M. Roussin. There is, however, an improvement with *Captain Carvallo*, by Denis Cannan. Mr. Cannan's abilities were, I think, first praised publicly by my colleague, Jan Stephens, who wrote appreciatively of *Max*, Mr. Cannan's first play, when it was acted in London by one of the Sunday evening companies. *Max* was a confused but promising work which made some impression when it was given later at the Malvern Festival of 1949. Mr. Cannan's technical advance in *Captain Carvallo* was very noticeable. *Captain Carvallo* was first presented at the Bristol Old Vic early in 1950, and came to the St. James's, with a different company, in August of the same year. In *Max*, a play in which an English soldier came to tell a German family about the death of their son in battle, one hardly knew what Mr. Cannan was aiming at. In *Captain Carvallo* one no more doubted what was Mr. Cannan's aim, than one questioned that he had achieved it. In *Captain Carvallo* Mr. Cannon was amiably and wittily the spokesman for Laodicea. *Captain Carvallo* was an officer in an invading army; and he carried around with him a pot of geraniums more prominently than firearms. He was billeted on the home of a fanatical clerical partisan who had a beautiful wife. The course of the plot called on the clergyman to change identities with another member of the local Resistance, a professor of biology whom Peter Finch (at the St. James's) played with dry and engaging wit: and patriotism required both of them to try and explode a bomb underneath Captain Carvallo's bed. Throughout the play the author preserved, with ease and grace, his own attitude intact. He did not, like Chesterton, regard war as romantic and splendid; he did not even, like Fry, regard it as evil. It merely seemed to him rather foolish, as the games of children might seem foolish to an overcultivated adult. He contemplated the activities of his characters with a tolerant and not unfriendly disdain, and smiled at their ideals of loyalty, heroism, and determination (which so often and so easily lead to personal treachery and murder) as things which he had himself discarded, without bitterness, long ago. *Captain Carvallo* had, in fact, an atmosphere of its own, a compliment that can be paid to few modern British plays. At the very end of the play, in the parting of the Captain and the clergyman's lovely wife, there was a charming touch of sentiment. But I suspect that this was put there by the accomplished London players, James Donald and Diana Wynyard, rather than by Mr. Cannan, for it had not been noticeable in the Bristol production.

The retreat from poetry began again in Roger MacDougall's *To Dorothy, a Son*, in which the humours of delayed childbirth were explored with industrious relish. Sheila Sim lay in bed the entire performance, urgently expecting a baby; and, as the distracted husband, Richard Attenborough rushed up and down stairs incessantly, chasing a joke and never catching it. But Yolande Donlan played a young lady named Myrtle of such complete inability to understand anything at all, of such total vacuity that in the end she became a creation of satisfying, if null, perfection; and the play ran for more than a year.

More in line with what we are looking for was Terence Rattigan's *Who is Sylvia?* I imagine that Mr. Rattigan had designed a play definitely poetic in conception, but that wit and frivolity kept breaking in. The serious Rattigan who wrote *The Browning Version* was in this play badgered by the lively young author of *French Without Tears*, to the eventual discomfiture of both. The central idea of *Who Is Sylvia?* was the same as that of Hardy's *The Well-Beloved* (which, as Agate would add at this point, Mr. Rattigan may nevertheless not have read). Mark, a polished young man in the Diplomatic Service, like the hero of *The Well-Beloved*, was all through his life seeking an ideal, which from time to time he found embodied in a different woman. In the first act, and at the end of the second act, when Mark, then middle-aged, was awkwardly discovered by his son at a party at which he would have done better not to be present, there were signs that Mr. Rattigan was going to treat his theme with poetic seriousness. But if such was Mr. Rattigan's intention, it soon broke down. His hero degenerated into an occasionally amusing philanderer, who fell in love with three of the most strident and unattractive young girls (all played by the same actress) that I have seen on the stage. Robert Flemyng was the diplomat. Mr. Flemyng has far too much integrity for this sort of part. In the last act the diplomat's wife was introduced. He and she were now old, and he had imagined that all her life she had been unaware of his peccadilloes. She had, of course, known of them all the time, and had regarded them with tolerant amusement. Miss Athene Seyler played this part. Never have I known so accomplished an actress brought into a play so late to such little purpose. *Who is Sylvia?* had some witty lines, but one could not help feeling that either the theme should have been treated differently, or else that it was hardly worthy of a dramatist of Rattigan's calibre.

It was its author's most disappointing play. *The Winslow Boy* and *The Browning Version* had been plays of seriousness and weight. *Adventure Story*, Mr. Rattigan's study of the corrupting influence of absolute power, was over-ponderous, but its aim at least was ambitious, whereas *Who is Sylvia?* was a clumsy return to a manner in which Mr. Rattigan had accomplished cleverer things in his youth. His next play, *The Deep Blue Sea*, was in consequence awaited with anxiety as well as hope. It seemed to me, when it came, the best thing that he had written.

One of the few points on which current dramatic criticism is agreed is that the methods of realism are now worn out. No longer, it is said, can great effects be produced by such ordinary everyday incidents as making a woman offstage bang a door. No longer can our emotions be powerfully reached by presenting in the theatre men and women just like ourselves, living in the same drab surroundings, and talking with our own flat, uninspired speech. Certainly the most vigorous new dramatic movements express themselves in verse, with richness of metaphor and imagery. Yet realism can hardly be written off completely whilst Mr. Rattigan uses its methods to produce such a play as *The Deep Blue Sea*. I doubt whether there was in the entire dialogue of this play a single distinguished sentence, let alone speech. Undoubtedly there was nothing in it that could be set alongside the passages from Fry which I quoted earlier on in this book. These had in themselves a beauty independent of the part they played in the dramas from which they were taken. But the speeches in *The Deep Blue Sea* were nothing except in their relation to the dramatic structure of the play, which they made articulate and moving. They derived their whole power, which was considerable, from the situations and the characters of which they were the expression. Mr. Rattigan loves drama more than he loves words.

In this play he chose a difficult theme: a woman's physical infatuation for a man, and that man not her husband. To Hester Collyer nothing mattered but her obsession for a young test pilot whom she had met during one of her husband's golfing holidays at Sunningdale. For her the physical side of love was what counted; all the rest was as the crackling of thorns under a pot. Upon this single point of Hester's being Mr. Rattigan concentrated the entire force of his drama, whose intensity he increased by preserving the unities of time and place. Now such a play as this seems to me to run three considerable dangers. It might be offensive: it might be painful: and it might be dull. These dangers Mr. Rattigan triumphantly avoided. How did he do it?

He certainly made no effort to gloss over his heroine's attitude towards life. He did not conceal at any point that her conception of the fulfilment of love was the same as Donne's notion of its 'right, true end'. At no moment of the play could the audience forget that for all those things in love—affection, comradeship, common intellectual interests—that are independent of the satisfaction of physical desire, Hester Collyer had no use. From this point of view, *The Deep Blue Sea* must be one of the frankest plays ever seen on a London stage. Yet, except for the test pilot's frequent employment of the word 'bloody', its language was extremely chaste. In it Mr. Rattigan demonstrated that a dramatist of quality can deal with the most delicate questions plainly and without subterfuge, and yet keep his dialogue entirely free from offensiveness.

The play began with Hester's recovery from attempted suicide; throughout the evening Hester was on the verge of tears; and Peggy Ashcroft presented her with a wan, white face unprettified by any touch of colour. The drab flat in Ladbroke Grove, with a ramshackle kitchen carved out of the sitting-room, to which her lover, Freddie Page, had brought her, offered nothing to beguile the eye, and the costumes were mostly shabby dressing-gowns and plus-fours the worse for wear. Towards the end of the play Hester blocked doorways and windows in methodical preparation for another attempt at suicide, and at few points during the evening was she far from despair. There is exhilaration in watching a man fighting bravely against adverse circumstances, however tragic. Hester, however, was defeated, not by circumstances, but by her own terrible weakness, And weakness affords no consolation.

Yet the play was never painful. It was never painful because Mr. Rattigan never lost sympathy for any of his characters. One of the marks of a dramatist of the first order is that he can always understand the viewpoint of every person in his play. Shaw says somewhere that the dramatist must do equal battle on behalf of all his characters, both those with whom he is naturally in sympathy and those with whom he is not. He must write as persuasively, as devotedly, as eloquently for the Inquisitor as for Joan, for the armaments manufacturer as for the major in the Salvation Army. Mr. Rattigan remembered this in writing *The Deep Blue Sea*. There is no villain in the play. Hester was not neurotic: she was a woman of fine mind, taste, and character caught in the grip of a terrible obsession. Freddie, though he was liable to forget Hester's birthday, and to leave her at weekends to go golfing, though he wasted his time in bar parlours and had a limited vocabulary, was yet a kindly, friendly creature who sincerely loved her, and wanted to behave decently, but who simply could not respond to the intensity of passion that was burning her body and her soul. Hester's husband, Sir William Collyer, a High Court judge, was hard and keen in mind: unsentimental: with, one was sure, a due appreciation of the importance of worldly success; yet he, too, at heart was compassionate, spoke without bitterness, and was ready at any moment, and on any terms, to receive Hester home. Throughout the evening, then, one was in the company of people who, despite their obvious failings, were entitled in many ways to respect, for whom one felt a warm liking and a deep pity. Mr. Rattigan put his characters in a situation of extreme disadvantage, a situation out of which their characters forbade them to come with easy victory, but a situation in which, on the whole, they did not do at all badly. There was nothing here to lower one's opinion of human nature, or to suggest that, when in a position from which there is no escape, it will disgrace itself. Such a play cannot be painful.

It might, however, be dull. For two and a half hours *The Deep Blue Sea* confined itself to a single aspect of life, an aspect of life of which perhaps the majority of men and women have no intuitive understanding—the overwhelming, irresistible, and unceasing urge of physical passion. This, coupled with the unity of scene and time, might have resulted in monotony. It did not, for the reason that truth lies in nuances. The play moved only within a narrow compass, but within that compass it discovered an immense variety of shades of emotion. In Miss Ashcroft's performance there were many sobs, but no one sob was like any of the others. As the judge, Mr. Roland Culver was frequently at a loss for the exact word he was seeking; but it was never the same word, and he was never twice at a loss to precisely the same degree. Dumas uses swashbuckling, treachery, duelling, seduction, battles, hair's-breadth rescues, royal and ecclesiastical ceremonies, feasts, pursuits, hunting, dances, and a score of other matters to make a vigorous and entertaining novel; Proust will find sufficient subject for a book in a young boy who suffers from asthma watching half a dozen girls playing on the sands at the seaside. Neither book is monotonous; neither is out of scale; the one has the wider view, the other the deeper. Both, in their place, are right and proper. *The Deep Blue Sea* was right and proper.

It was superbly acted. I do not see how any acting in the

quietist manner (none of the Barrault rhetoric and abandon here) could well be more moving than that of Miss Ashcroft and Mr. Culver. Their first scene together, after the judge had been brought round to Ladbroke Grove by a telephone call telling him of his wife's illness, was extraordinarily fine, and played with that restraint which can on occasion suggest enormous tensions. They stood in the centre of the stage, facing each other, Miss Ashcroft white and troubled but quite calm in misery, Mr. Culver with piercing eyes watching her. He stood perfectly still, not a muscle of his face moved; but there was not one inch of his wife, not one flicker of an eyelid, that he did not notice, and immediately evaluate in its bearing on the possibility of his persuading her to return to him. With a few simple words, a few indirect sentences, these players and their author created the entire relationship between Hester and her husband, its mutual respect, and liking, and even affection, and the pitiable truth that respect, liking, and affection, without passion, are not enough.

Almost every other scene in which these two players appeared was equally fine, notably that wherein Hester recounted the story of how she fell in love with Freddie Page. She spoke the last line of this story—'And from that moment I knew I had no hope— no hope at all'—with a sad smile, half pitying and half mocking herself, that was quite heart-rending. Freddie Page I did not think Mr. Rattigan handled so well as the other two chief characters. He made Page defend himself explicitly, whilst the judge and Hester did not speak one word on their own behalf. Yet, by his mastery of implication and suggestion, he made their unuttered defence overwhelming, his understanding of the terrible, but transfiguring, bondage of love complete and satisfying.

Less tragic in intensity, but more deliberately poetic in method was N. C. Hunter's *Waters of the Moon*, one of the big successes of the Festival of Britain. This excellent slight entertainment was an exercise in the Chekhov manner, a casual study of the inhabitants of a Devonshire private hotel, into whose private griefs and dissatisfactions descended one snowbound Christmas a dazzling lady from London, all brilliant smiles, and resplendent clothes, and gay, defiant courage, and carefree, thoughtless kindness. The play evoked comparisons it could hardly, as a piece of writing, expect to sustain. The final departure of the magnificent London visitor, leaving the hotel's guests behind her in the sunshine of a winter's morning to fall back into the depressions out of which she had momentarily awakened them, though it was slickly managed, was too like the parting of the officers—again in a garden —and again in sunshine—in the unmatchable fourth act of *Three Sisters* to leave one altogether comfortable. Besides, the play did not seem really true. It is too much a theatrical cliché that all inhabitants of private hotels and boarding-houses are miserable for us not to be put on our guard against a drama that too glibly accepts it. *Waters of the Moon* was superficially observed, its dialogue was without distinction, it conveyed no great depth of feeling, but it was a very capable Chekhov pastiche; and it gave splendid parts to Dame Edith Evans as the dashing London visitor, and Dame Sybil Thorndike as an elderly lady, once rich, accustoming herself only with difficulty to the comparative narrowness of boarding-house existence.

I found Mr. Rosenthal's second play, *Red Letter Day*, more rewarding than *Third Person*. It was a trifling affair, a comic treatment of the dismay that her fiftieth birthday may cause to a woman who lives in a country which dotes on youth as much as America does. It had at least one first-class humorous scene, that in which the heroine, determined to prove that she had some attractiveness left, desperately phoned up two old admirers, only to find that the first of them had been dead sixteen years, and the second was totally deaf. As this disappointed lady Fay Compton was admirable.

Mr. Rosenthal has proved himself a competent dramatist, but his work does not lift itself above the purely realistic plane. A fellow-countryman of his, Samuel Taylor, was more successful in getting off the ground in *The Happy Time*. There is some poetry in Mr. Taylor's conception of life, a conception that marries the body and the spirit in a gay, harmonious union. His play was about the instilling of this philosophy into a small boy in a French-Canadian family, and it had several charming scenes, including one in which his father, beautifully played by Peter Finch, gently and kindly broke to him some of the physical facts of life. *The Happy Time* was, however, ill received at its first night, being one of many plays and entertainments during the period under review which on the final fall of the curtain were greeted with boos from the gallery. Personally I always find the gallery's audible expression of disapproval an ordeal, though most of the hooted entertainments have been poor things enough. *The Happy Time*, however, was in a different class from these. I suspect that its bad reception was due chiefly to the fact that much of the play was inaudible beyond the first few rows of stalls.

On this note of the gallery's anger I end my survey of the recent British theatre. It is an ungrateful note, and undeserved. For the British theatre, in the immediate past, has rendered a good account of itself. In Sir Laurence Olivier it has welcomed a new management that sets itself the highest ideals, and sometimes achieves them. Sir Laurence's tenure of the St. James's has had startling fluctuations, and at Christmas, 1951, he allowed the theatre to be used for an entertainment of staggering ineptitude. But at this theatre he has also given his own productions of Shaw and Shakespeare, and of Christopher Fry's *Venus Observed*. This play and Eliot's *Cocktail Party* have firmly established the right of poets to enter the theatre by the front door of the great houses, instead of sneaking in by way of draughty suburban halls. Certain speeches in *Death of a Salesman*, *Point of Departure*, *Les Nuits de la Colère*, and *Figure of Fun* have shown that dramatists can bring the spirit of poetry even into prose plays, even in some cases into realistic prose plays. John Gielgud's production of *Much Ado About Nothing*, and the Barrault presentation of *Partage de Midi* seemed to me to afford, at all points, and on every level, the highest satisfaction the drama can offer. Miss Ashcroft and Mr. Culver in *The Deep Blue Sea*, Mr. Burton in the First Part of *Henry IV*, Miss Leigh in *A Streetcar Named Desire*, Mme Feuillère in *Partage de Midi*, and Mr. Knox in *Return to Tyassi* all gave performances which I do not hesitate to call great. Finally, between 1949 and 1952 the theatre introduced English people to the work of outstanding Continental dramatists like Salacrou and Roussin, and consolidated the position of Anouilh. It seems a good, in some ways even a striking, record.

INDEX

Ackland, Rodney: *After October*, 160; adaptation of *Before the Party*, 160–1
Adelphi Theatre productions, 93
Agate, James, 49, 132; *Ego*, 14–15
Ainley, Henry, 136
Aldridge, Michael, 42
Aldwych Theatre productions, 2, 125, 146, 154, 156
Alexander, Kathleen, 121, 125
Ambassadors Theatre productions, 86, 149
Ambrière, Francis, 30, 34, 35, 59, 68, 79
America: influence on English theatre, 45–6; modern literature and drama in, 118; war boom in theatrical world, 118–119; present day slump in, 119; temporary loss of self-confidence in, 120; present standard of play production in, 123–4
Anderson, Maxwell: *Winterset*, 120
Andrews, Harry, 140
Anouilh, Jean, 56, 172; personality of, 23–4, 44–5; difficulties with producers, 27–8; pessimism of, 30–1, 33–4; sense of pity, 36; *Ring Round the Moon (L'Invitation au Château)*, 22, 26, 28 ff.; *Antigone*, 22, 33; *Fading Mansions*, 22; *Ardèle*, 23, 34–6, 38, 39; *Eurydice (Point of Departure)*, 23, 36–9; *Le Voyageur sans Bagage*, 23, 39–43; *Romeo et Jeannette (Fading Mansions)*, 22, 23, 31, 33; *La Répétition*, 23, 24–6; *Colombe*, 24; *Le Bal des Voleurs*, 23, 26, 27–8
Apollo Theatre productions, 153
Aristotle, on tragedy, 93
Arts Theatre Club, 47; Competition, 99; productions, 99, 101, 117, 133, 148
Ascherson, Renée, 136, 147
Ashcroft, Peggy, 136, 168, 169–70, 172
Ashmore, Peter, 38, 147
Atkins, Robert, 139
Attenborough, Richard, 165
Attiwill, Ken: *Sayonara*, 45
Austen, Jane, 105–6

Baddeley, Hermione, 149
Bagnold, Enid: *Poor Judas*, 99–100
Baker, Stanley, 85
Bankhead, Tallulah, 149, 150
Banks, Leslie, 148
Banzie, Brenda de, 38
Barber, John, 34, 136

Barrault, Jean-Louis, 24, 25–6, 27, 32, 57, 59, 64, 67, 74, 75, 76, 77–8, 80
Barrie, Sir J. M., 34, 35; *Peter Pan*, 109–10
Barsacq, André, 26, 27, 30, 155
Baxter, Beverley, 80
Baxter, Jane, 49, 112, 114
Beaufort, John, 139
Beaumont, Hugh, 146–7
Beigbeder, Marc: *L'Homme Sartre*, 71–2
Belmonte, Juan, 96–7, 142
Bergner, Elizabeth, 49
Bernhardt, Sarah, 115
Best, Edna, 149
Birmingham Repertory Company, 27, 34, 36
Black, Kitty, 37
Blake, Grey, 11
Bloom, Claire, 28
Bogarde, Dirk, 38
Bolton, Guy: Adaptation of *Larger Than Life*, 20–2. *See also* Maugham, Somerset
Bouquet, Michael, 24
Brasseur, Pierre, 73, 75, 125
Brassillach, Robert, 89
Bridie, James: *Mr. Gillie*, 162–3; *Daphne Laureola*, 163 ,164; *The Anatomist*, 164
Brighton, Royal Theatre productions, 5, 11
Bristol Old Vic productions, 39, 40, 41, 164
Brook, Peter, 22, 28, 40, 104, 108, 128, 134
Brown, Ivor, 111, 151, 159
Brown, John Mason, 127
Browne, Wynyard: *The Holly and the Ivy*, 48–9, 52
Bull-fighting, 96–7, 141–3
Burton, Richard, 141–4, 172
Byron, John, 102

Campbell, Douglas, 145
Campbell, Mrs. Patrick, 148
Cannan, Denis: *Captain Carvallo*, 109, 164–5; *Max*, 164
Carey, Denis, 40
Carousel, 119
Casares, Maria, 26
Casson, Sir Lewis, 137
Cavanagh, John, 3
Chekhov, Anton, 49, 65; *The Three Sisters*, 146; *The Seagull*, 148; *Ivanov*, 148
Chesterton, G. K., 7
Church attendance, declining, 52–3, 54

Cinderella, 109, 110
Clare, Mary, 148
Claudel, Paul, 45, 73, 74; *Partage de Midi*, 16, 17, 27, 56, 74–9, 82; *Le Soulier de Satin*, 32, 74, 75
Clements, John, 149
Clergy, treatment of, in the theatre, 45, 46–8
Clunes, Alec, 133, 139, 146; as Arts Theatre competition judge, 99, 104
Cobb, Lee J., 124
Coliseum Theatre productions, 127
Colman, George: *The Clandestine Marriage*, 145
Comedy Theatre productions, 109
Compton, Fay, 161–2, 171
Cooper, Gladys, 157
Cookman, A. V, 111
Cotes, Peter, 152
Coward, Noel: *Fallen Angels*, 149; *Relative Values*, 156, 157; *Ace of Clubs*, 157
Criterion Theatre productions, 108, 117
Critics, differing tastes and standards of, 109, 111
Culver, Roland, 169–70, 172
Cummings, Constance, 51, 161

Dacqmine, Jacques, 75
Davies, Betty Ann, 114
Delany, Maureen, 49
Dent, Alan: on Joan Greenwood, 110; on John Gielgud, 116
De Quincey, Thomas, 76
Desailly, Jean, 68
Devine, George, 138
Dish Ran Away, The, 126
Donald, James, 165
Donat, Robert, 136
Donlan, Yolande, 165
Doone, Rupert, 90, 92
Dostoievsky, Fiodor: *Crime and Punishment*, 133
Drury Lane Theatre productions, 119, 153
Duchess Theatre productions, 48
Duke of York's Theatre productions, 20, 37, 49, 157
Dullin, Charles, 26, 91, 115
Dunnock, Mildred, 123, 124
Dussane, Beatrix, 68, 77, 87; *Notes de Théâtre*, 32, 55–6

Edinburgh, Lyceum Theatre productions, 5, 9, 40
Eliot, T. S., 45, 46, 56, 90; *The Cocktail Party*, 5–12, 108, 116, 117, 172; *Murder in the Cathedral*, 8
Eliott, Denholm, 16, 85, 117
Embassy Theatre, Hampstead, 152

Esch, José van den, 63, 68
Evans, Dame Edith, 163, 171
Evans, Maurice, 139
Evil, and creative impulse, 2
Existentialism, 71–2, 73

Feuillère, Edwige, 27, 75, 79–80, 81–2, 172
Feuillère, Pierre, 80, 81
Finch, Peter, 38, 163, 165, 171
Fitzgerald, Walter, 158
Flemyng, Robert, 10, 112, 114–17, 166
France: Resistance movement in, 89; Theatre: clarity of diction in, 26–7; neglect of scenery and grouping of actors, 27; during the Occupation, 32–3
Frank, Elizabeth, 110
Frazer, Sir James: *The Golden Bough*, 70–1
Freedley, George: *History of the Theatre*, 123
Fry, Christopher, 5, 13–14, 40, 56, 159; *Venus Observed*, 13–20, 172; *The Lady's Not for Burning*, 13, 15, 133–4, 141; *Phoenix Too Frequent*, 14; *A Sleep of Prisoners*, 56, 82–5; translation of *Ring Round the Moon*, 22, 29–30 (see also Anouilh); as Arts Theatre competition judge, 99, 104
Furse, Roger, 17, 151

Gabin, Jean, 23
Galsworthy, John, 56
Galtier-Boissière, Jean: *Mon Journal dans la Drôle de Paix*, 95
Gamelin, General, 88
Garrick Theatre productions, 153
Gassner, John, 86
German Occupation in Paris. *See* France.
Gide, André, 74; adaptation of *The Trial*, 56, 57
Gielgud, John, 38, 40, 77–8, 81, 104, 114, 115, 128, 132–7, 139, 172
Gignoux, Hubert, 38
Gingold, Hermione, 149, 150
Giraudoux: *Amphitryon 38*, 26, 90
Globe Theatre productions, 22, 30, 134
Goldner, Charles, 95
Gordon, Colin, 99
Green, Julien, 1–2, 6, 74
Greene, Graham, 90
Greenwood, Joan, 109–10
Griffith, Hugh, 37, 141
Group Theatre productions, 89–90
Griffith, Hugh, 37, 141
Group Theatre productions, 89–90
Guinness, Alec, 11, 115, 116, 139, 146; interpretation of *Hamlet*, 128–32
Guth, Paul, 73
Guthrie, Tyrone, 61, 145; *Top of the Ladder*, 60–1

Gwynn, Michael, 140

Halstan, Margaret, 113, 114
Hammond, Kay, 149
Hankin, St. John: *The Return of the Prodigal*, 133
Hardy, Robert, 137
Hardy, Thomas, 17; *Far From the Madding Crowd*, 27; *The Well-Beloved*, 166
Hare, Robertson, 156
Harris, Robert, 100
Harrison, Rex, 12
Hastings, Charlotte: *Bonaventure*, 161
Hastings, Hugh: *Seagulls over Sorrento*, 108, 109, 153, 159–60
Haye, Helen, 41, 50
Hayes, George, 38
Haymarket Theatre productions, 108, 132, 148, 153
Heggen, Thomas: *Mister Roberts*, 46, 127
Helpmann, Robert, 151
Hentschel, Irene, 148
Herlie, Eileen, 148, 149
Hinton, Mary, 92
Hordern, Michael, 101
Hudd, Walter, 147
Hunt, Hugh, 145
Hunter, Ian, 158
Hunter, N. C.: *Waters of the Moon*, 108, 109, 153, 170–1
Huxley, T. H., 54

Irving, Laurence, 137

Jackson, Sir Barry, 138
James, Henry, 118
Jarvis, Alan, 90
Jay, Ernest, 100
Jeans, Isabel, 34
Jeans, Ursula, 10, 117
Johns, Glynis, 162
Johnson, Celia, 147
Jonson, Ben: *Bartholomew Fair*, 128
Jouvet, Louis, 26, 72
Justin, John, 51

Kafka, Franz: *The Trial*, 57
Kazan, Elia, 123, 125
Kemp, T. C., 29, 81
Kempson, Rachel, 61
Kemsley, Viscount, 78
Kerridge, Mary, 61, 162
Keynes, Lord, 53
King-Wood, David, 93
Knox, Alexander, 49, 52, 172

Lafront, M. A.: *La Corrida*, 96
Lambert, J. W., 111, 146, 153

Landis, Jessie Royce, 22
Laval, Pierre, 93, 95
Léautaud, Paul, 75, 102–3
Lee, Bernard, 159
Le Gallienne, Eva, 122
Lehmann, John, 90
Leigh, Vivien, 126, 151, 172
Leighton, Margaret, 12, 147, 148
Levy, Ben: *Return to Tyassi*, 49–52
Lind, Cherry, 110
Lister, Moira, 99
Livesey, Roger, 117, 146
Lomas, Herbert, 49, 52
Lonsdale, Frederick: *The Way Things Go*, 162
Lovell, Roderick, 161
Lyric Theatre productions, 153
Lyric Theatre, Hammersmith, productions, 37, 38, 148

MacDougall, Roger: *To Dorothy A Son*, 165
MacOwen, Michael, 83
Macrae, Arthur: adaptation of *Figure of Fun*, 154
Madren, Peter, 46
Mallison, Miles, 61
Mallet, Robert, 102, 103
Malvern Festival plays 164
Mann, Thomas, 2, 4; *Dr. Faustus*, 2
Marlowe, Christopher: *Tamburlaine*, 145, Marcel, Gabriel, 56
Manolete, 141, 142–3 146
Marquet, Mary, 24
Marhall, Herbert, 29
Mary Had a Little . . ., 109, 111, 126
Massigli, Monsieur and Madame, 80, 87
Materialism, 45
Maugham, Somerset, 56; *Theatre*, 20. See also Bolton: *Larger Than Life*, and Ackland: *Before the Party*.
Messel, Oliver, 22, 153
Metro-Goldwyn-Mayer production: *Quo Vadis*, 146, 150
Miller, Arthur: *Death of a Salesman*, 121–2, 124
Miller, Joan, 152
Mills, John, 60, 61
Mitchell, Yvonne, 91
Montague, Bertram, 110
Morehouse, Ward: *Matinée Tomorrow*, 118–19
Morgan, Charles: *The Voyage*, 52
Morris, Colin: *Desert Rats*, 108; *Reluctant Heroes*, 108
Morton, Clive, 114
Moseiwitsch, Tania, 140

Muni, Paul, 121, 125

Naismith, Lawrence, 21-2
Nathan, George Jean, 5, 86, 122, 123
Navar, Tonia, 24
Nesbitt, Cathleen, 7
New Boltons Theatre productions, 152
New Lindsey Theatre productions, 45, 152
News-Chronicle, on Peter Pan, 110
New Theatre productions, 5, 89, 91, 128, 133, 144, 149
New Torch Theatre productions, 152
New York: productions, 86; Alvin Theatre, 126, 127; Morosco Theatre, 122
Ney, Marie, 136
Nicholls, Anthony, 3
Nicholson, Nora, 114
Norden, Christine, 110
Novello, Ivor, 139

Obey: Lucrece, 90
Odets, Clifford: Rocket to the Moon, 22
Oklahoma!, 119
Old Vic Theatre productions, 128, 133, 138, 145-6
Olivier, Sir Laurence, 13, 16, 77, 115, 116, 128, 133, 138, 144, 150-2, 172
Opéra, 30

Page, Tilsa, 50
Pagnol, Marcel, 23
Paris: the Theatre in, 87 ff.; classical tradition, 90; Antoine Theatre productions, 71; Atelier Theatre productions, 24, 25 26, 30; Bouffes-Parisiens productions, 155; Comédie des Champs-Elysées productions, 34; Marigny Theatre productions, 24, 25, 57, 67, 75; Théâtre Sarah Bernhardt productions, 91
Payne, Laurence, 41
Péguy: Jeanne d'Arc, 32
Phoenix Theatre productions, 121, 125, 132, 134
Pinero, Sir Arthur: The Schoolmistress, 148; The Second Mrs. Tanqueray, 148-9
Piper, John, 90
Popesco, Elvire, 66, 155
Porel, Jacqueline, 153
Porter, Eric, 36
Portman, Eric, 98
Priestley, J. B., 56
Princes Theatre productions, 149
Pryse, Hugh, 85

Quatre Saisons, Compagnie des, 26
Quayle, Anthony, 128, 134, 136, 138-9
Quéant, Gilles: Théâtre de France, 114
Quincey, Thomas de, 76

Radine, Serge: Anouilh, Lenormand, Salacrou, 31, 34, 44
Rattigan, Terence, 56, 147; Who is Sylvia? 165-6; The Browning Version, 166; French Without Tears, 166; The Winslow Boy, 166; Adventure Story, 166; The Deep Blue Sea, 166-70, 172
Redgrave, Michael, 128, 139-40, 146
Reed, Herbert, 90
Réjane, Gabrielle, 115, 116
Religion, in the contemporary Western European Theatre, 53, 56
Relph, George, 16, 34
Renaud, Madeleine, 24, 27, 61, 64, 67, 78, 80. See also Barrault, Jean-Jacques.
Repertory Players, the, 89
Richardson, Sir Ralph, 104-6, 116, 128, 133, 138, 139, 144, 147
Riscoe, Arthur, 156
Robson, Flora, 132, 135
Rose, George, 135
Rosenthal, Andrew: Third Person, 117; Red Letter Day, 171
Rouleau, Raymond, 124
Roussin, André, 49, 172; Nina, 66-7, 155-156; The Little Hut, 153-4; Bobosse (Figure of Fun), 154-5
Rowntree, B. Seebohm and Lavers, G. R.: English Life and Leisure, 47-8, 52-3
Roy, Derek, 110
Rutherford, Margaret, 28

St. Denis, Michel, 138
St. James's Theatre productions, 13, 60, 74, 80, 148, 150, 164, 172
Sainthill, Loudon, 141
Salacrou, Armand, 61-2, 63, 108, 172; Les Nuits de la Colère, 61, 64-6, 67-9; Un Homme Comme les Autres, 62; Histoire de Rire, 62, 64, 65; L'Archipel Lenoir, 63; La Terre est Ronde, 64
Sanchez, Manuel Rodriguez. See Manolete.
Sartre, Jean-Paul, 32-3, 56, 69; and politics, 86; and the Occupation, 89; Les Mouches, 32, 89, 90-3; Le Diable et le Bon Dieu, 57
Saville Theatre productiosn, 148, 153
Savoy Theatre productions, 153, 156
Sayers, Dorothy: The Nine Tailors, 162
Scala Theatre productions, 109
Scofield, Paul, 24, 28, 137, 138
Scott, Hutchinson, 40
Seyler, Athene, 166
Shakespeare, William: cycle of historical plays at Stratford, 139 ff.; King Lear, 98, 134; The Winter's Tale, 128, 132, 134-5; Antony and Cleopatra, 128, 150-2; Hamlet, 128, 146, 147, 149; Julius Caesar,

134; *Measure for Measure*, 134; *Much Ado About Nothing*, 134, 135–7; *Henry IV*, 138, 140, 141; *Richard II*, 139–40; *The Tempest*, 141; *Othello*, 145; *Midsummer Night's Dream*, 145; *Twelfth Night*, 146; *Merry Wives of Windsor*, 146; *Henry V*, 146; *Macbeth*, 148
Shaw, George Bernard, 56; *Caesar and Cleopatra*, 128, 150–2; *Man and Superman*, 149
Shaw, Glen Byam, 138
Sherek, Henry, 6, 49, 108
Sheriff, R. C.: *Home at Seven*, 104
Shiner, Ronald, 159
Sim, Alastair, 163
Sim, Sheila, 165
Sitwell, Sacheverell, 141
Sophocles: *Electra*, 128
South Pacific, 119
Squire, Ronald, 34, 36
Stannard, Heather, 16–17, 18
Steevens, George, 131
Steinbeck, John: *Of Mice and Men*, 120
Stephens, Jan, 164
Stock, Nigel, 159
Storks Don't Talk, 109, 111, 126
Storm, Lesley: *The Day's Mischief*, 157
Strachey, Lytton, 60
Strand Theatre productions, 109
Stratford Memorial Theatre, 128, 134, 138, 139
Strode, W. Chetham: *Background*, 163–4
Strindberg, August, 34
Stuart, Aimée: *Lace on Her Petticoat*, 86–7
Sundstrom, Frank, 57, 59
Sundstrom, Jacqueline, 57, 60
Swanson, Gloria, 155

Taylor, Samuel: *The Happy Time*, 171–2
Ten Men and a Miss, 156
Tennent, H. M., Organisation, 108, 146
Tetzel, Joan, 153
'Théâtre Engagé, le,' 86 ff.
Thorndike, Dame Sybil, 171
Times, The, on *Peter Pan*, 109–10; on *Cinderella*, 110
Tolosa, Pavo, 143
Townley, Toke, 61
Trewin, J. C., 111, 159

Tutin, Dorothy, 137

Unity Theatre productions, 87
Ustinov, Peter, 108; *The Love of Four Colonels*, 82, 98–9; *The Moment of Truth*, 93–8; as Arts Theatre Competition judge, 99, 104

Valentin, Monelle, 23
Vattier, Robert, 26, 155
Vaudeville Theatre productions, 34
Vershinin, 65
Vigny, Alfred de, 102

Waddington, Patrick, 49
Wallace, Henry, 104
Walpole, Hugh: *The Old Ladies*, 148
Ward, Ronald, 148–9
Watling, Peter: *Rain on the Just*, 108, 112; *Indian Summer*, 108, 109, 112–17
Webb, Alan, 107
Webber, C. E.: *Right Side Up*, 100–1
Wells, H. G., 55
Wherry, Daniel, 46
White, Leonard, 85
Whitehall Theatre productions, 108
Whiting, John, 147; *Saint's Day*, 40–1, 47, 99, 101–2, 103, 104, 106, 109; *A Penny for a Song*, 106–7, 108, 109
Wilder, Thornton: *Our Town*, 120
Will Any Gentleman?, 156
Williams, Emlyn, 3; *Accolade*, 2–5
Williams, Tennessee: *A Streetcar Named Desire*, 121, 125–6
Willman, Noel, 3
Winter Garden Theatre productions, 57
Winter, Keith: *The Rats of Norway*, 122
Wolfit, Donald, 115, 138, 145
Wooland, Norman, 151
Worsley, T. C., 112
Worth, Irene, 12
Wyndham's Theatre productions, 98, 104
Wynyard, Diana, 132, 135, 136, 137, 165

Youth, in the Theatre, 108

Zetterling, Mai, 38